Governpreneurship

Establishing a Thriving Entrepreneurial Spirit in Government

Robert D. Hisrich

Thunderbird School of Global Management, USA

Amr Al-Dabbagh

Al-Dabbagh Group, Saudi Arabia

Edward Elgar

Cheltenham, UK • Northampton, MA, USA

Published by
Edward Elgar Publishing Limited
The Lypiatts
15 Lansdown Road
Cheltenham
Glos GL50 2JA
UK

Edward Elgar Publishing, Inc.
William Pratt House
9 Dewey Court
Northampton
Massachusetts 01060
USA

A catalogue record for this book
is available from the British Library

Library of Congress Control Number: 2012942516

ISBN 978 1 78195 162 0 (cased)
         978 1 78195 228 3 (paperback)

Typeset by Servis Filmsetting Ltd, Stockport, Cheshire
Printed and bound by MPG Books Group, UK

Contents

Figures

Tables

About the authors

Robert D. Hisrich

Robert D. Hisrich, Ph.D., is the Garvin Professor of Global Entrepreneurship and Director of the Walker Center for Global Entrepreneurship at Thunderbird School of Global Management (USA), the world's leading school of global business. He received his BA from DePauw University, his MBA and Ph.D. degrees from the University of Cincinnati, and honorary doctorate degrees from Chivash State University (Russia) and the University of Miskolc (Hungary). Hisrich was a Fulbright Professor at the International Management Center in Budapest, Hungary. He was named a Professor in Budapest at the Foundation for Small Enterprise Economic Development, where he also held the Alexander Hamilton Chair in Entrepreneurship.

Dr. Hisrich himself is a global entrepreneur who has been involved in the founding of more than a dozen companies including H&B Associates, a marketing and management consulting firm.

He has written over 350 articles and authored or co-authored 30 books including: *Corporate Entrepreneurship; Technology Entrepreneurship: Creating, Capturing and Protecting Value; International Entrepreneurship: Starting, Developing and Managing a Global Venture* (second edition); *Entrepreneurship: Starting, Developing, and Managing a New Enterprise* (translated into thirteen languages and in its ninth edition); *The 13 Biggest Mistakes that Derail Small Businesses and How to Avoid Them* and *The Woman Entrepreneur.*

Dr. Hisrich has instituted academic and training programs around the world. Not only highly respected and sought after in the academic sector, his expertise has been tapped by top corporations, governments and governmental agencies.

Amr Al-Dabbagh

After having served two highly-acclaimed four-year terms in government as Governor of the Saudi Arabian General Investment Authority (SAGIA) (KSA), with a rank of Minister, His Excellency Amr Al-Dabbagh is now focused on achieving three targets. As Chairman and CEO of Al-Dabbagh Group, the fifty-year old corporate platform, he leads the '20 × 20' goal to make Al-Dabbagh Group a top 20 global family business by 2020. As Founding Chairman of the Stars Foundation, the philanthropic platform, he leads a '20 × 20' goal to support the lives of twenty million disadvantaged people by 2020 in the Under Five Mortality Rate (U5MR) countries as defined by UNICEF. As steward of the family heritage, he leads the 'Club 32' initiative to empower the thirty-two members of Al-Dabbagh family's third generation, including his own five children, to become global leaders in the fields they love most. For His Excellency, the corporate platform 'ensures earning,' the philanthropic 'ensures giving,' and Club 32 ensures the 'continuity and sustainability' of earning and giving by endowing Club 32 members with the skills and traits needed to become responsible stakeholders of the three platforms, and thereby responsible global citizens.

Foreword

When I took office in 1993, I promised the American people I would make the federal government work better and cost less – that I would, in effect, 'reinvent government.' One of the first initiatives I launched, which would go on to become the longest running governmental reform program in history, was the National Performance Review (NPR), later renamed the National Partnership for Reinventing Government. The NPR set out to create a more efficient and effective government by employing the principles the private sector had refined to increase performance and deliver the right conditions in which innovation and human potential could flourish. In short, we set out to make the government more entrepreneurial – more results-oriented, performance-based, and customer-focused.

I asked Vice President Al Gore to lead the NPR, and knowing we had no time to waste, gave him just six months to come back to me with a full report. On September 7, 1993, he handed me a document detailing 1250 specific actions to improve the government's ability to serve the American people. The report established four simple principles that would modernize government: (1) putting customers first; (2) cutting red tape; (3) empowering employees to get results; and (4) cutting back to basics. These four principles, though expanded upon in this book, are the cornerstones of entrepreneurial organizations, and ideally, entrepreneurial governments.

By the time my Presidency drew to a close less than eight years later, the NPR's achievements had quieted all skeptics. In that time, we saved $136 billion for the American people; we reduced the federal workforce by more than 400 000 to its smallest size in 40 years; we eliminated 640 000 pages of internal agency rules and 16 000 pages of unnecessary federal regulations; we committed to more than 4000 customer service standards across 570 organizations; we presented Vice President Gore's 'Hammer Award' to more than 68 000 employees for having saved, or found more efficient uses for, more than $53 billion; and we established 350 'reinvention labs' to pilot new ways of doing business. Not coincidentally, the public's trust in government more than doubled during this same time period.

My administration proposed four principles of government entrepreneurship in our reinvention program, while the authors of *Governpreneurship* provide in six chapters a comprehensive study of the subject. Chapter 7 concludes the book with four case studies to better understand government entrepreneurship in different types of situations: an agency, a country, a city, and a hospital.

I've known the focus of the first study (and co-author of this book), Amr Al-Dabbagh, for more than a decade, and have been a strong admirer of his professional and humanitarian work. His achievements during the eight years he led the Saudi Arabian General Investment Authority speak for themselves, and the 'Ten Golden Rules of Governpreneurship' he derived from the process are essential knowledge for anyone seeking to create a dynamic public sector organization.

After more than 20 years in public office and ten years traveling the world for my Foundation, I've concluded that the best outcomes occur when a strong, effective private sector works together with an innovative, entrepreneurial government to promote the economy. I know that as you read this book, you'll gain invaluable insights about the type of government that will succeed in the twenty-first century.

William Jefferson Clinton, 2012

Foreword

I assumed leadership at a time of global recession, and yet Malaysia subsequently managed to create an entrepreneurial revolution of sorts by enhancing small business. Malaysia needed to create new markets for its products and services as the traditional markets at the time were affected by the global recession. Much like today, albeit on a much smaller scale, the world had become poorer and things produced by the country at the time had more difficulty penetrating the market than they had in the past. I was determined to place the Malaysian economy in a better position relative to the real business of producing goods and supplying services, and concentrate on perfection and precision. I was determined for Malaysia to demonstrate its capacity.

Planning for development and preparing master plans according to sector requirements has been an integral part of Malaysia's approach to development. Malaysia has gained much experience from studying methods of privatization in other countries and has made certain adjustments to such an approach, which identified the services and bodies open to privatization efforts by the private entrepreneurial sector. At the genesis of such efforts, privatization progressed fairly well in terms of numbers. The sale of government interests in companies had generated revenues, which were also earned from lease payments, and had exceeded expectations. In doing so, Malaysia has been able to champion alternatives, which on the one hand allows it to share in strong growth market economy as defined by our own characteristics, as well as gain significant global political latitude. This has allowed Malaysia to challenge and question the prevailing accepted norms. As a result of such strategic planning, Malaysia has been able to manifest other possible active forms which have been deduced from indigenous traditions, practices, and knowledge.

I commend the contributions contained in this work, which is intended to bring forth the topic of entrepreneurship in government and governmental agencies perhaps as a direct response to the global financial 'meltdown' and the fact that the world is beginning to recognize that the role of many governments and their agencies may need to be redefined. Consequently, there is great opportunity for the aforementioned agencies to examine their current systems and, like Malaysia did in the preceding decades, perhaps learn from the experiences of other countries such as Malaysia, and offer viable alternatives which will not only fulfill the tenets of their own culture, but will also satisfy the global needs and requirements of others.

His Excellency, Tun Dr Mahathir Mohamad, Former Prime Minister
of Malaysia, 2011

Preface

Starting and operating a new venture in one's own country or globally, or being involved in corporate entrepreneurship involves considerable risk and energy to overcome all the obstacles involved; yet, even more risk and energy is involved in governpreneurship – establishing entrepreneurship in a government or government agency. It involves overcoming the inertia, rigidity, rules and regulations and bureaucratic nature of almost all governmental organizations to create something new – a new way of doing things, a new system and/or a new service. Governpreneurship becomes increasingly important in an era of economic downturn, reduced sources of revenue, and increased demand and expectation from constituencies.

While entrepreneurship has traditionally been viewed as a private sector phenomenon, corporate and social entrepreneurship have developed in a number of different domains such as not-for-profits, for-profits and public sector organizations. Entrepreneurship is a universal concept that can be applied in small- and medium-sized enterprises (SMEs), large national and multinational organizations, as well as social ventures, enterprises, communities and even governments. It is not limited to a select group of people: any person with the right orientation, decision making framework, drive and motivation can develop an entrepreneurial perspective and mindset. This perspective and mindset identifies a need and transforms a creative and innovative idea to fill that need.

In organizations and governments, entrepreneurs challenge existing assumptions and look to generate value in more innovative and creative ways. Entrepreneurs change the way things are done by identifying opportunities and successfully filling them. Through this challenge and change renewal occurs.

To fully cover this topic of Governpreneurship (entrepreneurship in government), the book is divided into seven chapters and four case histories.

Chapter 1, 'Entrepreneurship in the public sector', discusses the differences between government entities, corporate entrepreneurship and entrepreneurship, and develops a framework for public sector entrepreneurship and its challenges. Chapter 2, 'The government entrepreneur', focuses on government innovation, the significant roles in government entrepreneurship and of course the characteristics of one. Formulation and managing policy innovation is the focus of Chapter 3. After discussing approaches to and stages in policy innovation, approaches, different frameworks and how to understand the policy landscape are presented. Chapter 4, 'Locating and fostering innovation', discusses how to create an innovative public culture, the influences of media and the benefits of contracting services. The chapter concludes with programs fostering entrepreneurial innovation and provides some examples of governments encouraging innovation. Chapter 5, 'Managing the internal and external politics', discusses these two important impacts on government entrepreneurship as well as how change can occur from outside the government. The important concepts of developing the plan and building the coalition are the topics of Chapter 6. The aspects, benefits and obstacles to creating a coalition are discussed with particular attention being paid to public–private partnerships. The book concludes with funding the venture (Chapter 7). Following a presentation of methods of financing, cost-savings activities, funding examples of public–private partnerships and venture capital, the chapter and book conclude with presenting some innovative funding programs.

To illustrate the aspects of government entrepreneurship discussed in these seven chapters, four case histories are presented. The first case history features government entrepreneurship at the national level—the country of Ireland. The Celtic Tiger discusses the basics of the country's economic development and evolution. Governpreneurship is seen throughout the various activities and aspects of the government of Singapore, the second case history. The third case history deals with entrepreneurship in the public sector of the Kingdom of Saudi Arabia. Following a presentation of the development and operation of Saudi Arabia General Investment Authority (SAGIA), the case history concludes with the ten golden rules for entrepreneurship in the public sector. The last case history, HUG – Geneva University Hospital is a unique example of government entrepreneurship in a state-owned hospital

Many individuals—corporate executives, government officials, entrepreneurs and professors from all over the world—have made this book possible. Our special thanks go to: the research assistants Stephanie Arthur, Rebecca Knowles, David Kralik, Katie Nehlsen and Debra Wheat for their timely research, writing and editing; Professor Claudine Kearney for her comments and initial ideas on this manuscript; the two hundred or more colleagues at SAGIA, the true governpreneurs and stars who made SAGIA's success possible; our case writers Patricia Kavanagh, Katie Nehlsen, and Raphael H. Cohen; and our editors and editorial assistants. Our utmost appreciation goes to Carol Pacelli without whom this book would never had been prepared in a timely manner.

To:

- my parents, Dr. Lloyd and Ella, who sent me on this journey;
- my wife and companion, Tina, for her total love, understanding and support;
- my family: Kelly and her husband, Rich; Kary and Katy for teaching me so much;
- my grandchildren: Rachel, Andrew and Sarah, who teach me about loving, simplicity and laughter; and
- a beautiful Golden Retriever, Kaiya, whose intelligence and love go beyond understanding.

Robert D. Hisrich

To:

- His Majesty, King Abdullah bin Abdulaziz, whose trust and empowerment unleashed the governpreneur in me;
- my father, who is my role model;
- my mother, who is the source of my values and ethics;
- my wife, who is the source of my strength; and
- my children, who are the source of my joy and happiness.

Amr Al-Dabbagh

   May each of you always think entrepreneurially in all that you do.

1. Entrepreneurship in the public sector

CHAPTER OBJECTIVES

- To introduce the concept of entrepreneurship and provide an overview of entrepreneurship in public sector organizations.
- To discuss the core concepts and develop a framework for entrepreneurship in public sector entrepreneurship.
- To identify the challenges and solutions of public sector entrepreneurship.

INTRODUCTION

If small- and medium-sized enterprises (SMEs) and large organizations can be entrepreneurial, what about organizations outside the private sector? Can entrepreneurship occur in public sector organizations such as government and governmental agencies?

Public sector entrepreneurship becomes even more important when public revenues are reduced and public services are questioned. The degree to which entrepreneurship can be achieved in the public sector depends to a large extent on the organization's internal and external environments. While there is no ideal model for achieving public sector entrepreneurship, this book outlines some ways to encourage and manage entrepreneurship in the public sector.

While entrepreneurship has traditionally been viewed as a private sector phenomenon, entrepreneurship is really a universal concept and can be applied not only in SMEs and large organizations but also in government and other public sector organizations. Public sector organizational managers should undertake their public mission, goals and objectives entrepreneurially by implementing flexible, innovative strategies. Government and other public sector managers need to provide vision and leadership while developing an entrepreneurial culture within their organization.

To facilitate the development of entrepreneurship, governmental organizations need to focus on support, resources, rewards and flexible organizational structures. This support facilitates and promotes entrepreneurial activity in the organization and champions innovative thinking. Simultaneously, bureaucracy and bottlenecks are eliminated to reduce the barriers. Public sector organizations can benefit from understanding such aspects of entrepreneurship as opportunity recognition and evaluation, developing plans for new concepts and assessing and managing risks.

This first chapter provides an overview of public sector entrepreneurship, identifies the key differences between public and private sector entrepreneurship and develops and discusses a framework for public sector entrepreneurship. Challenges in developing entrepreneurship in the public sector, together with approaches for addressing these challenges are presented. The chapter concludes with a discussion of alternative government structures for public sector entrepreneurship.

ENTREPRENEURSHIP: AN OVERVIEW

There are many definitions of entrepreneurs and entrepreneurship in both the private and public sectors, and many questions have not been fully answered. Who is an entrepreneur? What is entrepreneurship? What is the process of entrepreneurship? Who is the public sector entrepreneur? What is public sector entrepreneurship? What is the process of public sector entrepreneurship?

The term entrepreneurship refers to the efforts of an individual who accepts risks to translate a vision into a successful enterprise. Some have focused on the creation of new organizations. Others have felt that entrepreneurship is about wealth creation and ownership. Others feel that entrepreneurship is about discovery and addressing opportunities. A broad, all-inclusive definition of entrepreneurship is 'the process of creating something new with value by devoting the necessary time and effort; assuming the accompanying financial, psychic and social risks and uncertainties and receiving the resulting rewards of monetary and personal satisfaction'.[1]

Corporate entrepreneurship 'is the process by which individuals inside organizations pursue opportunities independent of the resources they currently control; this involves doing new things and departing from the customary to pursue opportunities'.[2] It creates a new spirit of entrepreneurship and innovations and encourages employees to think and act like entrepreneurs by giving them the freedom and flexibility to pursue their ideas. It can result in the creation of new things or renewal and innovation in the organization.

Corporate entrepreneurship usually has two major aspects: new venture creation within the existing organization and the transformation of the organization through strategic renewal. This renewal can involve formal or informal activities to create new businesses or processes. Renewal has many aspects, such as redefining the business concept, reorganization or introduction of system-wide changes. It often involves the creative redeployment of resources, leading to new products or services or new ways of doing things.

While the term entrepreneurship is mostly associated with private sector activity, the concept has also been applied to the public sector. Drucker felt that entrepreneurship was as much a public sector as a private sector phenomenon.[3] He regarded entrepreneurship as perceptiveness to change and the entrepreneur as one who searches for change, and responds to it. While there is indeed a need for the public sector to become most innovative and dynamic, the need for strong entrepreneurial leadership makes the realization of public entrepreneurship more challenging. Public sector entrepreneurship creates value for citizens and addresses social opportunities.

A comparison of the three types of entrepreneurs in the private sector, corporate and public sectors in Table 1.1 indicates that the entrepreneur is creative, proactive and innovative. This provides innovation through identifying and developing opportunities. Successful entrepreneurs and entrepreneurial activities are unique in public sector organizations with larger, hierarchical and more rigid organizations. The following is the definition of public sector entrepreneurship used in this book:

> Public sector entrepreneurship is an individual or group of individuals undertaking activities to initiate change by adapting, innovating and assuming risk, and recognizing that personal goals and objectives are less important than generating results for the organization.

PUBLIC SECTOR ENTREPRENEURSHIP

Public sector organizations are often large, hierarchical entities facing captive demand, enjoying somewhat guaranteed sources and levels of financing, and having some distance from the influences of voters, stakeholders and political institutions. The more the government organization is bureaucratic and conservative, the less entrepreneurial government employees are apt to be.

As a result of the global economy, governments are increasingly looking to foster entrepreneurial thinking and activity. Some governments are now attempting to realign their public sectors with the changing global

Table 1.1   *Comparison of private, corporate, and public entrepreneurs*

	Private (Independent) Entrepreneur	Corporate Entrepreneur	Public Sector Entrepreneur
Objectives	Freedom to discover and exploit profitable opportunities; independent and goal orientated; high need for achievement	Requires freedom and flexibility to pursue projects without being bogged down in bureaucracy; goal orientated; motivated but is influenced by the corporate characteristics	An individual who is motivated by power and achievement; undertakes purposeful activity to initiate, maintain or aggrandize, one or more public sector organizations; not constrained by profit
Focus	Strong focus on the external environment; competitive environment and technological advancement	Focus on innovative activities and orientations such as development of new products, services, technologies, administrative techniques, strategies and competitive postures; Concentrate on the internal and external environment	Aim to create value for citizens by bringing together unique combinations of public and/or private resources to exploit social opportunities; learns to use external forces to initiate and achieve internal change
Innovation	Create value through innovation and seizing that opportunity without regard to resources (human and capital); produces resources or endows existing resources with enhanced potential for creating wealth	A system that enables and encourages individuals to use creative processes that enable them to apply and invent technologies that can be planned, deliberate, and purposeful in terms of the level of innovative activity desired; instigation of renewal and innovation within that organization	Public managers are entrepreneurial in the way they take risks with an opportunistic bias toward action and consciously overcome bureaucratic and political obstacles their innovations face

Table 1.1   (continued)

	Private (Independent) Entrepreneur	Corporate Entrepreneur	Public Sector Entrepreneur
Opportunity	Pursues an opportunity, regardless of the resources they control; relatively unconstrained by situational forces	Pursues opportunities independent of the resources they currently control; doing new things and departing from the customary to pursue opportunities	Uses every opportunity to distinguish their public enterprise and leadership style from what is the norm in the public sector; understand the business as well as supporting the opportunity for business growth and development
Risk taking	Risk taking is a prime factor in the entrepreneurial character and function; assumes significant personal and financial risk but attempts to minimize them	Moderate risk taker; recognizes that risks are career related	Calculated risk taker; takes relatively big organizational risks without taking big personal risks
Character and Skills	Self-confident; strong knowledge of business	Self-confident; strong self-belief that they can manipulate the system; strong technical or product knowledge; good managerial skills	Self-confident; high tolerance for ambiguity; strong political skills

Source: Kearney, C., R. D. Hisrich and F. Roche (2007) A conceptual model of public sector corporate entrepreneurship. *International Entrepreneurship and Management Journal*, **4** (3), 295–313.

environment. They are emphasizing new 'public managerialism' and discontinuous reforms that challenge traditional mindsets and include the need for innovation and entrepreneurship.[4]

An example supporting Drucker's definition of entrepreneurship is Lee Kuan Yew, the first Prime Minister of Singapore. Following Singapore's declaration of independence in 1959, the Prime Minister faced the task of transforming the small island nation into an independent and self-sustaining economy. The Prime Minister innovatively pursued a series of economic policies that did not follow the tradition of forging trade relations with neighboring countries. Instead, he pursued an aggressive campaign to attract new resources into the nation through foreign direct investment. The legacy of Lee's entrepreneurial approach to economic development continues to attract vast amounts of economic wealth into Singapore, as is discussed in the case study in Appendix 2.

Private sector organizations are affected by their external environment. One aspect of this that has been the rapidly changing is the nature of the relationships between public officials and their constituencies. Entrepreneurial behavior is now viewed as one way to develop innovative solutions to satisfy the needs and expectations of their constituencies.

Public sector entrepreneurship is similar to some extent to entrepreneurship in large corporations – corporate entrepreneurship. The public sector and large corporations often have formalized hierarchies, established stakeholder groups with competing demands, deeply entrenched cultures, detailed rules and procedures, and a fairly rigid system of financial controls, budgeting and employee rewards. Managers in the public sector and large corporations focus more on internal developments and on the actual process than the outcome. This approach can inhibit entrepreneurship and innovation.

DIFFERENCES BETWEEN PUBLIC AND PRIVATE SECTOR ENTREPRENEURSHIP

The emergence of the entrepreneurship phenomenon in the public sector has raised some interesting questions regarding the responsibility of public managers and politicians. Public sector entrepreneurs need to understand this political authority when designing and implementing policies. Public sector entrepreneurs need to be civic-minded and have the public interest in mind. In the case of Singapore, this is exemplified by a 'top-down' approach to entrepreneurship, a strategic approach that includes: governmental policies to reduce barriers to foreign direct investment, subsidies for firms or researchers in targeted industries, emphasis on creative thinking and 'think tanks' at public universities, and the recruitment of foreign professionals into the state to mentor the next generation and fuel entrepreneurial growth in the business sector.

Some of the differences between the public and private sectors are that the public sector:

- has greater diversity and conflicting, multiple objectives;
- has lower scores on organizational commitment and job satisfaction;
- can be lower in prestige and social status;
- has less decision-making autonomy and flexibility, and more constraints;
- has a higher concentration of authority with established centralized procedures;
- has lower incentives;
- has salaried managers who do not share in the organization's profits;
- is not constrained by the profit motive of the private sector;
- can more easily obtain large amounts of funding; and
- is free of any private enterprise restrictions.

These differences in public sector entrepreneurs reflect the following differences between public and private sector organizations:

- have no profit motive but instead social and political objectives;
- receive funds indirectly from an involuntary taxpayer;
- have problems in identifying the organization's stakeholders and constituencies; and
- are subject to public scrutiny.

Entrepreneurship in the public sector, unlike the private sector, relies less on particular individual attributes and more on a group desire. Personal qualities and motivations become less important than being able to operate at the institutional level. The differences between public and private sector entrepreneurship in Table 1.2 indicate the key differences with respect to the level of diversity in objectives, diversity in decision making, authority, risk/rewards, motivation, availability of funding, different restrictions in growth and levels of independence.

FRAMEWORK FOR PUBLIC SECTOR ENTREPRENEURSHIP

The pillars of public sector entrepreneurship in Figure 1.1 present the framework for public sector entrepreneurship in this book. There are two major pillars – external and internal environments. Each has its own attributes.

Table 1.2   Differences between public and private sector entrepreneurship

	Public Sector Entrepreneurship	Private (Independent) Entrepreneurship
Objectives	Greater diversity and multiplicity of objectives; greater conflict among objectives	More clearly defined goals and objectives; greater consistency among objectives
Decision making	Less decision making autonomy and flexibility; more constraint on procedures and operations; subject to public scrutiny; major decisions have to be transparent	Greater degree of flexibility and autonomy in the decision making process; more participative and independent in their decision making
Authority	More authoritarian; more centralized or centrally controlled	More democratic; more decentralized
Risk/Rewards	Risk and reward trade-offs favor avoiding mistakes; lower financial incentives; does not share enterprise's profits	Identifies risk factors and aims to minimize them; calculated risk taker; invest personal capital in the business; higher financial incentives; profitability is fundamental to generate income
Motivation	Lower commitment and job satisfaction	Greater level of commitment and job satisfaction
Funding and profit	Not constrained by narrow profit; easier to obtain funding for risky projects; easier to raise capital; does not have a profit motive, instead they are guided by political and social objectives	Can be constrained by narrow profit; more difficult to access and obtain funding for risky projects; difficult to raise capital; profit oriented
Restrictions	Restrictions on growth and power that face the private sector are not applicable to the public sector	Can be restrictions on the growth and power of the enterprise
Independence	Obtains independence by overcoming dependencies	Obtains independence by avoiding or minimizing dependencies

Source: Adopted from Kearney, C., R. D. Hisrich and F. Roche (2007) Facilitating public sector corporate entrepreneurship process: a conceptual model. *Journal of Enterprising Culture,* **15** (3), 275–279.

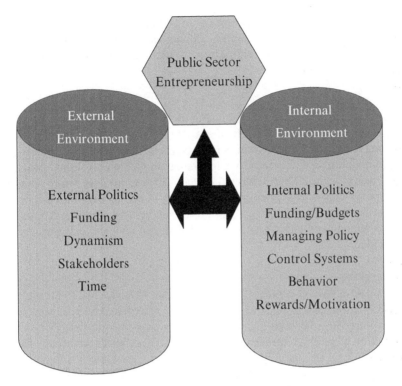

Figure 1.1 The pillars of public sector entrepreneurship

Dimensions in Public Sector Entrepreneurship

There are many dimensions that make up public sector entrepreneurship including venturing, renewal, innovation, risk taking and proactivity.

Venturing
New business venturing is a most important characteristic of corporate entrepreneurship and can result in a new business creation within an existing organization. In both large and small corporations, new venturing can include the formation of autonomous or semi-autonomous units or organizations, internal venturing, corporate start-ups and corporate venturing. This is also an important aspect of public sector entrepreneurship.

Renewal
This reflects the transformation of organizations through the renewal of key ideas. Renewal is achieved through the redefinition of the organization's

mission and requires developing or adopting new organizational structures for innovation and change. Public sector entrepreneurship needs
to emphasize strategy reformulation, reorganization and organizational
change.

Innovation
Innovation is a process that begins with seeing an opportunity, developing an innovation and introducing a new product, process or service in
the marketplace. Innovativeness reflects a tendency to support new ideas,
experimentation and creativity while departing from established practices
and technologies. These innovations can include process improvements,
new services and new organizational forms. Public sector innovation supports and encourages redesigning and restructuring the process to enhance
the efficiency and effectiveness in the delivery of new and existing services
provided.[5]

Risk taking
The issue of risk is central to entrepreneurial behavior. Risk-taking pro-
pensity varies according to the institution. Bozeman and Kingsley state,
'Characteristics of high-level public sector jobs means that risk-taking
behavior of public managers may be subject to greater scrutiny.'[6] Given
the high level of visibility for public sector employees risk taking is less
attractive in the public sector. Although risk-taking decisions are not
always desirable in the public sector, public organizations need to encourage risk taking because their policy environment is never entirely predict-
able and stable. According to Kearney, Hisrich and Roche, 'Public sector
risk taking is reflected in investment decisions and strategic actions in the
face of uncertainty and political obstacles.'[7]

Proactivity
Proactiveness is concerned with implementation, which is doing what
is necessary to bring the entrepreneurial concept to fruition. Public
sector proactivity is action-orientated, change-oriented with a focus on
overcoming potential problems that affect the public sector. It involves
a high level of commitment, perseverance, flexibility, adaptability and a
willingness to take responsibility for failure. Proactivity often involves a
creative interpretation of rules and skills at networking and leveraging of
resources.

In November 1994, the partisan divide in the United States Congress
changed for the first time in 40 years from the Democratic to the
Republican Party, led by Newt Gingrich, who would become the new
Speaker. Gingrich's campaign that made him Speaker, the Contract with

America, is a model for public sector proactivity. The Contract with America was action-oriented because in the words of Gingrich, it said, 'if you elect us this is what we'll do and this is our contract'.[8] It was change-oriented because it set out to elect a new group of individuals who would pass legislation that polling data confirmed a majority of Americans were in support of including 'making Congress subject to the same laws it passes on America'. In Gingrich's view, the problem in the public sector that needed to be overcome was a large, unresponsive government. To overcome these challenges, they had to shrink the size of government. In his address to the nation after 100 days in office as Speaker, Gingrich noted that, 'We cut congressional committee staffs and budgets by 30 percent . . . we are going to sell one congressional building and privatize at least one congressional parking lot.'[9] Gingrich's speech also resonated tones of commitment and perseverance when he noted, 'While we've done a lot, this contract has never been about curing all the ills of the nation; 100 days can't overturn the neglect of decades.'[10] Finally, there were also lessons about taking responsibility for failure when he noted, 'As promised, we introduced a constitutional amendment on term limits. We failed,' but later would use this as a rallying cry for persistence when he noted, 'I pledge to you that term limits will be the first vote of the next Congress. So keep the pressure on, keep your hopes up.'

External Environment

The external environment significantly influences public sector entre-preneurship. Managers in the public sector need to monitor the external environment and modify their organization's goals and objectives in light of new requirements. Strong political leadership, clear policy direction and effective communication not only allow public sector entrepreneurs to implement change, but enable them to identify and develop new ways of doing things. The external environment consists of five aspects: external politics, dynamism, funding, stakeholders and time.

External politics
Political environment is a fundamental dimension of the external environment having significant impact on both public and private sector organizations. The external environment of a public organization has numerous political considerations, political constraints, frequent changes in policy and short time-horizons. The views of opinion leaders, legislators and interest groups are sometimes more important than the economic issues of private sector organizations. Public sector organizations need to be able to adapt to political environmental factors affecting their organization.

Dynamism

Dynamism, the level of environmental predictability, is manifested in the variance of the rate of market and industry change and the level of uncertainty about forces that are beyond the control of individual organizations. Dynamic environments provide more opportunities for the entrepreneurial organization, while hostile environments provide a strong incentive for organizations to pursue innovation as a source of competitive advantage. Increased dynamism will lead to different approaches in managing the public sector organization.

Funding

Funding can stimulate or constrain entrepreneurship in the public sector. It is sometimes easier to raise capital in the public sector than in the private sector, especially for risky projects that satisfy political and social objectives. Like in the private sector, inadequate funding inhibits public sector entrepreneurship. Since there are greater challenges and budgetary restrictions in most public sector organizations during times of economic instability, public sector organizations can face complex demands from their constituencies, reductions in budgets and greater regulatory constraints.

Stakeholders

Public sector organizations have a variety of stakeholders. Open communication and transparency are needed within the internal organization and with the external constituencies. A public sector organization is responsible to a large number of stakeholders, which leads to greater complexity in managing these relationships. For change to occur within the public sector organization, the emphasis needs to be on results rather than process, which needs to be clearly communicated to the different stakeholders.

Time

Short-term budgets and planning horizons occur within the public sector resulting in difficulty thinking outside of day-to-day pressures on how things could be improved. Excessive concern for short-term results is a barrier to public sector entrepreneurship. Public sector managers and leaders need to provide vision and leadership while developing an entrepreneurial culture within their organizations.

Randal O'Toole, the author of *The Best-Laid Plans: How Government Planning Harms Your Quality of Life, Your Pocketbook and Your Future*, argues that 'as soon as a government plan is written, people who benefit from the plan form special interest groups to insure that the plan does not change no matter how costly it proves to be to society as a whole'.[11] O'Toole's example is perhaps most applicable in countries where citizens not only have the right to organize, but also have free, fair and frequent elections. This is because it is difficult to plan ahead when one doesn't know if they will have a job in the near future. Additionally, if a new leader assumes office, he or she often feels empowered to change an existing plan on the assumption that he or she has a 'mandate' for leadership and bringing about their own vision.

Thus, a great example of a successful long-term government-planned project is the Chinese Qinghai–Tibet Railway. Some may argue that planning for the railway began on 22 December 1899 when Sun Yat Sen published 'the Current Map of China', calling for a railway to be built from Shanghai to Tibet. The thesis for this plan was that the 'ultimate way to solve the Tibet issue was to establish a united community of all ethnic groups of China, in a bid to resist imperialist aggression'.[12] In 1955, Mao Zedong ordered engineers to examine the study but efforts to find a solution were stalled for years. Three years after Mao's death in 1979, a 500-mile track from Xining to Golmud went online.[13] By 2006, having overcome difficulties related to high elevation and mountainous terrain, Sun's plan finally came to fruition when the final 1142 km rail line was completed.

Internal Environment

There are no criteria that characterize a typical internal environment for a public sector entrepreneurial organization. The internal environment has the following aspects: internal politics, funding/budgets, managing policy, control systems, behavior and rewards/motivation.

Internal politics

Internal politics in public sector organizations can restrict entrepreneurial activity. The political cycle puts pressure to achieve quick results that can help achieve a larger share in the next round of appropriations; these results may be possible only so long as political allies remain in power. Greater latitude needs to exist in budgeting, expenditures and operational prioritization in public sector organizations. This results in many public sector employees focusing on internal politics and controls rather than on developing innovative ways to solve the needs of their stakeholders.

Funding/budgets

Another obstacle in the internal environment is inadequate resources, which can result from funding decisions made at a higher political level. When funding is not dependable and there is rapid change in social and environmental factors, the bureaucratic framework can fail to provide the flexibility, motivation or incentives for public sector entrepreneurship to occur.

Managing policy

It is important for policy makers to recognize that public sector entrepreneurship can be stimulated or constrained by the policy established. Policies and regulations need to be established that encourage and support both private sector and public sector organizations to engage in entrepreneurial activities.

Control systems

Management control systems help ensure that resources are obtained and used effectively and efficiently in the accomplishment of the organization's objectives and help provide direction for the innovative efforts of the organization. Too much control on behavior and resource utilization can undermine employee creativity as well as their motivation to experiment and take risks. It is not about more or less control, but the type and amount of control.

Behavior

Entrepreneurial organizations focus on encouraging creative behavior among employees and as a result benefit from the development of new products, processes or systems. One challenge for organizations in fostering entrepreneurship is the difficulty in identifying potential entrepreneurs who will initiate this creative behavior.

Rewards/motivation

Rewards enhance the motivation of individuals to engage in entrepreneurial behavior. Rewarding employees for success goes beyond the financial aspects to include recognition and feedback. Providing a salary and good benefits does not guarantee high morale or job satisfaction in an organization. Employees need to own their jobs and to receive regular recognition and feel appreciated to be truly satisfied. If good performance is not recognized and rewarded, there is no incentive for employees to take risks. It is not surprising that public sector employees are not very innovative given the typical reward systems in place.

Government, unlike the private sector, is not able to offer its employees additional lucrative forms of non-salary compensation such as year-end bonuses and stock ownership plans. Stewart Liff, the author of *Managing Government Employees*, has studied this issue and reached similar conclusions. He notes that, 'Many members of the public believe that government employees are overpaid, while others feel that government employees have a level of job security that does not exist in the private sector. To then issue large bonuses to these same individuals would be an extremely difficult sell, especially during an era when we have unprecedented deficits in many branches of government.'[14]

CHALLENGES FOR PUBLIC SECTOR ENTREPRENEURSHIP

In order to pursue effectively entrepreneurship in the public sector, certain obstacles need to be overcome such as: multiple and ambiguous goals; limited autonomy; over-cautious managerial behavior; reward systems that discourage risk taking; short-term orientation; and limited ability to motivate subordinates. Successful public sector entrepreneurs are not over-whelmed by constraints and do not waste time complaining about them, but instead find ways to get around or transform them into positive situations.

Organizations in both the public and private sector experience challenges when attempting to be entrepreneurial. The incentives, combined with societal perceptions of the public sector, make it more difficult for entrepreneurship to develop. Often the requirement to work within the bureaucratic structure and policies is the most significant obstacle to innovation. Overcoming the barriers of structures, rules, regulations and procedures, allow public sector entrepreneurship benefits such as improved customer services and satisfaction, better internal processes, improved communication and better employee relationships.

OVERCOMING THE CHALLENGES OF PUBLIC SECTOR ENTREPRENEURSHIP

In public sector organizations, entrepreneurship takes on distinct characteristics and has a number of obstacles and constraints not found in the private sector. To overcome these, unique approaches to organizational design and management are needed to facilitate entrepreneurship.

To date, there has been no formal analysis of the elements and instances of entrepreneurship and innovation in the public sector. The challenges facing the public sector entrepreneur include multiplicity and ambiguity of goals, limited autonomy, political interference, high visibility, skewed rewards systems and short-term orientation. Sometimes these challenges can, in fact, facilitate entrepreneurial behavior.

There are three aspects of overcoming the challenges of establishing public sector entrepreneurship in any governmental organization. First, there is a need to establish a vision reflected in the mission statement of the organization that delineates clear unambiguous goals and encourages independent thinking and autonomy. This helps eliminate the confusion resulting from non-prioritized multiple goals and directions from politicians and government bureaucrats. This, coupled with the autonomy to act, provides the landscape for governmental entrepreneurship to occur. Government entrepreneurs need to feel empowered to think creatively and do their job as efficiently and effectively as possible.

Second, since it is necessary to invest in both long-term and short-term projects, an appropriate reward system needs to be established. The reward system should be a combination of economic and non-economic rewards that compensates innovative thinking and actions. This should help minimize fear of failure and its repercussions. Particularly important is to reward success along the way in long-term projects and programs even when the originators are no longer involved.

Finally, the success of the government entrepreneurship needs to be communicated both internally and externally. Internally through the social media, organization newsletter and special events, the success of the government entrepreneurship should be celebrated. This celebration should continue with the external media by skillfully managing the relations with the press. This involves frequent meetings, press releases and openness avoiding the usual smoke-and-mirrors approach. Employing each of these can help overcome the challenges allowing government entrepreneurship to occur.

Clearly, governmental entrepreneurial structures need to support the discovery and address opportunities in innovative ways. Gore's report on the National Performance Review (1993) suggests four principles of entrepreneurship for the government:

1. reduction of red tape;
2. promotion of customer satisfaction;
3. empowerment of employees; and,
4. promotion of cost efficient performance.

Keeping a simple, short, principles-based, reform-oriented focus may be the most beneficial way that one can bring about entrepreneurship in government. In 1998, the National Performance Review listed accomplishments including:[15]

  - Reduction of red tape: The elimination of 16 000 pages of regulations by working in voluntary partnership. The National Performance Review noted that, at the EPA, their efforts 'eliminated 7.8 million tons of solid waste; prevented the release of 80 million metric tons of carbon dioxide; and saved nearly 1.8 billion gallons of clean water. And, through their voluntary efforts, EPA's partners also saved lots of money – $3.3 billion.'

- Promotion of customer satisfaction: Published more than 4000 customer service standards for more than 570 organizations and programs.
- Empowerment of employees: The introduction of 'Hammer Awards' designed to recognize 'significant contributions in support of reinventing government principles' by employees such as Judith Spencer who built a secure electronic system by partnering with commercial suppliers to renegotiate the Federal Telephone Contract (FTS-2001) without paper and saved $1.5 million dollars.
- Promotion of cost efficient performance: Saving nearly $200 billion through legislative or administrative action by streamlining bureaucracy, reinventing federal procurement, reengineering through the use of information technology, reducing intergovernmental administrative costs and changes to individual agencies.

Since conflict can exist between public entrepreneurship and policy and regulations, socially oriented entrepreneurship emphasizing public participation provides a solution by offering a program of action that makes these more compatible. An environment needs to be established in the government organization that allows government entrepreneurs to be found and encouraged to operate.

Morris and Jones[16] suggest that a successful public sector entrepreneur has several characteristics:

- a mix of power and achievement motivation;
- an ability to work strategically;
- beginning with small steps;
- strong political and external networking skills;
- calculated risk taking;
- self-confidence; and,
- an ability to tolerate and use ambiguity as a source of discretion.

PUBLIC SECTOR ENTREPRENEURSHIP AND GOVERNMENT STRUCTURE

Bureaucracy, a classical organization of government, is a formal organizational structure characterized by division of labor; hierarchy and position based on expertise. In a highly formalized system, there is less flexibility in how individuals can behave within the system.

Excessive formalization along with rules, regulations and procedures result in bureaucratic behavior. Formalization may detract from organizational performance as it inhibits adaptability, open communication and rapid response. These bureaucratic characteristics inhibit an organization's ability to foster entrepreneurship. The higher the level of bureaucratization, the greater the potential conflict with entrepreneurship. Bureaucracy generally results in more formal procedures and less flexibility and risk-taking. It usually has a lack of rewards or incentives for successful innovations and significant penalties for violation of established procedures.

Implementing an appropriate organizational structure is needed for establishing an entrepreneurial culture. The organizational structure also provides the administrative mechanisms by which ideas are evaluated, chosen and implemented. A public sector entrepreneurial posture can struggle or flourish depending on the particular organizational structure. Khandwalla[17] states that, 'Wherever there is a strong [entrepreneurial] orientation there ought to be an organic orientation. Risk taking managements often seize opportunities and make commitments of resources before fully understanding what actions need to be taken. Unless management is flexible, the organization will not be able to adapt itself to the evolving situation.' Slevin and Covin[18] found that the combination of entrepreneurial postures and organic structures are associated with higher performance than the combination of entrepreneurial postures and mechanistic structures. There is a strong relationship between an organization's entrepreneurial capacity and structural formality, structural differentiation and decentralization, control mechanisms and the number of layers in the organizational hierarchy.

Public sector managers usually have less freedom to react and have the burden of hierarchy (rules and red tape) without the freedom and power to manage their subordinates. Minimal hierarchy is often viewed as a structural attribute of entrepreneurship. For entrepreneurship to occur in the public sector there is a need for greater flexibility and adaptability as high levels of rigidity and red tape prohibit the development of an entrepreneurial culture.

Flexibility can be mandated in a top-down environment, but our research suggests a more organic approach by creating an environment where new business can develop as the example with the Government of Malta will illustrate. The World Economic Forum's Global Competitiveness Report 2010–11 ranks Malta 11th out of 139 countries for 'financial market development', two years earlier it was in 34th position. The rate of FDI flow may have played a big part in Malta's rapid rise in global competitiveness. In an interview with The Banker, Kenneth Farrugia, chairman of FinanceMalta, which promotes Malta as an international financial center, noted that FDI at the end of June 2010 was EU11.9 billion, which was nearly double from the previous year.[19] One of the biggest sources of FDI has been the aviation industry. In April 2010, Prime Minister Lawrence Gonzi spoke at the Abu Dhabi Chamber of Commerce and noted that, 'SR Technics, a leading global provider of aircraft maintenance, repair and overhaul services and part of Mubadala Group, chose Malta over 53 other locations to build its new maintenance facility. A key factor in this choice was the ready availability of a competitive and highly skilled workforce.' James Stewart, the CEO of SR Technics, would add that, 'We looked at the country's political stability, and we looked at the economic stability . . . The training facilities we saw there are probably the best we've seen in terms of hands on skills . . . When you put everything together it was clear that Malta had the right balance.' Flexibility is important and so is creating an environment of certainty. While Stewart acknowledged that 'although Malta doesn't have the lowest cost of some of the places the company looked at, such as those in Eastern Europe or on the fringe of Europe, the long term prospects were good'.[20] The FDI contract, a $40 million project that will create 350 new jobs in its initial phase, was negotiated in 6 months in part to the Minister of Finance, Economy and Investment, Tonio Fenech, and his admission that it 'would not have been possible without the government's flexibility and quick responsiveness when comes to making decisions to support foreign investment'.[21] Michael Bonello, the governor of the Central Bank of Malta, would add another reason for the success of his country's ability to attract FDI. In an interview with The Banker, Bonello noted, 'Close cooperation between industry and academia has been an important factor behind the strong FDI inflows. Sectors where such cooperation has produced particularly good results include the insurance, pharmaceutical and aircraft maintenance industries.'[22]

PUBLIC SECTOR TRANSFORMATION TOWARDS ENTREPRENEURSHIP

The following are several ways a public sector organization can transform itself into a more entrepreneurial organization:

- Competitive strategy: Develop a competitive strategy that brings about greater levels of competition and incentives to increase efficiency and effectiveness, utilization of resources, more constituency orientation, encourage entrepreneurship and enhance employee motivation and morale. This competitive strategy can be intensified through Public–Private Partnership Agreements discussed later in this book.

- Structure/formalization: Reduce the bureaucracy and formalization by developing a decentralized structure and decision-making process, delegating authority and autonomy, and encouraging and rewarding innovative behavior at all levels.
- Goals and objectives: Establish clearly defined goals and objectives. Identify the desired outcomes in relation to the actual outcome and evaluate any deviation between them, taking corrective action in a timely manner.
- Constituency orientation: Focus on the needs, wants and expectations of a diverse group of constituencies and develop a business model to provide customer satisfaction, with a focus on resource utilization and value creation. Monitor and evaluate constituency satisfaction to improve efficiency and quality of service.
- Budgets/spending: Monitor and control the spending of public finances in ways that are innovative and can be defined in terms of constituency and the generation of innovation, wealth and prosperity for the country.
- Long-term orientation: Develop a long-term approach, anticipating potential problems and developing alternative strategies and contingency plans for the future.
- Partnership agreements: Work with the private sector to develop public and private sector partnership agreements and develop more creative solutions to problems and utilization of resources.

Public sector entrepreneurship provides a more flexible, dynamic, innovative and creative approach to meeting the needs of the public. How this can be accomplished is discussed in the remainder of this book and in case studies at the end.

NOTES

1. Robert D. Hisrich, Michael P. Peters and Dean A. Shepherd, *Entrepreneurship*, 10th edn. (Chicago, IL: McGraw-Hill/Irwin, 2010).
2. Robert D. Hisrich and Claudine Kearney, *Corporate Entrepreneurship* (New York: McGraw-Hill, 2012).
3. Peter F. Drucker, *Innovation and Entrepreneurship: Practice and Principles* (London: Butterworth-Heinemann, 1985).

4. Organisation for Economic Co-operation and Development (OECD), *Governance in Transition: Public Management Reforms in OECD Countries*, (Paris: OECD, 1995) and Organisation for Economic Co-operation and Development (OECD), *Ministerial Symposium on the Future of Public Services*, (Paris: OECD, 1996).
5. Claudine R. Kearney, Robert D. Hisrich and Frank Roche, 'Facilitating public sector corporate entrepreneurship process: a conceptual model', *Journal of Enterprising Culture* (2007b), **15** (3), 282–283.
6. Barry Bozeman and Gordon Kingsley, 'Risk culture in public and private organizations', *Public Administration Review* (1998), **58**, 110.
7. Claudine R. Kearney, Robert D. Hisrich and Frank Roche, 'Facilitating public sector corporate entrepreneurship process: a conceptual model', *Journal of Enterprising Culture* (2007b), **15** (3), 283.
8. http://pennpoliticalreview.org/2011/03/qa-with-newt-gingrich/.
9. Newt Gingrich, Transcript of address to the nation on 7 April 1995.
10. Newt Gingrich, Transcript of address to the nation on 7 April 1995.
11. http://www.cato.org/pub_display.php?pub_id=8831.
12. http://news.xinhuanet.com/english/2009-05/18/content_11395609.htm.
13. http://www.wired.com/wired/archive/14.07/chinarail. html?pg=1&topic=chinarail&topic _set=.
14. Stewart Liff, *Managing Government Employees* (New York: Amacom Press, 2007), p. 124.
15. http://govinfo.library.unt.edu/npr/accompli/index.html.
16. Michael H. Morris and Foard F. Jones, 'Entrepreneurship in established organizations: the case of the public sector', *Entrepreneurship Theory and Practice* (Fall 1999), 71–91.
17. Pradip N. Khandwalla, *The Design of Organizations* (New York: Harcourt Bruce Jovanovich, 1977), p. 426.
18. Dennis P. Slevin and Jeffrey G. Covin, 'Juggling entrepreneurial style and organizational structure: how to get your act together', *Sloan Management Review* (Winter 1990), 43–53.
19. Michael Imeson, 'Malta's success story', *The Banker*, 1 April 2011, 55–56.
20. http://www.timesofmalta.com/articles/view/20100218/business/sr-technics-malta-is-the -right-place-to-be-ceo-says.294557.
21. https://opm.gov.mt/srt_invtf?l=2
22. 'Malta: a European financial hub', *The Banker* (Special Report: 31 March 2010).

BIBLIOGRAPHY

Bozeman, Barry and Gordon Kingsley (1998), 'Risk culture in public and private organizations', *Public Administration Review*, **58**, 109–118.

Drucker, Peter F. (1985), *Innovation and Entrepreneurship: Practice and Principles*, London: Butterworth-Heinemann.

Gore Jr., Albert (1993), *From Red Tape to Results: Creating a Government that Works Better and Costs Less*, Washington DC: Government Printing Office.

Hisrich, Robert D., Michael P. Peters and Dean A. Shepherd (2010), *Entrepreneurship*, 10th edn., Chicago: McGraw-Hill/Irwin.

Hisrich, Robert D. and Claudine Kearney (2012), *Corporate Entrepreneurship*, New York: McGraw-Hill.

Kearney, Claudine, Robert D. Hisrich and Frank Roche (2007a), 'A conceptual model of public sector corporate entrepreneurship', *International Entrepreneurship and Management Journal*, **4** (3), 295–313.

Kearney, Claudine, Robert D. Hisrich and Frank Roche (2007b), 'Facilitating public sector corporate entrepreneurship process: a conceptual model', *Journal of Enterprising Culture*, **15** (3), 275–299.

Khandwalla, Pradip N. (1977), *The Design of Organizations*, New York: Harcourt Bruce Jovanovich.

Morris, Michael H. and Foard F. Jones (1999), 'Entrepreneurship in established organizations: the case of the public sector', *Entrepreneurship Theory and Practice*, Fall, 71–91.

Organisation for Economic Co-operation and Development (OECD) (1995), *Governance in Transition: Public Management Reforms in OECD Countries*, Paris: OECD.

Organisation for Economic Co-operation and Development (OECD) (1996), Ministerial Symposium on the Future of Public Services, Paris: OECD.

Slevin, Dennis P. and Jeffrey G. Covin (1990), 'Juggling entrepreneurial style and organizational structure: how to get your act together', *Sloan Management Review*, Winter, 43–53.

2. The government entrepreneur

CHAPTER OBJECTIVES

- To understand the need for government entrepreneurship.
- To understand the unique dynamic created in the government for entrepreneurship.
- To understand the need for and problems in government innovation.
- To understand the specific challenges faced by government entrepreneurs.
- To explain the types of roles critical for government entrepreneurship.
- To understand the qualities and behaviors of a successful government entrepreneur.

INTRODUCTION

In the past, the government had a significant advantage over the private sector in the market for public services offered. For example, in the United States, large government programs such as the Social Security Administration (SSA) or the Centers for Disease Control and Prevention (CDC) are examples of successful initiatives that brought together the right mix of departments and talent to serve public needs.

With the passing of time, the structure of society has changed, and governments are now facing a much more competitive arena for tax revenue than ever before. This has forced governments to reevaluate and consider other tactics. Government entrepreneurship is one way for governments to innovate and reinvent themselves.

One of the factors for success is the perception of whether a new concept will work. Government entrepreneurship is ready for this discussion and there are arguments for both sides. One argument holds that entrepreneurship is the solution to the inefficiencies common to the public sector, a way of making it more 'businesslike'; this position also assumes a positive outcome from entrepreneurial efforts. The opposite argument is that the conflicts are too great, that typical entrepreneurial behaviors cannot adjust to the bureaucratic norms of the public sector; it also argues that the image of the entrepreneur is that of a rogue, one who takes on an outsider's view. This is difficult for an internal staff to do yet is necessary to create innovative approaches to existing problems. As Llewellyn et al. (2000, pp. 163–171) found in their research, 'If you even mention the word entrepreneurship people tend to associate it to business and then are re-active in thinking the public service ethos and entrepreneurship don't go hand-in-hand.' The system will have to consider this perception if it attempts to employ corporate entrepreneurship.

Despite careful attention to try to differentiate itself, in this sense, the public sector must look to the private sector as a model. Innovation is a key – and necessary – way of life for the private sector. However, as highlighted in Chapter 1, the public sector is a unique entity, and the administration and the government entrepreneurs must decide issues of structure and ways of working together in order to create a model for public sector entrepreneurship that is just as unique as the entity itself.

This chapter highlights the need for government entrepreneurship and helps explain the unique dynamic created in the public sector for it. Several types of challenges facing entrepreneurs and other stakeholders in this space are presented, and two types of roles that can lead to success are explained. This chapter concludes with a look at the characteristics of an entrepreneur that can be success factors for working in the public sector.

THE DYNAMICS OF PUBLIC SECTOR ENTREPRENEURSHIP

In most people's minds, the public and private sectors are vastly different entities and in many ways, this is true. Yet the people who work within these worlds are not always set in that one particular mold. Whether a person becomes an entrepreneur because he/she is 'born' that way (the elusively defined 'entrepreneurial spirit') or because he/she is trained as an entrepreneur (more and more entrepreneurship programs are popping up by demand, for all ages all over the world (Arthur et al., 2011), he/she is going to bring that approach to her work regardless of the context. Whether he/she is allowed to succeed depends greatly on how well a synergistic system for operating can be established. As seen in Chapter 1, the challenges within the public sector make this more difficult, but it is a challenge that can be dealt with. Understanding how entrepreneurship works in the private sector and understanding how to adjust to the unique qualities of the public sector will be necessary for the government entrepreneur.

Many of the challenges found within the internal environment (Internal Pillar outlined in Chapter 1) can be categorized as what most people would call 'bureaucracy'. Although this system does provide certain advantages (e.g. a clearly constructed, objective compensation schedule), most bureaucratic elements are viewed negatively. These are also perceived as barriers to success for government entrepreneurs.

In addition to the considerable Internal Pillar challenges, there are those in the external environment (pillar) as well, which also have an impact on the government entrepreneur. For example, the government as an entity established to serve the public can easily find itself at odds as to which segments of the public are going to be served at a given time. It may even face paralysis regarding making strategic choices out of fear of having them 'considered as discrimination'. These choices may be in direct conflict with what the government entrepreneur believes is important or attainable at any given time.

Even if decisions are made – despite agreed upon satisfaction levels between decision maker and government entrepreneur – maintaining the right client relationships can also be a challenge. In the private sector, relationships are built based on mutual incentives and gains; however, public sector services are traditionally heavy handed, not necessarily designed according to specific client-oriented needs. The hope would be, though, that as public sectors continue to operate in a more competitive space, there would also be a shift to a more client-oriented framework, one in which the government entrepreneur could play a significant role because of the interpersonal skills and focus that he/she brings to the institution.

The reality is that the public sector system of operating at the macro level is not going to change drastically. It has been designed as such for particular reasons (e.g. legal mandates), and changes made at the macro level are very difficult and time-consuming.

The dynamic that this rigid system creates for the government entrepreneur is a contradictory one: the same space is being occupied by both risk-taking and risk-adverse entities. It also puts the government entrepreneur in an awkward position: he/she is torn between the political institution that pays his/her salary and the clients (the public community) served by that institution's programs/ventures.

So what can be done to remedy this challenging situation? Changing the public sector environment as a whole into one that looks like the private sector is not going to work. Nor, should it necessarily be the goal. Peirce and Kruger (1993, pp. 52–70) point out that bureaucracy is

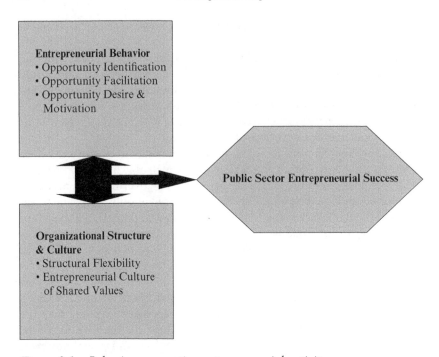

Figure 2.1   Behaviors promoting entrepreneurial activity

also common in large, private companies and the subsequent challenges exist for entrepreneurs in that space as well. Most researchers point out that role specificity is important. Two main types of management roles should be considered: one to serve a program manager function (likely, the government entrepreneur) and one responsible for managing the administration's policies and bureaucracy. Striking a balance between the managerial roles that are necessary for the system to function is essential for dealing with this unique dynamic. Admittedly, though, this balance is often hard to create and maintain and will take a commitment from everyone involved.

Three main elements of entrepreneurial behavior in a government, indicated in Figure 2.1, are opportunity identification, opportunity facilitation and opportunity desire and motivation.

Opportunity Identification

The first element, opportunity identification, is the awareness of conditions that need to change for the organization and individual managers to be able to develop something new and entrepreneurial. Opportunity identification involves having unconstrained relationships and networks, being well informed and having access to acquired information, having the necessary resources to make decisions and achieve desirable outcomes. In an entrepreneurial-driven government organization, individuals throughout the government organization not only believe they should but also are encouraged and permitted to: associate with key people, network both formally and informally inside and outside the organization, have access to information and can freely identify entrepreneurial opportunities.

Opportunity Facilitation

The second element, opportunity facilitation, is the way the government organization and the individual managers seek to adopt change. The two approaches to initiate change are challenging – questioning the assumptions and directions of the government organization and having managers as coaches rather than authority figures. When employees in the governmental organization not only believe they should but also are encouraged to freely and supportively challenge any other employees in the organization and respect each other noting areas of specialization not authority, they can undertake tasks necessary to facilitate opportunities within the organization. While opportunity facilitating is only possible if opportunities have first been identified, it does not necessarily achieve desirable outcomes unless there is appropriate rewards/motivation.

Opportunity Desire and Motivation

The third element, opportunity desire and motivation, involves the overall willingness to change and locus of desire and motivation to pursue opportunity. Perry (1996, pp. 5–22) defined public sector motivation as 'an individual's predisposition to respond to motives grounded primarily or uniquely in public institutions and organizations'. Efforts to enhance the performance of governmental organizations partly depend on the ability to successfully reward/motivate public sector employees.

Entrepreneurially orientated motivation usually relies on some form of compensation for results. Compensation in governmental organizations usually takes the form of intrinsic versus extrinsic rewards. Being able to identify and facilitate opportunities, having the desire and motivation to pursue them and being rewarded for so doing establishes an entrepreneurial climate in a governmental organization.

GOVERNMENT INNOVATION

Innovation indicates the presence or absence of entrepreneurship in a government organization. Innovation is a key part of the entrepreneurial process whereby new ideas are put into practice. Schumpeter identified innovation in fast-changing environments as the essence of entrepreneurial behavior, stating that:

> We call entrepreneurs not only those 'independent' businessmen in an exchange economy who are usually so designated, but all who actually perform the function by which we define the concept, even if they are 'dependent' employees of the company, like managers, members of boards of directors and so forth . . . On the other hand, our concept is narrower than the traditional one in that it does not include all heads of firms, managers or industrialists who may operate an established business, but only those who actually perform the function.

There are generally five types of innovation: developing new products and services, developing new methods of production, identifying new markets, discovering new sources of supply and developing new organizational forms.

Innovation can be identified as creating something 'new'. It can be a sequence of activities that introduce a change in a social unit with the objective of benefiting the unit or the wider society. Government innovation is a political process that activates organizations to launch a significant new public project that changes rules, procedures and structures that are related to the communication and exchange of information within the organization and between the organization and its external stakeholders. While these projects do not require the invention of something entirely 'new', they often require that the public government organization redesign the processes through which it serves its clients.

An example of government process design can be found in the ways in which motor vehicle registration centers have changed over the last 10 years to institute operational efficiency by segregating complexity to ensure that customers wait in line for a specialist that can best serve their needs. One such example can be found in the state of Rhode Island. In 2010, the state opened a new three-story Department of Motor Vehicle (DMV) building in the city of Cranston with each floor dedicated to specific operations and administrative functions, allowing for more efficient operations and better customer service. A press release announcing the opening noted that, 'The first floor is home to Operator Control, the Disability Placard Office, the Plate Office, the Accidents Office, an ATM machine and a café operated by the Services for the Blind. The second floor is dedicated to all license and registration transactions, as well as a separate area for written exams and includes an ATM machine. The third floor contains automobile dealer and commercial driver license transactions, as well as the title research office. Administrative offices are located on all three floors.'[1]

Innovation is perhaps the most pressing challenge facing governments today. Drucker stated, 'innovation is the specific function of entrepreneurship . . . it is the means by which the entrepreneur either creates new wealth producing resources or endows existing resources with enhanced potential for creating wealth'. Essentially, innovation is the effort to create purposeful, focused change in the economic and social environments.

Kanter (1988, pp. 169–211) outlined four major innovation tasks which correspond to the innovation process as it unfolds over time:

1. Idea generation and activation of the drivers of the innovation.
2. Coalition building and acquisition of the power necessary to move the idea into reality.
3. Idea realization and innovation production turning the idea into a model – a product or plan or prototype that can be used.
4. Transfer or diffusion – the commercialization of the product, the adoption of the idea.

Government entrepreneurship can only occur in an organization that encourages and supports innovation. There are several ways to facilitate innovation in a government organization:

- Ensure resources are available for innovation.
- Open communication occurs at all levels throughout the organization.
- Decentralized structures are in place to provide open access to innovation role models and coaches.
- Cohesive work groups are operant with open constructive conflict resolution approaches that integrate and develop individual creativity.
- Low staff turnover occurs.
- Personnel policies are instituted that reward and motivate innovative behavior.
- Effective mechanisms are developed to deal with environmental uncertainty and the ability to adapt change.

Innovation in government generally has not been thought of as a critical aspect of growth and development. Generally, the government is

recognized as being a more complex open system, an impediment to innovation. The media's and opposition parties' interest in exposing public
sector failures is also an impediment to innovation as is the fact that their
policy environment is filled with uncertainty. The need for risk taking and
experimenting by allowing flexibility and accepting potential failure can
be in conflict with the traditional values such as due process and accountability. In comparison to private sector managers, government managers
report lower organizational commitment, lower satisfaction of work
needs and lower job satisfaction. This reflects to some extent the inflex-
ibility of personnel policies and procedures, and the weak link between
performance and rewards. The incentive and motivation to be innovative
in the government has been low and the associated risk is high due to
public scrutiny.

BARRIERS TO PUBLIC SECTOR INNOVATIONS

A number of key barriers to innovation that are particularly prevalent in
the government have been identified by Mulgan and Albury (2003). These
include:

- Delivery pressures and administrative burdens: limited time to
  dedicate to thinking due to election cycles about how to do things
  differently or innovation in delivery service that might be more time
  and cost effective.
- Short-term budgets and planning horizons: inability to think outside
  of day-to-day pressures on how things could be improved is
  exacerbated by short-term budget and planning horizons.
- Poor rewards and incentives to innovate: the tradition of higher
  penalties for failed innovations than rewards for successful ones
  remains within the civil service.
- Culture of risk aversion: the primary concerns of accountability,
  standards and continuity induce a culture of risk aversion which
  impedes and blocks.
- Poor skills in active risk or change management: while opportunity
  and motivation may be present, there is a relative paucity of skills in
  change and risk management.
- Reluctance to close down failing programs or organizations: it is
  extremely unlikely that public sector organizations will cease to exist
  as a consequence of not being innovative.
- Technologies available but constraining cultural or organizational arrangements: innovation is often impeded because there

is a resistance to embedded innovation within the organizational fabric.

CHALLENGES FOR THE GOVERNMENT ENTREPRENEUR

The government – with its reporting systems, fiduciary responsibilities and other bureaucratic functions – by nature of its entity creates challenges for a government entrepreneur. A few overarching areas in which challenge occur are the following:

- Time: When asked about the effectiveness of government, people will often express sentiments such as 'nothing ever gets done'. The highly complex procedures required are time-consuming, especially for larger, macro-level initiatives. However, as any entrepreneur knows, opportunity costs can be high in business. In the services industries, especially, delays can be costly, both financially and from a human-need perspective. It is even possible that losing time when serving public needs can create new problems. For public sectors serving the public through its programs and ventures, this can be detrimental on many levels – not the least of which is public perception of its priorities and capabilities.
- Analysis: In government agencies, everything needs to be analyzed and quantified; fiduciary responsibilities and complex legal regulations tie the public sector's hands and are uncompromisable. In the United States, the need for analysis can often slow good legislation down from being swiftly enacted and create division among political parties who disagree on the conclusions of the analysis. For example, in Washington DC there are two agencies which play sometimes dueling roles in analyzing the budgetary impact of new legislation, the Congressional Budget Office (CBO) and the Office of Management and Budget (OMB). In February 2011, the OMB and CBO both had a chance to analyze President Obama's budget and disagreed by $1.7 trillion dollars on the impact on the US economy.[2] Yet for a government entrepreneur, this becomes a challenge because not everything that is important for the job is easily quantifiable. Managing these requirements and finding a means of quantifying qualitative information takes time away from program creation and management, which is the strength of the entrepreneur and which is necessary for a successful venture – in either the private or public sectors.

- Risk: The government – whether made up of publicly elected officials or inherited through family lineage – has a responsibility to use public-sector money carefully and with discretion. This necessarily makes the administration more risk-adverse because the number and weight of the stakeholders is so great. The importance of this to the public sector is understandable, yet at the same time, it can significantly limit the risk allowed the government entrepreneur. Understanding where entrepreneurship fits into the system is important because involved in that should be a discussion of what types and level of risks are acceptable and how this balances with accountability (Llewellyn et al., 2000).
- Corruption: Despite the numerous anti-corruption policies and oversight agencies that exist on the international stage, government entrepreneurs may still be faced with corruption or unethical business practices, from within their own organization/public sector or within a potential project partner's. As the anti-corruption and transparency in business movement gains strength, corruption will become less and less of a major issue; however, change happens slowly, so a successful entrepreneur should be prepared for this.

Some specific challenges faced by entrepreneurs in the public sector are outlined from Morris and Jones (1999) in Table 2.1.

Llewellyn et al. argue that 'bureaucratic and entrepreneurial tendencies coexist' just as much in the public sector as the private and that there is always an 'uneasy balance' in its practice. Several of the obstacles – such as red tape, limited rewards, limited autonomy and interference from politicians – are ones that can likely be worked out through the right balance between the program manager and the administrative manager. The authors also suggest that taking the time to determine what function these roles play is important for each public sector institution. A cookie-cutter approach is not likely to work, so each organization must determine for itself 'the function of enterprise as the vital motor for change, growth, and innovation' (Llewellyn et al., 2000).

Another consideration important for the government entrepreneur is the environment in which he/she works, particularly the directives that come down. In the political system, this is especially important and can change greatly over time. As mentioned, the government leaders are elected by the public; therefore, their incentives may change depending on the election cycle and, thus, their appetite for entrepreneurial activity will change or serve different purposes. Eusepi and Wilson (2008, pp. 39–54) explain this phenomenon through differentiating what they call 'long-chain' and 'short-chain' models.

Table 2.1   Developing entrepreneurial behavior in the government

Opportunity Identification ● Active ● Time Frame ● Key Focus	Organizational Competencies ● Active search for dynamism ● Long term orientation ● Structural and cultural changes for entrepreneurial success Individual Competencies ● Active drive and motivation ● Future orientation ● Transformation from past behavior
Opportunity Facilitation ● Structure ● Human Resources ● Leadership	Organizational Competencies ● Concise, defined structural change ● Effective human resource policies for change, recruitment, motivation, training and development ● Environmental scanning Individual Competencies ● Adaptation to embrace change ● Excelled drive and motivation ● Moderate level of risking taking with the focus on innovative opportunities to do better
Opportunity Desire and Motivation ● Motivation and Desire to Change ● Drive to Achieve ● Intrinsic and Extrinsic Motivation	Organizational Competencies ● Drive to change ● Long term strategy to change ● Focused and goal orientated Individual Competencies ● Individual desire to change ● Overcome past concerns ● Focused and motivated to achieve

Source: Morris, Michael H. and Foard F. Jones (1999), 'Entrepreneurship in established organizations: the case of the public sector', *Entrepreneurship Theory and Practice*, **24** (1), 71–90.

In the long-chain model, the view toward innovation becomes somewhat negative. The politician is incentivized to maintain the status quo rather than creating great changes. He has been elected and the risks to him of failing at new ventures become greater in his mind than the rewards that could possibly come from innovation. In this model, Eusepi and Wilson suggest that innovation may only be encouraged if 'he/she sees external shocks coming'. They explain this through the dichotomy between political and economic goals and posit that this creates what can be called a 'political dis-entrepreneur'.

Conversely, the 'short chain' is the model of thinking which can be seen to come as an election cycle approaches, in which maintaining the status quo may lose importance over the need to show progress and profit. This position champions the more traditional entrepreneurial model (Schumpeter's famous 'creative destruction' model) that supports innovation and even profit-generation. For the government entrepreneur – the program manager and advocate – the models in these cycles have direct impact on his/her work; therefore, understanding these political motivations and knowing how to adjust to them is important.

Entrepreneurship in the public forum can establish itself in two different ways: from top down or from bottom up (Peirce and Kruger, 1993, pp. 52–70). This means that the ideas for projects can come from someone higher in the hierarchy or from the government entrepreneur. If from the former, the government entrepreneur has to be flexible to any underlying objectives for the assignment. He/she will need to create his/her own autonomy for managing the project since it is likely going to contain constraints in many forms (Peirce and Kruger, 1993). Throughout history, there are many examples of entrepreneurs who were placed in positions with decision-making power (e.g. Mary E. Switzer [US, mid-twentieth century] or Friedrich Althoff [Germany/Prussia, early twentieth century]). For entrepreneurs such as these, having both autonomy and control over the resources is much easier. For others, this is harder and skills in negotiation and influencing are necessary.

Ideas can also come from the government entrepreneur. Some argue that this method will not work because in a bureaucratic system, it is much harder to push something up the hierarchy than it is to have it be pushed down. Additionally, in government entrepreneurship, limitations dictate that the venture fit clearly and transparently into the larger goals of the system; for a government entrepreneur who is not in an upper position in the hierarchy, he/she probably will not know enough about the overall system to be able to make this judgment. A successful government entrepreneur must either integrate into the system sufficiently to contribute directly or be flexible to the tasks assigned and able to work with the inherent constraints.

TWO SIGNIFICANT ROLES IN GOVERNMENT ENTREPRENEURSHIP

The program manager and the administrative manager roles may change in nomenclature, but the essence of the roles is important. The mindset of each is aligned with the function played within the organization.

Program Manager

The program manager is the government entrepreneur who is the primary advocate for the initiative. The impetus is to get things done. Action is of upmost importance, without much time spent questioning. As Ferman and Levin (1987, pp. 187–199) note, 'Contemplation . . . is secondary to action'. The program advocate is the one who is going to push the project forward; inaction, procedural delays and too much questioning can compromise the forward momentum, and the success of the project as a whole.

Administrative Manager

The administrative manager role can be filled by many different people within an organization, as long as the person has influence or responsibility for policy making itself or ensuring that the goals and regulatory provisions of the institution are not compromised. This role has the big-picture view of the public sector in mind and must weigh the work of the program manager against the whole: Does it fit in? Where? How?

Ferman and Levin argue that although a balance between these roles must exist, the role that the administrative manager represents must dominate, the entrepreneurial venture must align and further the larger goals of the administration in the end. Thus, it is somewhat of a false balance. The balance becomes more of a synergistic effort, with each role clear in its position and responsibility, and having a strong communication method in place with the other. Establishing this relationship is critical from the beginning because as the program is developed and more constituents, external partners and clients are included, the entrepreneurial venture gets much more complex and hard to manage and control. The potential failures are hard enough to manage in the private sector, but in government, the stakes are usually much higher.

Because the governmental system has so many restrictions that are inflexible, the administrative manager plays a significant role in massaging the system so that it will be open to innovation and flexibility as much as is possible.

Having a strong leader and a good planning system are considered relevant characteristics of an entrepreneurial organization. A successful administrative manager, will work closely with the government entrepreneur to support his/her work to positively affect the overall goals of the institution. Since the limitations placed on this role challenge the government entrepreneur in ways unlike that faced by private sector entrepreneurs, what factors can help make a government entrepreneur successful?

CHARACTERISTICS OF A GOVERNMENT ENTREPRENEUR

The nature of the external environment within which public sector agencies often work can lend itself well to governmental entrepreneurial efforts. Turbulence and crises create the need for action that can be served well by those well equipped to handle them and to create appropriate, innovative solutions. Those individuals who can identify these external moments and can work with the institution to create an effective solution will be the most successful.

Morris and Jones (1999, pp. 80–85) describe the successful government entrepreneur in seven dimensions:

1. Primary motive: power motivated and achievement motivated; may think in grandiose terms; not constrained by profit motive.
2. Time orientation: end goals of 10–15 years; begins with impressive short-term success, then implements long-term plan as series of short-term programs.
3. Skills: strong political skills; able to develop power sources beyond those formally assigned; adept at using public relations and the media to advantage.
4. Attitude toward system: tends to redesign or restructure the system to accomplish his/her own ends.
5. Focus: learns to co-opt or use external forces to accomplish internal change; builds constituencies of support among politicians, unions, the private sector, the media and the community.
6. Risks and failure: calculated risk-taker; takes big organizational risks without taking big personal risks by managing the process by which risky decisions are made; tends to deviate from rules only slightly at first, then progressively more; since failure is harder to define, will manage events to promote positive outcomes.

7. Courage and destiny: self-confident, optimistic, bold; high tolerance for ambiguity; uses ambiguity as a source of managerial discretion.

Similarly, Ferman and Levin also highlight five characteristics and behaviors of successful government entrepreneurs. First, good government entrepreneurs have the interpersonal skills necessary to build coalitions. They can seek out the constituencies needed for the creation and approval of the initiatives . . . and can influence them to become willing partners in the effort. The time taken in this process is well worth it because there will be time when their help is needed either to move the program forward or to defend it to naysayers along the way.

Second, all entrepreneurs have fortitude in the face of adversity, but this characteristic is particularly important for government entrepreneurs because of the extra constraints inherent in the government. The authors reference Albert Hirschmann's 'Hiding Hand' strategy for economic development in which he urged executives to 'willfully ignore the limitations at hand and extend their reach beyond constraints'.

One significantly challenging situation confronting a government entrepreneur may be corruption. Corruption and anti-ethical behavior comes in many forms. In the case of bureaucrats, however, corruptive behavior is often found in the three areas over which they have control: administrative procedures, regulation of business activity and rule making. An action guide produced by the Russian Organization for Small and Medium Entrepreneurship (OPORA) and the Russian Information Science for Democracy (INDEM) suggests that businesses should be aware of ways in which public sector officials may try to derail their work through audits of business conduct, administrative issues such as permits and biased rule making that creates barriers to success. Being familiar with the anti-corruption policies in the countries in which one is working, with the specific businesses that have reputations for ethical/unethical practices, and with the resources available (globally, regionally and locally) to report and combat corruptive practices is good risk management practice for any government entrepreneur.

Third, it is important to know how to deal with limitations. Having the flexibility to work with the restraints of the public entity is important. These restraints can take different forms, including those connected with budget or decision making for underlying and contradictory political reasons. The government entrepreneur needs to remember that public opinion matters very much in this space, and sometimes this can lead to conflicts between what the best big-picture decision is and what the best immediate decision is.

Another type of restraint is one imposed by the particular program itself. As Mary E. Switzer, a well-known entrepreneur who worked within the federal bureaucracy, found during her last job as Commissioner of Social and Rehabilitation Services, an approach for solving problems in one program may not work well in the context of another (Berkowitz, 1980, pp. 79–81). The needs of each venture, the particular role entrepreneurship will fill and the methods for addressing the needs are all important.

One of the tactics in which successful government entrepreneurs have gotten around limitations such as this is to understand how to plan small, quantifiable programs that have a quick turnaround for showing success. Nowhere is this more important and evident than in government disaster relief programs, which directly affect the lives of people in times of significant stress and basic human needs. In the aftermath of the Hurricane Katrina disaster, public opinion polls captured Americans' disapproval of President Bush's poor handling of the disaster relief. The President's approval ratings dipped below 40 percent in a poll released by the Associated Press.[3] Compare this with a Newsweek poll released shortly after the 9/11 terrorist attacks which, despite the tragedy, many have commented was an orderly disaster relief response. In the aftermath of the 9/11 attacks, 89 percent of Americans approved of the Bush's handling of the crisis.[4]

Having small, quantifiable programs are important because all the key stakeholders need to see the benefits to the venture quickly and in ways they can understand and support – whether they are voting members of the community or influential members of the media. Having this, the government entrepreneur can then scale up the program, if necessary, and will not have the same resistance continue using resources and time without having accountability for them.

Fourth, the government entrepreneur needs to know how to identify and use talent appropriately, especially if there are weak financial reward systems in place – as is more common in the public sector than in the private sector – being able to use interpersonal skills to influence buy-in will be very helpful. Seeking out the hidden talent in current employees can be a way to tap into the current pool, and hiring the right skills for the position is another. Because people are not usually going into the public sector with the expectations for large salaries and bonus structures, creating another sense of value is important. For example, Gordon Chase, who headed New York City's Health Services Administration from 1967–73, convinced his employees that 'what they were doing was the most important thing in New York' and inspired them to be better managers than they thought they were (Berkowitz, 1980, pp. 79–81). The value that government entrepreneurs add to the public sector system should also be taken into account as far as their performance assessment goes. Going hand-in-hand with nurturing talent on the front end is acknowledging the value of this talent on the back end. Since governmental entrepreneurial ventures are often designed with long-term goals in mind, measuring the entrepreneur's efforts based on common performance indicators made in the short term may give a false impression of the entrepreneur's value as an employee and as a driver for the system (Llewellyn et al., 2000, pp. 163–171). Aligning performance evaluations and rewards with the carefully crafted stages for the program's development may help avoid this problem.

Fifth, the government entrepreneur can be most successful knowing how to create the best organizational structure for the program needs, both now and in the future. The government entrepreneur needs to be a visionary and also have a sound understanding of public sector processes and help establish the best structure from both a theoretical and practical perspective.

Finally, government entrepreneurs need to develop individual competencies to be successful. These include:

- Drive, energy and motivation to change
- Drive to achieve
- Future and change oriented
- Challenging the past
- Focus on opportunity to excel
- Utilize core competencies by being innovative and creative
- Take moderate risks and be proactive.

NOTES

1. http://www.ri.gov/press/view/12041.
2. Erik Wasson, 'Obama frames plan as thrifty, but with prudent investment', *The Hill*, 15 February 2011.
3. Will Lester, 'President's approval dips below 40 percent for the first time', Associated Press, 10 September 2005.
4. Joseph Curl, 'Whatever it takes; President promises to eradicate the evil', *The Washington Times*, 16 September 2001.

BIBLIOGRAPHY

Arthur, Stephanie, Angel Cabrera and Robert D. Hisrich (2011), 'The importance of education in the entrepreneurial process: a world view', Working paper,

Walker Center for Global Entrepreneurship, Thunderbird School of Global Management.

Berkowitz, Edward (1980), 'Mary E. Switzer: the entrepreneur within the federal bureaucracy', *American Journal of Economics and Sociology*, **39** (1), 79–81.

Borins, Sandford (February 2001), 'The challenge of innovating in government', PricewaterhouseCoopers Endowment for the Business of Government.

Borins, Sandford (2002), 'Leadership and innovation in the public sector', *Leadership and Organization Development Journal*, **23** (8), 467–476.

Drucker, Peter F. (1985), *Innovation and Entrepreneurship: Practice and Principles*, London: Butterworth-Heinemann.

Eusepi, Giuseppe and Edgar J. Wilson (2008), 'How to make a dis-entrepreneur of the Schumpeterian entrepreneur: the impact of institutional settings on growth', *Public Choice*, **136**, 39–54.

Ferman, Barbara and Martin A. Levin (Autumn 1987), 'Dilemmas of innovation and accountability: entrepreneurs and chief executives', *Policy Studies Review*, **7** (1), 187–199.

Johnson, David (2001), 'What is innovation and entrepreneurship? Lessons for larger organizations', *Industrial and Commercial Training*, **33** (4), 135–140.

Kanter, Rosabeth Moss (1988), 'When a thousand flowers bloom: structural, collective and social conditions for innovations in organizations', *Research in Organizational Behavior*, **10**, 169–211.

Llewellyn, Nick, Alan Lawton, Charles Edwards and Geoff Jones (October 2000), 'Entrepreneurship and the public sector: issues and applications', *Entrepreneurship and Innovation*, 163–171.

McClelland, David C. (1961), *The Achieving Society*, Princeton, NJ: D. Van Nostrand.

McClelland, David C. (November/December 1965), 'Achievement motivation can be developed', *Harvard Business Review*, **43**.

Miller, Danny (July 1983), 'The correlates of entrepreneurship in three types of firms', *Management Science*, **29**, 770–791.

Morris, Michael H. and Foard F. Jones (1999), 'Entrepreneurship in established organizations: the case of the public sector', *Entrepreneurship Theory and Practice*, **24** (1), 71–90.

Mulgan, Geoff and David Albury (October 2003), 'Innovation in the public sector', Strategy Unit, Cabinet Office.

OPORA and INDEM (2007), Business without Corruption: An Action Guide, Moscow: OPORA and INDEM.

Peirce, W.S. and P. Kruger (1993), 'Entrepreneurship in a bureaucracy: the case of Friedrich Althoff', *Journal of Economic Studies*, **20** (4/5), 52–70.

Perry, James L. (1996), 'Measuring public service motivation: an assessment of construct reliability and validity', *Journal of Public Administration Research and Theory*, **6**, 5–22.

PricewaterhouseCoopers (2008), 'Confronting corruption: the business case for an effective anti-corruption programme', accessed 23 July 2012 at: www.pwc.com/anti-corruption.

Schumpeter, Joseph A. (1934), *The Theory of Economic Development*, Cambridge, MA: Harvard University Press.

van Mierlo, J. G. A. (2002), 'Public entrepreneurship as innovative management strategy in the public sector: a public choice approach', originally presented at the 65th Annual Conference of the Southern Economic Association, November 1995.

3. Formulating and managing policy innovation

CHAPTER OBJECTIVES

- To understand the prerequisites and stages of policy innovation.
- To understand the approaches to sound policy innovation.
- To understand the different frameworks available and the open method.
- To provide some examples of some approaches to policy innovation.

INTRODUCTION

Every organization must innovate and needs at least one core competence of innovation in today's hypercompetitive world. Innovation is much more than invention. It is creating a technology that creates value for market(s). While value has multiple definitions, each successful company must establish the value proposition for each innovation and its core competency. A value proposition is the story that a venture shares with its market concerning the benefits provided by the innovation and the company as a whole. YouTube's value proposition, for example, is broadcast yourself.

Value propositions are important because they communicate what the venture intends to provide which helps guide the decision-making process. Procter & Gamble's (P&G) value proposition is touching lives, improving life. This serves as a guide for scientists and product developers at P&G for structuring their research and development efforts and investment. This has resulted in the company introducing hundreds of new products to markets around the world each year. These same principles apply to governments and governmental agencies.

When the word innovation is mentioned, most of us think of the private sector – and it should not be a surprise given that private-sector innovation is the root of more than 87 percent of economic growth in the United States.[1] But, as we have seen both in earlier chapters and just in everyday interactions with the government and governmental agencies, innovation is needed just as much in the public sector.

PRE-REQUISITES FOR POLICY INNOVATION

James Brian Quinn (1985, pp. 73–84) evaluates the managerial practices and innovation approaches of successful large companies and their smaller counterparts in his multi-year research study. He uncovered the following primary factors leading to innovative technology policy:

- Developing a deep understanding of and response to customer demand;
- Having a strong commitment to their objective;
- Being pioneers and good problem solvers allows them to persevere despite the setbacks, frustrations and ambiguities that accompany innovations;
- Perseverance is key;
- Solutions are adopted wherever they can be found and this unencumbered approach removes limits on imagination and increases motivation;
- Undeterred by delays, willing to experiment, test, recycle and try again with little time lost and can gain timing and performance advantages; and
- Able to foresee tangible personal rewards if they succeed.

In addition, interviews and secondary sources were used and crosschecked to establish the management patterns of several outstanding innovative large companies in Europe, the United States and Japan. The following are the most important patterns for successful innovation within the organizational context according to Quinn:

- atmosphere and vision;
- orientation to the market;
- small, flat organizations;
- multiple approaches;
- developmental shoot-outs;
- small teams of engineers, technicians, designers and model makers with no intervening organizational or physical barriers to developing a new product from idea to commercial prototype stages; and
- interactive learning.

STAGES OF POLICY INNOVATION

There are four main stages of policy innovation:

- Establishing the issue or problem;
- Developing possible solutions;
- Contesting possible solutions;
- Institutionalizing, implementing and refining the preferred solution.

During each stage of the innovation process, the resolution must be codetermined by the capacity of players to keep their arguments alive through persistence, persuasion and power, which are influenced by the different frames that are created through narratives, stories and data. This evidence, and the theories that make sense of the evidence, are then woven together with the many implications and possible outcomes, into a discourse intended to persuade others and therefore lead not only to policy creation, but adoption, implementation and institutionalization.

POLICY (AND ITS CREATION) IS DYNAMIC AND LOCATION SPECIFIC

With vastly differentiated institutional structures in governments and governmental agencies, policy measures, regulations and implementation procedures that fit one system cannot simply be applied directly to another.

Shulin Gu (1999) discusses policy specifically within the framework of economic development, but his cautions can be extrapolated to all forms of policy creation: 'Any piece of policy should not be regarded as fixed and universally applicable. In contrast, policy is country [or jurisdiction]-specific. A workable policy runs an adaptive process in interactions with the system to which it aims to introduce a change. Adjustment over time with the operation of the system gives the possibility to the policy process to get system-fitness that is definitely needed in the management of historical transition.'

Gu's approach rejects the notion that any single policy package can be universally applicable in different circumstances, but rather advocates for a policy process that fosters the most basic principles and makes them the focus. These principles include:

- Promoting knowledge inflows and enhanced learning;
- Creating innovative dynamics;
- Facilitating the development of knowledge networking;

- Analyzing local situations;
- Leveraging the appropriate technology, institutions and human capital through policy rather than pitting them against one another;
- Interaction between policy maker and all levels of the organization or institution affected.

The National Innovation Systems for Developing Countries (NIS) approach that Shulin Gu discusses positions a policy maker as part of the system rather than one distinctly separate from the system he/she is trying to change. The policy maker's role has been described in many ways. While he/she is part of a dynamic system, it is often quite different than simple conventions. According to Gu, a policy maker is often not very free when it comes to making decisions because of the restrictions of the institutions and the status of the system. Gu compares the policy innovator to the firm innovator and concludes, 'A policy initiative may incur unperceived response just like a firm innovator has to deal with uncertain outcomes from his innovative action'. With limited knowledge and various impediments to making decisions, a successful policy maker must be aware, adaptive and not easily deterred.

Gu highlights the science and technology policies of Korea and Taiwan to further explain how paths and patterns within policies are country specific. Even though Korea and Taiwan share similarities in the foundations of their policies, the means of innovation and other activities are distinctly different. Korea's technology policy gives priority to what are termed 'strategic industries' such as the automobile, shipbuilding, machinery and microelectronics. The country's fiscal measure and policy are used to promote large Cheabols (large, usually family-owned, business groups) in the procurement of foreign capital goods, paying fees and investing in in-house R&D activities. Taiwan has more of a dual approach to technology policy. The government provides direct intervention and financial support to large-scale, technologically complex upstream sectors, typically intermediate good sectors. Their policies also focus on securing infrastructure services, offering technical support to small- and medium-sized firms and to efforts attempting to increase knowledge-spillovers and spin-offs.

While Gu admits that there are no easy solutions to keep a policy initiative in a positive learning process, he does reflect on how the 'inertia of institutions tends to deter necessary reform initiatives until a big shock comes to press for change'. He discusses how sometimes the internal consensus within a society is the necessary condition for change and sometimes it must be coupled with or replaced by a third-party outsider assisting with the urgency to change. However, this can further complicate the picture as it is often hard to determine who the external third party should be, how they should be involved and to what extent. Co-evolution is one way for governments to pave appropriate pathways for change. This may require putting local policy makers in a broader context to accomplish a long-term movement such as in the international policy arena; in this area, policy makers could garner support for local, state or national initiatives through international partnerships, coalitions or lessons.

APPROACHES TO INNOVATION POLICY

Innovation policy is increasingly informed from the perspective of a national innovation system (NIS). Dodgson contends that policy prescriptions tend to be fairly uniform in practice despite the fact that research findings emphasize the importance of national differences in the framing conditions for innovation.[2]

Justifications for innovation policy by organizations such as the Organisation for Economic Co-operation and Development (OECD) generally refer to notions of market failure with the United States being frequently portrayed as the best model for international emulation. This is due to the focus of the United States on the commercialization of public sector research and entrepreneurship. Dodgson and Hughes feel that empirical evidence supporting the hypothesis that the 'free market' can be relied upon to promote innovation is limited, even in the United States. The authors examine how the global financial crisis provides new opportunities to consider alternatives as well as developing a broad framework for NIS analysis that involves free market, coordination and complex-evolutionary system approaches.

Australia is a particularly interesting example. While Australia has a successful economy, the country faces productivity and innovation challenges. Based on the country's NIS as well as the government's response to it, the policy making in the country is being refocused with new approaches to coordination and complex-evolutionary thinking. The approaches emphasize the importance of systemic connectivity, evolving institutions and organizational capabilities. In spite of this new approach, the predominant logic behind policy choices remains one of addressing market failure and the primary focus of policy attention continues to be science and research rather than demand-led approaches. The major conclusion of the research is that systems failure, rather than just market failure, must be developed in order to make further improvements in the policy-making arena.

DIFFERENT FRAMEWORKS UNDERLYING THE MODES OF ORGANIZATION

The state and the market have long been recognized as the key modes of social organization that form the foundation for democratic society; however, the failure of these governance modes to solve complex public problems has engendered new approaches. Keast, Mandell and Brown (2006, pp. 27–50) feel that the failures of the old systems to fully address societal issues is what led the way for networks and the network governance mode to come to be. 'While inextricably inter-related, each of these modes is underpinned by differing operating frameworks which are grounded in contrasting rule systems, moral orders and rationales and each requires different actors, institutional arrangements and strategies.' As a result of the dynamic nature of adoption and utilization, the current policy arena contains aspects of all three governance modes. In addition, these modes often appear in crosscutting, hybrid governance forms leading to even further governance complexity. Keast et al. refer to this as the 'crowded' policy domain in which differing governance arrangements, policy prescriptions, participants and processes compete with each other to cause overlap and confusion. In the worst cases, these clashes thwart the potential for, and implementation of, positive service delivery and efficiency.

The authors feel that policy and decision makers need 'to effectively isolate, select and mix and match governance aspects of each of the three modes and thereby orchestrate the varying, and often competing, elements of these modes residing in the policy domain into harmonious collective action'. For without acknowledging the differences, and selecting optimal mixes of these ways of looking at the various issues, it would be difficult to cultivate meaningful dialogue and interaction even between the most favorable elements.

THE OPEN METHOD OF COORDINATION IN INNOVATION POLICY

The application of the open method of coordination (OMC) has not yet gone very far in innovation policy. Kaiser and Prange (2004, pp. 249–266) feel that the multi-level character of innovation policies and the diversity of national innovation systems are hurdles to applying the OMC in the policy area. They claim that these two peculiarities of innovation policies prevented 'vertical policy coordination' and 'horizontal policy learning', which have both been espoused as the main goals of applying the OMC.

They further feel that OMC is only likely to constitute a valuable mode of governance if:

- National and regional specificities are carefully taken into account;
- Actors at each territorial level are considered during the entire policy process; and
- Qualitative benchmark indicators are developed which consider the diversities of national innovation systems and regional idiosyncrasies.

The innovation policy development of the European Union was the basis for their research since there are significant variations among EU member states and regions in terms of legislative and budgetary systems. This complex system has many different policies, institutions and national coordination mechanisms. In the EU, vertical coordination (and the problems that often accompany it) differentiates innovation policy from other policies, such as social or employment policy. Increasing transaction costs are one example of how vertical coordination problems in one policy area often increase with the number of administrative levels and the degree of sub-national autonomy. Innovation policy is also different from other policy areas because it is often the case that private organizations, not the government, are the main players. In this context, Kaiser and Prange indicate how member states, regions or even local clusters must compete for critical resources, such as knowledge, foreign research and development investments, or human resources, not only with other member states but also with innovation markets around the world. Innovation policies are faced with the problem that there is a tension between market coordination and political coordination.

AN ACTOR–NETWORK THEORY ANALYSIS: POLICY INNOVATION FOR SMOKE-FREE PLACES

Some issues that governments or societies face defy conventional analysis and management because of their complexity and often convoluted nature. Issues such as the tobacco epidemic are major challenges for policy implementers, for example. Young, Borland and Coghill chronicled the evolution of indoor smoke-free regulations, a tobacco control policy innovation and identified the key attributes of those jurisdictions that successfully pursued this innovation and those that to-date have not.[3] The authors employed the actor–network theory (ANT), a comprehensive framework for the analysis of fundamental system change that can be applied to a variety of complex policy issues such as other public health issues, global food distribution or climate change, and proves especially helpful in overcoming some systemic barriers to other complex transnational problems.

Their research highlights how systems change their structures and processes within limits defined by their response repertoire. The potential for structural or procedural change becomes constrained over time, as systems are usually unable to change their functions (what they do) from within. This is especially true when their activities take place within a context of polarization and stalemate, as was the case with the tobacco control domain.

This example helps to explain why fundamental, innovative change requires action outside of the existing system structures to be successful. Young, Borland and Coghill (2010) define these external actors as both those who believe the system is not delivering and internal groups or individuals acting outside their system roles. These external perspectives offer fresh ideas and views for redesign or analysis because they are not structured into the system and can act as a network to affect the change.

MANAGING RISK THROUGH INNOVATION POLICY

Throughout the last few decades, public policy and public management methods have been very concerned with the management of risk. Risk by definition is quantifiable, or at the very least something that can be 'managed'. In contrast, according to Matthews (2009), 'the preparedness perspective places far more emphasis on the need to deal with uncertainty – challenges that cannot be easily quantified, accurately forecasted or managed'. Although the distinction between risk and uncertainty is not always easily defined, it is often the area where policy makers find themselves working. The preparedness perspective stresses the key role of governments in managing the economic, social, environmental and national security consequences of this substantive uncertainty and offers five complimentary principles for giving preparedness a more integral role in innovation policy:

- Being more realistic and honest about limitations to forecasts and predictions, particularly in complex systems environments where simple cause and effect do not apply.
- Making a more explicit distinction between risk and uncertainty, and doing more to understand the grey area between the two, again

giving due recognition to the inherent unpredictability of complex systems.

- Putting more effort into demonstrating how science translates uncertainty into risk and in so doing increases our levels of preparedness.
- Adopting 'preparedness friendly' guidelines for research funding and performance evaluation that utilize 'risk-facilitating' portfolio-based investment methods.
- Doing more to specify how preparedness outcomes are reflected (in the short term) in greater accuracy in the estimated Net Present Value of economic assets and also (in the very long term) the challenge of being fairer to future generations.

UNDERSTANDING THE POLICY LANDSCAPE

As is the case in making change in any organization, it is important to understand both the context and landscape in which innovation policy is trying to be created and implemented. It is crucial to figure out who the key players are – both internally and externally – and to identify their motivations and needs. It is also important to assess their alliances, background and future orientation as well as their key strengths, resources and willingness to collaborate. Creating a stakeholder map and keeping it up to date will be instrumental in being able to best leverage your understanding of both the context and the space.

In addition to understanding the players, it is important to understand the history of related policy attempts at innovation that have both failed and succeeded. Being armed with the lessons and best practices from previous attempts in your jurisdiction and other comparable ones will prove invaluable as you begin to navigate the process.

It is also necessary to understand both where innovation policy is needed most and within what arena there is the most readiness for innovation. Adjusting your strategy to start in a place or with a topic that is more likely to succeed may help you to achieve small wins and gain momentum rather than being stopped in your tracks with a failed attempt at innovation in an area not yet ready to accept change – even of the necessary type.

Much of the current literature discusses how the increased complexity of social problems and the current lack of resources to fight them have increased the need and the urgency for innovation within governments. There is also avid discussion surrounding the changing face of the financial landscape and how governments must adjust in order to operate within these new constraints and realities. Adapting to these changes will require innovation and an entrepreneurial spirit both within and in conjunction with governmental agencies. Kohli and Mulgan (2010) argue still more urgency emerges from fiscal pressures. As money gets tighter, public agencies must find more efficient ways to operate – whether it is conducting the census, administering social security, improving workplace safety or tackling crime, public-sector productivity matters just as much for future prosperity in these days of fiscal tightness as private-sector productivity. There is also a growing sense of responsibility among the corporate and NGO sectors to help address some of these social problems in a way that is mutually beneficial. The Bill and Melinda Gates Foundation is an example of an NGO working alongside government to address social problems. The Gates Foundation, together with Rotary International, the United States Government, the United Kingdom and Japan, has for several years contributed $200 million in the fight to eradicate polio worldwide.[4] In January 2012, the Government of India announced a year of no new cases of children being paralyzed by polio. If these trends continue, India is expected to be removed from the list of polio-endemic countries.[5] Aligning these needs, interested players and motivations will increase the odds for success in creating policies that foster collaboration and innovation.

Finding the right way to tackle societal issues or creating a strategy for innovative policy development is rarely straightforward. However, as Kohli and Mulgan point out, this usually requires a cycle of coming up with new ideas, testing whether they actually work and scaling up the ideas that are most effective.

There is often a great deal of talk about innovation in the public sector, but most often the stereotypes and typical laundry list of red tape, layers of complication and deep rooted systems prevail when it comes time to turn talk of innovation into action. There are few examples of innovation institutionalized in government budgets, roles, systems and processes. As Kohli and Mulgan candidly point out, it is even rarer to find officials, politicians or government workers who are aware of the full range of tools that they could be using to accelerate the development and spread of better ideas.

Although Kohli and Mulgan do admit that some of the most innovative creations of the twentieth century did develop within public institutions, they are quick to point them out as exceptions. They and offer the following reasons why innovation is harder in the public sphere:

- The private sector offers strong financial rewards for innovation, but the public sector often discourages new thinking among its employees. New ideas almost always involve some risk – and if something fails in government, political leaders and staff know they are likely to be asked why funds were wasted. The real incentive in government is to keep doing things in the proven and safe way – even if that means better, more efficient methods are not identified.

- The way money is allocated to public-sector organizations can dampen the desire to innovate. The budgeting and appropriations process focuses on programs that are shrinking or growing, with little attention paid to the stock of programs that form the baseline. Programs with limited efficacy that fly below the radar are often left alone. It can be easier as a program manager to maintain the status quo than devise better ways of running a program.

- Political leaders are encouraged to push for ideas that are popular with voters, sometimes at the expense of more effective proposals. And voters often reward decisions to increase investment in teachers or police officers, even when there may be ways to make current investment more efficient without added expense. In 1997, President Bill Clinton called on Congress to fund 100 000 more teachers. But in testimony before the House Education Committee, Chester E. Finn of the Hudson Institute assessed the Clinton plan and noted that the private board which would screen the new teachers had a very complex and costly process having been around for a decade and spent millions of federal dollars only to be able to certify 500 teachers. The problem, Finn noted, was that 'the board itself (dominated by teachers' union representatives) is still ambivalent about branding certain teachers as superior to others'.[6] There are much weaker incentives for solutions that are not immediately popular, but may be more effective. Raising awareness of public health problems is unlikely to be immediately popular, for example, but could yield better results than more popular measures such as increasing investment in facilities or clinicians.

- Public-sector culture often rewards people for turning the gears of bureaucracy rather than improving the overall machinery. There is often a strong culture of 'this is the ways things are done around here', especially in functions that service citizens or internal customers. There is little incentive without market competition for public organizations to place themselves in their customers' shoes. There is only one passport provider. And, strong labor rights can reinforce cultural barriers to innovation because unions often must ratify even small changes to working practices. In February 2010, a Rio Tinto mine in Boron, California, locked out 540 hourly workers after the International Longshore and Warehouse Union Local 30 refused to ratify a new contract. The *Los Angeles Times* noted that the company offered the union, 'a 2 percent wage increase, an annual performance bonus, a $4000 signing bonus and 80 percent coverage of healthcare costs'. At issue was the ability for Rio Tinto to 'hire more nonunion employees and, more importantly, change the seniority system so that it can promote people based on skill and performance rather than just years of service'.[7] The improved job security enjoyed by union-protected workers can help raise morale, but it may also reduce their incentive to innovate.

• Government promotions rarely reward innovative staff. The most valued skills are handling political crises well; crafting documents that win headlines; or steering relations with key stakeholders. While these are important, they are not skills that focus on improving outcomes for society or citizens. It is hardly surprising that junior workers seek to emulate the former skill set and become less focused on innovation.

• Outside government, a great deal of innovation occurs through collaboration. Academics build on each other's work to advance new ideas. So-called 'open source' innovation is increasingly common in business, especially in the technological area. Businesses have always looked to competitors for ideas of better products or services. Yet in government, there is the tendency to be secretive and develop new products in-house. There are exceptions: New Zealand uses a wiki – or collaboratively edited website – to rewrite police legislation and the city of Seoul has tapped thousands of citizens' ideas in implementing public policy. But there is generally a deep-rooted cultural aversion to admitting that government may not have all the answers.

NEW APPROACHES TO CREATING INNOVATIVE POLICY

Three new approaches to creating innovative policy will be discussed: policy innovation consulting, the Mowat Centre for Policy Innovation and a conference on policy innovation.

Policy Innovation Consulting

Policy Innovation (PI) is a strategic management consulting firm that helps state and local governments and their public, private and not-for-profit partners govern smarter. PI helps government officials diagnose problems and design solutions that result in increased revenue, reduced expenses, less risk and/or improvements in service quality.

As indicated on their website,[8] PI encourages its clients to focus on the following approaches to foster innovation:

- Systems: A group of interacting, interrelated and interdependent components that form a complex and unified whole. Most public service delivery takes place in systems. And while state and local governments cannot control entire systems, the part of the system they do control needs to be the focus of intervention and improvement.
- Metrics: The old saying that which gets measured gets improved holds for government activities. Metrics are the measures used to gauge performance. Without them it is impossible to know how well (or poorly) the organization is doing. And, impossible to set and hit performance targets.
- Analytics: Sophisticated analysis and use of data to enable fact-based decision making at every level of an organization are key. State and local governments and their partners often are data rich and data poor at the same time. Vast sums of data exist, but are often inaccessible. State and local government executives have the potential to make decisions that are informed by data much more easily and cost-effectively than ever before.
- Results: Citizens across the globe are demanding that their national and subnational governments focus not on the inputs to public service production and delivery but on the outputs of the production process. Increasingly, they are demanding to know if those outputs are improving the lives of the citizens they serve. And higher levels of government are beginning to link funding to specific programmatic outcomes.
- Tools: Public, private and not-for-profit organizations need devices to produce and deliver necessary public services. With advances in technology, online and analytical tools can help executives deliver these services better, faster and cheaper.

The Mowat Centre for Policy Innovation

The Mowat Centre for Policy Innovation[9] is an independent, non-partisan public policy research center located at the University of Toronto School of Public Policy and Governance that undertakes collaborative applied policy research and engages in public dialogue on Canada's most important national issues. The Centre proposes innovative, research driven public policy recommendations, informed by Ontario's reality. The Centre believes a prosperous, equitable and dynamic Canada requires strong provinces, including a strong Ontario, and strong cities.

As explained on their website, the 'Mowat Research Model' is the Mowat Centre's collaborative approach to knowledge development. It ensures that the Centre's research, findings and recommendations are timely, relevant and informed by a realistic understanding of government, service delivery and Canadian society. Mowat Centre researchers begin by identifying a topic and outlining the scope, objectives, deliverables and terms of reference for each research project. The Mowat Centre identifies a lead academic researcher for each project and convenes an initial meeting to prepare a prospectus on the research. This meeting would include the lead researcher and three to four partners, comprised of government officials, thought leaders and practitioners from the non-profit or private sector. The project partners are actively engaged throughout the project. They help inform the project scope by providing input into the project prospectus, and provide feedback and advice as the research is conducted and materials are drafted. The Mowat Centre is also committed to leveraging new and emerging technologies in the policy development process.[10]

A Conference on Policy Innovation

Criterion Conferences of Australia hosted the Policy Innovation: Applying New Ideas & Improving Processes to Produce Better Outcomes conference in July 2010 in Canberra. It was labeled as 'A practitioners guide to policy innovation' and was officially sanctioned by the Australian Prime Minister Julia Gillard who believes 'policy innovation is crucial to ensuring we achieve desired outcomes and meet future challenges'.[11]

The conference theme centered on 'Policy Innovation: The Application of New Ideas and New Ways of Doing Things to Produce Better Outputs and Outcomes'. The conference tackled issues of how to innovate amid more immediate pressures taking precedence over desires to improve processes, think 'outside the box' and develop more forward-looking, creative policy advice.

The Policy Innovation Conference featured a series of presentations from a selection of departments already on the path to innovation as well as presentations from some of the leading thinkers in this area. Delegates learned to foster innovation in their own departments, enhance their own innovation performance, and develop more innovative policy that better prepared them to address the significant challenges they face. The key results of the conference included:

- An understanding of the importance of innovation in the current context in Australia;
- How departments can build cultures of innovation;

- What can be done to enhance innovation performance on the individual and departmental levels.

NOTES

1. Nathan Rosenburg, *Innovation and Economic Growth* (Paris: OECD, 2004), accessed 23 July 2012 at: http://www.oecd.org/datao-ecd/55/49/34267902.pdf.
2. James Brian Quinn (1985), 'Managing innovation: controlled chaos', *Harvard Business Review*, **63** (3), 73–84.
3. http://www.policyinnovation.com/index.cfm.
4. http://www.gatesfoundation.org/annual-letter/2011/Pages/ending-polio.aspx.
5. http://www.washingtonpost.com/world/eradicating-polio-in-india/2012/01/12/gIQA4bt0tP_graphic.html.
6. Chester E. Finn Jr. and John M. Olin Fellow, Testimony, Hudson Institute House Education Administration Education Proposals, 13 March 1997.
7. David Kelly, 'Borax mine workers locked out in labor dispute', *Los Angeles Times*, 1 February 2010.
8. http://www.policyinnovation.com/index.cfm.
9. http://www.mowatcentre.ca/.
10. http://www.mowatcentre.ca/the-mowat-research-model.php.
11. http://policy-innovation.com/index.php.

BIBLIOGRAPHY

Dodgson, Mark and Alan Hughes (2009), 'Systems thinking, market failure, and the development of innovation policy: the case of Australia', Centre for Business Research, University of Cambridge Working Paper No. 397.

Gu, Shulin (1999), 'Implications of national innovation systems for developing countries: managing change and complexity in economic development', United Nations University, Institute for New Technologies.

Kaiser, Robert and Heiko Prange (2004), 'Managing diversity in a system of multi-level governance: the open method of co-ordination in innovation policy', *Journal of European Public Policy*, **11** (2), 249–266.

Keast, Robyn L., Mryna Mandell and Kerry A. Brown (2006), 'Mixing state, market and network governance modes: the role of government in "crowded" policy domains', *International Journal of Organization Theory and Behavior*, **9** (1), 27–50.

Kohli, Jitinder and Geoff Mulgan (July 2010), 'Capital ideas: how to generate innovation in the public sector', a product of CAP's Doing What Works project in conjunction with The Young Foundation and the Center for American Progress.

Matthews, M. (November 2009), 'Giving preparedness a central role in science and innovation policy', FASTS Policy Discussion Paper, Canberra, ACT: FASTS.

Valente T.W. (2005), 'Models and methods for innovation diffusion', in P.J. Carrington, J. Scott and S. Wasserman (eds) *Models and Methods in Social Network Analysis*, Cambridge: Cambridge University Press, pp. 98–116.

Wilden, A. (1972), *System and Structure: Essays in Communication and Exchange*, London, England: Tavistock.

Young, David, Ron Borland and Ken Coghill (July 2010), 'An actor–network theory analysis of policy innovation for smoke-free places: understanding change in complex systems', *American Journal of Public Health, American Public Health Association*, **100** (7), 1208–1217.

4. Locating and fostering innovation

CHAPTER OBJECTIVES

- To understand the difficulties in innovation in government.
- To understand the principles of creating a culture that embraces change.
- To illustrate innovation in the education sector through examples.
- To illustrate city-level innovation through examples.
- To explain how to engage the community.

INTRODUCTION

Creativity, the ability to develop new ideas, solutions or products/services, leads to invention, which in turn can lead to innovation, a new idea being in the market. Creative ideas often occur when creative people look at established practices, products or solutions and think of some new and different.

Creative ideas can occur in all sectors including government. A successful government generates cost-effective new ways of thinking and doing things. This occurred in Barcelona, Spain, where an old Olivetti plant that used to make typewriters and employed around 3000 workers was converted into a brightly painted, exposed-beam facility housing young professionals talking business in a variety of languages. The old plant reopened in 2006 as a high-tech business incubator. This four-story concrete/glass structure hosts start-up companies, provides seminars to students and young professionals on such topics as creating a business plan, and provides linkages to the investment community. The converted factory in downtown Barcelona hosts over 50 start-up companies that create everything from bicycle helmets with built-in air bags to the latest video games.

Similarly, Singapore is spending over $10 billion on a mega development called One North to integrate research and development complexes and provide living laboratories for advanced materials, biotech and medical services. Seoul, Korea, near an old railway depot, has created the Digital Media City to house 120000 workers and 2000 companies by 2015.

WHY IS IT SO HARD TO INNOVATE?

Stephen Goldsmith, the deputy mayor of New York City, former two-term mayor of Indianapolis, and author of *The Power of Social Innovation*, a thought and practice leader, has a lot to share about how (and why) to foster innovation in the public sector.[1] As part of a collaborative 3-week series exploring the re-invention of the social infrastructure of cities, published in partnership with the Advanced Leadership Initiative at Harvard University, Goldsmith reflects on why it may be so difficult to cultivate innovation within the public sector. He points out that although 'the economy has changed dramatically over the last century, we still basically manufacture government the way we did 75 years ago'. He faults this disconnect between past rules and governing models and present needs as the main hurdle to actually solving some of today's most formidable challenges. Goldsmith highlights how modern problems need collaborative solutions and faults these antiquated systems and their legacy of 'regularity morass' for thwarting true collaborations among the needed sectors.

Goldsmith goes on to explain that today's convoluted regulatory system that suffocates most of the city governments is largely a product of Progressive-era reformers reacting to the real abuses of power by government officials. Their appropriate reaction to corruption at the time engendered laws designed that have now grown into counterproductive regulations that restrict innovative thinking. He argues removing these counterproductive rules and adapting governing models in order to adapt to current realities. He offers the example of how public services are increasingly delivered by 'networks' of private companies, non-profits and government officials working together, and highlights that 'government must abandon its hierarchical workforce structure and embrace a structure that empowers lower-level employees with the training and discretion they need to better manage these networked relationships'.

The time has come for city and country governments to recognize that citizens worldwide be given greater flexibility to adapt successfully to our changing world. Government's unique strengths as a facilitator of social innovation and networked government need to be unleashed to ensure a vibrant urban future. By sharing increasingly robust information with the public and by opening two-way channels of communication and new platforms for collaboration, governments and citizens can work together to address even the most daunting challenges. Government must be able to leverage its core competencies, such as policy-making authority and powerful incentive programs, and needs to create a structure that allows them to do this that provides the highest amount of public value.

WHAT DOES INNOVATION LOOK LIKE?

Innovation is not something for which a blueprint can be drawn, but there are cycles and stages that tend to occur in its development. The Center for American Progress believes that innovation – whether it is in the private or public sector – follows six basic stages in some configuration.

Every organization needs to innovate and needs at least one core competence of innovation in today's hypercompetitive world. Innovation is much more than invention. It is creating a technology that creates value for market(s). While value has multiple definitions, each successful organization must establish the value proposition for each innovation and its core competency. A value proposition is the story that an organization shares with its market and constituencies concerning the benefits provided by the innovation and the company as a whole. YouTube's value proposition is – broadcast yourself.

Value propositions are important because they communicate what the organization intends to provide; this helps guide the decision-making process. Procter & Gamble's (P&G) value proposition is touching lives, improving life. This serves as a guide for scientists and product developers at P&G for structuring their research and development efforts and investment. This has resulted in the company introducing hundreds of new products to markets around the world each year. These same principles apply to government and governmental agencies.

Figure 4.1 depicts a six-stage cycle of social innovation. These six stages are: (1) prompts, inspirations and diagnoses; (2) proposals and ideas; (3) prototyping and pilots; (4) sustaining; (5) scaling and diffusion; and (6) systemic change. While these stages are not always sequential, there needs to be a feedback loop created between each one.

CREATING A PUBLIC CULTURE THAT EMBRACES CHANGE

Stephen Goldsmith discusses five basic principles to help encourage a public culture that embraces rather than condemns change:[2]

- Create an environment and attitude of continuous innovation. An elected leader needs to create a culture of continuous innovation that encourages public employees to identify a problem or generate solutions. This strategy has been employed with success around the world, including in the United Kingdom where the Prime Minister's Delivery Unit aggressively identifies and advocates for change.

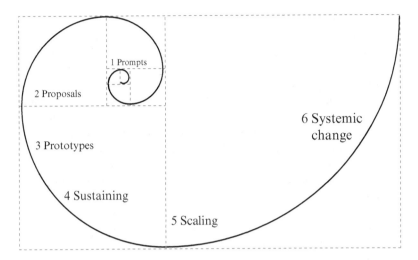

Notes: Innovation in the private sector follows a process from invention to wide adoption
of new goods or services. Social innovation follows a similar cycle and there are six stages
from inception to impact.

These stages are not always sequential – some innovations can jump a stage or two – and
there can be feedback loops between them:

1. Prompts, inspirations, and diagnoses. Solutions derive from problems. The impetuses
for social innovation are therefore often social problems: funding crises, systemic failures,
tragedies. These prompts can be founts of creative inspiration, but must be accurately
diagnosed in order to identify the root causes of particular problems. New technologies or
knowledge can also sometimes act as prompts.

2. Proposals and ideas. Once a problem or a new possibility is understood, social innovators
set about generating ideas for solutions.

3. Prototyping and pilots. This is the testing stage. Whether through controlled trials or just
running an idea up the flagpole and seeing if anyone salutes, the refining and prototyping
process is critical for social innovation. Ideas are battle-tested, supporting coalitions
emerge, internecine conflicts get smoothed out, and success benchmarks become formalized.

4. Sustaining. Here, the training wheels come off and the road to long-term viability is
paved. That means finding revenue streams, writing supportive legislation, and assembling
the human and technical resources to put the air beneath the wings of innovation. The idea
often has to become simpler at this stage.

5. Scaling and diffusion. The idea takes off here, reaping social economies of scale through
expansion, replication, and diffusion. There is no profit motive to drive social innovation
across the globe like in the private sector. Social solutions often require government
intervention and public–private partnerships to grow.

6. Systemic change. This is the end-game of social innovation. An idea, or many ideas
in concert, become so entrenched that they give birth to new modes of thinking, new
architectures, and ultimately entirely new frameworks.

Source: Robin Murray, Julie Caulier-Grice, and Geoff Mulgan, *The Open Book of Social
Innovation* (United Kingdom: Young Federation/NESTA, 2010), accessed at http://www.
youngfoundation.org/files/images/Open_Book_of_Social Innovation.pdf.

Figure 4.1   The six-stage cycle of social innovation

Ultimately, the chief executive must be willing to accept the risks, both real and perceived, and embrace change. He/she needs to encourage subordinates to generate ideas, assess feasibility, build business cases, coordinate implementation, track results and help make successful reforms stick.

- Create dedicated innovation teams. A dedicated change unit is trusted to interact with agency heads and other key officials, but neither manages nor is managed by those units they seek to influence. Boston Mayor Tom Menino created the Office of New Urban Mechanics to focus on innovation. Menino chose to create dedicated teams to deliver on his key reforms. These dedicated teams have been the drivers of success:
  - in promoting sustainability through PlaNYC
  - in combating poverty through the Center for Economic Opportunity; and
  - in maximizing agency efficiency through the Mayor's Office of Operations.
- Continuous and transparent measured results. Performance measures drive change month-by-month, quarter-by-quarter, year-by-year, performance data helps identify targets for improvement. For example, in New York City Hall's 'bullpen', senior officials work in sight of large television monitors that constantly scroll performance data. When an agency's numbers drift above or below the norm, they are noticed. Each deputy mayor's computer also has an icon through which they can access performance data for their agencies and give insight on where they need to intervene or innovate.
- Never cover up failure or mask mediocrity. Given the compatibility of the press, the temptation to sweep imperfection under the rug is understandable. This should not be done. As painful as negative press may be, a cover-up is infinitely worse. Use the discomfort to spur positive change.
- Relentlessly seek ideas for innovation. Within any bureaucracy, many great ideas remain locked inside front-line employees. Tap into this resource. New York City has launched an internal 'idea market' to capture these ideas. The forum was off to a slow start because employees with good ideas do not want to risk being seen as offering criticism of their managers. The city is trying to nurture a culture of innovation, encouraging employees who share their ideas despite such trepidation.

THE INFLUENCE OF AND INTERACTION WITH THE MEDIA

In today's age of constant news and myriad media outlets, the media is a stakeholder that is usually at the table. It plays an important role in not just reporting on innovations that occur in and outside of government, but helps shape the way the general public views the government and its innovative activities.

POTENTIAL BENEFITS OF CONTRACTING SERVICES

The failing education sectors around the world represent some of the most challenging social, economic and policy challenges. Some governments have responded – to varying degrees – to these challenges by introducing market-based policies that emphasize choice, managerial autonomy for schools and accountability for results. Contracting with the private sector for the delivery of ancillary services such as catering and school transport is relatively common in the education sector. A more recent trend has governments contracting with the private sector for the delivery of core education services. While such contracting is not yet widespread, there are a number of examples in operation in the United States and around the world, and the contract and charter school movements are significantly increasing.

Norman LaRocque provides an overview of international examples of contracting with the private sector for the delivery of educational services, professional services and the provision of educational infrastructure and highlights some lessons from various international experiences that can be applied to government initiatives in the design and delivery of various services.[3]

There are several reasons for organizations contracting out delivery services. Proponents argue that contracting may have a number of benefits over traditional methods of service procurement. Contracting may:

- Improve the quality of spending by lifting the efficiency of service delivery and by allowing better targeting of spending;
- Allow governments to take advantage of specialized skills that might not be available in a government agency;
- Allow governments to overcome operating restrictions such as inflexible salary scales and civil service restrictions;
- Allow governments to respond to new demands and facilitate the adoption of innovations in service delivery and experimentation;

- Permit economies of scale regardless of the size of the government entity;
- Allow governments to focus on those functions for which it has a comparative advantage;
- Increase access to services, especially for those groups who have been poorly served under traditional forms of service delivery; and
- Increase transparency of government spending by making the cost of services more visible.

It should also be noted that contracting has a number of drawbacks, including that it can be more expensive than traditional procurement methods, could foster corruption or result in a loss of government accountability and control.[4]

Some typologies for contracting in education are indicated in Table 4.1. A description and example of each contracting form is provided. For example, operational contracts are government contracts with a private sector provider to operate an existing public service using public infrastructure. Examples include contract schools (United States) and concession schools (Bogotá, Colombia), the latter is discussed in-depth in the next section.

EXAMPLES OF CONTRACTING INNOVATION FROM THE EDUCATION SECTOR

Two examples of contracting innovation – private management of public schools and concession schools in Colombia – are discussed below.

Private Management of Public Schools

One area of increasing private participation is the private management of public schools. There are various models of private management of public schools employed by governments in a number of developed and developing countries. LaRocque highlights three examples of structures that could be applied to more than just the delivery of education services if done thoughtfully and provide models that could be emulated for other governmental programs:

Privately Managed Public Schools and Charter Schools in the United States

These schools are privately managed, but they remain publicly owned and publicly funded. Students usually do not pay fees to attend these schools.

Table 4.1 *Typology of forms of contracting in education*

Contracting form	Description	Examples
Management contracts	Government contracts with private sector to *manage* an existing public service using public infrastructure	Contract schools, USA
Operational contracts	Government contracts with a private provider to *operate* an existing public service using public infrastructure	Contract schools, USA Concession Schools, Bogotá Fe y Alegría, Latin America/ Spain
Service delivery contracts	Government contracts with a private provider to deliver a specified service/ set of services using private infrastructure	Government Sponsorship of Students in Private Schools, Côte d'Ivoire Alternative Education, New Zealand Educational Service Contracting, Philippines
Provision of infrastructure	Government contracts the private sector to design, build, finance and operate educational infrastructure such as classrooms and school hostels	UK Private Finance Initiative 'New Schools' Private Finance Project, Australia Public Private Partnerships (P3) for Educational Infrastructure, Nova Scotia, Canada J. F. Oyster Bilingual Elementary School, Washington DC Offenbach Schools Project, County of Offenbach, Germany Montaigne Lyceum, The Hague, Netherlands
Auxiliary services contracts/ professional services	Government contracts the private sector to undertake education-related functions such as school review, schooling improvement or curriculum development	Contracting out of Local Education Authority (LEA) functions in the United Kingdom (UK) Pitágoras Network of Schools De La Salle Supervised Schools Sabis Network of Schools

Source: Norman LaRocque (October 2005), 'Contracting for the delivery of education services: a typology and international examples', Program on Education Policy and Governance Conference, Harvard University, accessed at http://www.innovations.harvard. edu/showdoc.html?id=9189.

Figure 4.2   Direct and indirect management contracts

Typically, private sector operators are brought in to operate the worst performing schools in a given school district. The private management of public schools in the United States typically takes one of two forms. The first usually has the local school board contracting directly with an external management organization (EMO) to manage a public school while the second involves having EMOs manage charter schools either as the holder of the school charter or under contract to the organization that holds the school charter (see Figure 4.2).

Under both the indirect and direct management models, the government pays the private sector operator a fixed amount per student (usually equal to the average cost of educating a student in the public sector) or is paid a fixed management fee and must meet specific performance benchmarks. The main difference between these models is how much of the management and operations are turned over to the contracted agent, such as who employs the teachers and manages the social services provided. Chicago, Philadelphia and Denver represent some of the most contracted schools in the United States and demonstrate how this type of innovative public–private partnership can use resources more efficiently to improve failing schools (see Figure 4.3).

Colegios en Concesión (Concession Schools) in Bogotá, Colombia

In Colombia, the City of Bogotá has introduced the Colegios en Concesión (Concession Schools) program, where the management of some public schools is turned over to private institutions with proven track records of delivering high-quality education. The Concession Schools model

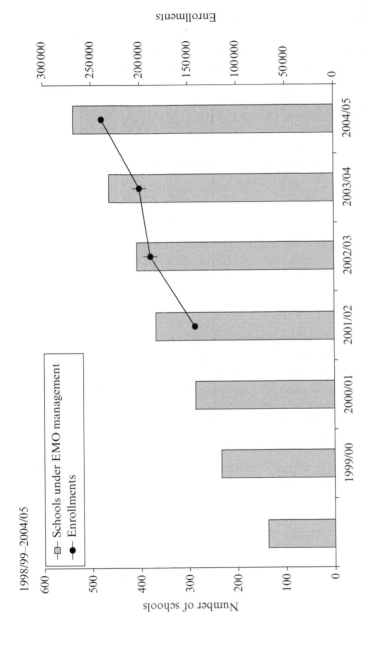

Source: Molnar, A. et al. (2005) *Profiles of For-Profit Education Management Companies: 2004–2005. Education Policy Studies Laboratory,* Arizona State University, Tempe, Arizona.

Figure 4.3 Number of schools under EMO management and enrollments, USA

was developed in the late 1990s and the first schools began operating in 2000. There are currently 25 schools (serving over 26 000 students) being operated by private managers under the Concession Schools model. The program was expected to grow to approximately 45 000 students in 51 schools (about 5 percent of public school coverage in Bogotá). However, a change in the mayoralty has reportedly stopped the program's expansion.

LESSONS FROM CITY LEVEL INNOVATION INITIATIVES

Lessons from innovation initiatives in such cities as Rio de Janeiro and New York City are discussed below.

Rio de Janeiro

As mayor of Rio de Janeiro, Eduardo Paes faced a great deal of skepticism and backlash when he introduced many technological innovations to modernize public management. Critics were especially tough on his proposals to spend money on technology. Investments in technology were so low for so long that technological blackouts were common. Today, technology is at a high enough level to provide the mayor the ability to follow the everyday activities of the municipality on a dashboard. All departments have specific software and innovative processes to make their task more efficient. They progressively increase the IT share of their municipal budget because as Paes reflects in his blog,[5] 'they know the value technology can bring to raise efficiency and improve the quality of services to citizens'. The city uses some of these allocated funds to train government staff in new technologies and bring in new talent with technological knowledge and IT experience to serve in management and policy-making roles.

At the center of their technological innovations program is the Command and Controlling Center (CCC), which Paes describes as, 'a situation room with upscale technology that gathers information produced by several departments of the municipal administration to monitor the city and focus on predicting and mitigating extreme natural events, mainly storms and flooding'. Imbedded in the program is a partnership with IBM, Oracle and Samsung. The CCC represents a new approach to civil defense and crisis management, involving not only public authorities and servants but also engaging the media, citizens and all stakeholders involved with issues relating to managing the crisis. The activities outlined in the emergency plan go from analyzing the images on the screens inside the situation room to teaching people living in low-income communities how to help their neighbors in a crisis situation.

When discussing the challenges to fostering innovation, Eduardo Paes reports that it is subverting the pervasive culture of thinking 'within the box' that gives him the most trouble. He discusses how coordinating with, working across or sharing among sectors is not a tradition in Brazil and that the biggest challenge in implementing the CCC is getting the city's various stakeholders to work as a team. This will be a universal challenge in establishing entrepreneurship in government given the usual rigidity and silos.

New York City

New York City is collaborating with multiple sectors to create a modern governing structure that elevates performance, enhances discretion and employs analytics. The NYC Simplicity is the newest in a growing line of innovations New York City is undertaking to increase transparency in its governance. The initiative relies on innovative handheld technology as it seeks to remove the regulatory barriers that inhibit government innovation and entrepreneurship by reorganizing government around the needs of residents and businesses. New York City mayor, Stephen Goldsmith, believes, 'Sharing government information publicly and creating forums to capture public feedback is another important way to improve public service delivery.' Other initiatives include their BigApps competition, the NYC DataMine and a 311 service request map, which plots information from the more than 19 million annual 311 calls on a street-level map.[6]

The New York City model also personifies Goldsmith's belief in the 'wisdom of crowds'. He explains, 'In order to further disrupt the barriers to information-sharing, New York City has launched two specific online platforms to take advantage of collaboration opportunities.' Next in line is 'Change by Us', a public platform that will enable community-based organizations and residents to collaborate on projects designed to make neighborhoods more environmentally sustainable. Goldsmith hopes the 'free flow of information will break open the siloed decision making that often prevents technically proficient bureaucrats from maximizing their effectiveness because they lack sufficient detail about individual and neighborhood problems'.

ENGAGING THE COMMUNITY ON HIGH IMPACT PROJECTS

According to Cities of Service,[7] in May 2011, ten US cities launched efforts to engage volunteers strategically to address the most pressing needs in their communities such as at risk youth, city beautification, education, drug addiction and health. Seven of these cities – Atlanta, Austin, Baltimore, Baton Rouge, Houston, Little Rock and Orlando – have publically announced their 'high-impact service plans'. All ten cities are recipients of Cities of Service Leadership Grants, funded jointly by the Rockefeller Foundation and Bloomberg Philanthropies. The 2-year grants enable cities to hire Chief Service Officers to work closely with mayors to develop and implement these service strategies.

The high-impact service plans personify the concept called 'impact volunteering', which was pioneered by Cities of Service. The volunteer strategies target community needs, use best practices and set clear outcomes and measures to gauge progress. Cities of Service is a bipartisan coalition of mayors who have committed to work together to engage citizens in a multi-year effort to address pressing city needs through impact volunteerism. Founded in September 2009, the coalition includes more than 100 mayors, representing more than 49 million Americans across the United States.

PROGRAMS CURRENTLY FOSTERING ENTREPRENEURIAL INNOVATION

Several programs are noteworthy in fostering entrepreneurial innovation. Two of these are discussed below – The Ash Center for Democratic Governance and Innovation and the Project on Municipal Innovation (PMI).

The Ash Center for Democratic Governance and Innovation

The Roy and Lila Ash Center for Democratic Governance and Innovation at the John F. Kennedy School of Government, Harvard University, advances excellence and innovation in governance and public policy through research, education and public discussion.[8] Last year the center recognized 173 government programs for their newly created Bright Ideas program – designed to recognize and share creative government initiatives around the country with interested public sector, nonprofit and academic communities. Bright Ideas hopes to complement the long-standing Innovations in American Government Awards Program[9] by providing government agencies with a collection of new solutions that can be adopted today. This new program serves to recognize promising government programs and partnerships that government officials, public servants and others might find useful when faced with their own challenges. This year's cohort of Bright Ideas addresses a range of pressing issues including poverty reduction, environmental conservation and emergency management. The Bright Ideas are showcased on the Ash Center's Government Innovators Network, an online marketplace of ideas and examples of government innovation for policy makers and practitioners where innovative ideas are proposed, shared and disseminated.

Project on Municipal Innovation

In response to unprecedented budget deficits and the impending explosion of unfunded pension liabilities, the Project on Municipal Innovation (PMI)[10] was developed to create a peer-learning network of urban policy directors, to identify and promote best practices and to support the implementation of innovative ideas in cities across the country. PMI was established with support from Living Cities,[11] a collaborative of 22 of the world's largest foundations and financial institutions.

The Urban Policy Advisory Group (UPAG) – a forum of 30 of the largest and most creative cities and urban counties in the United States – is central to the PMI. It provides its members with regular access to leading policy experts and fosters ongoing collaborative discussions. One of its main goals is to help speed the adaptation and replication of innovative ideas while helping to identify and solve critical questions related to pragmatic policy deployment.

Technical assistance, a critical component of the PMI mission, facilitates the development and broad diffusion of innovative ideas in urban areas. Public policy experts are engaged to provide in-depth, on-site consultation to UPAG member cities. By providing technical assistance, they hope to close the gap between research and practice. PMI's technical assistance program promotes the adoption of innovative public management strategies with an emphasis on forming new partnerships between the public, private and philanthropic sectors. PMI carefully examines its technical assistance efforts to identify sources of success and barriers to implementation. These critical lessons are then disseminated through the project's website, which also includes 'state-of-the-field' reports and implementation blueprints.

PRACTICAL EXAMPLES OF GOVERNMENTS FOSTERING INNOVATION

The Center for American Progress acknowledges that spurring innovation within the public sector requires government-wide action, as well as specific interventions within agencies. Their newest report highlights a number of examples from around the world as proof that governments can foster creative ideas despite the many barriers they encounter.[12] Some of these practical examples include:

- Having an interactive online forum where staff can suggest and comment such as the Transportation Security Administration's IdeaFactory, which had 11 000 ideas posted in its debut year. In addition to generating great ideas, these types of forums help manage internal bureaucracy and provide a process for questioning potentially outdated policies. The main challenge for an online interactive forum is ensuring that ideas are catalogued, reviewed, responded to and acted upon in a timely manner; otherwise, the forum may actually demotivate rather than spur innovation.[13]
- Creating a way to share the burden of updating manuals and work policies through programs like DropBox, Google.Docs or Wikis. The US Army's field manual wiki has hundreds of soldiers now participating in the task previously reserved for a handful of editors. Similarly, the US Education Department has developed a special website, the Open Innovation Portal, that encourages collaboration among education professionals to tackle difficult educational problems. It is important to have a system in place for checks and balances on information, but getting the general work force involved not only shares the workload, but also shares the responsibility. This keeps staff up-to-date on the policies and procedures as well as limits the recreations of the wheel syndrome that often happens throughout different departments or agencies.[14]
- Creating a physical space conducive to innovation creation. Denmark's Ministry of Economic and Business Affairs, the Ministry of Taxation and the Ministry of Employment joined forces to create MindLab, a physical space designed specially to be promote innovative thinking – with neutral colors, easy-to-move furniture, plenty of whiteboards and a special workshop zone. Within MindLab, the collaborative team challenges traditional thinking and bureaucracy, challenges each other's thinking and experiments with the objective in mind.[15]
- Emulating the corporate version of innovation scouts within the public sector. The Young Foundation in the United Kingdom employed an experienced investigative journalist to scan for promising new projects and see what elements could be adapted or replicated. Unlike the private sector where technology is protected by

intellectual property, agencies in the public sector can work much more openly together toward solutions particularly when the culture is simultaneously and shared across departments, agencies, states, or countries that face similar challenges.[16]

- Utilizing proven creativity generation techniques. The US Navy utilized the 'Deep Dive' approach, first pioneered by the human-centered design firm IDEO, to brainstorm rapidly new ways of thinking. Other techniques that can easily be adapted for the government space include brain writing, collective notebooks or focus groups.
- Bringing in outside facilitators to unleash the creative talents of public sector staff. This can be an effective way to identify the ideas that often sit untapped in public sector organizations. The process is not that expensive, and in some cases, organizations might be able to develop their own internal capacity to help facilitate creative brainstorming sessions. Innocentive[17] is a commercial organization that works with companies to identify scientific problems that need a solution and posts them online. It then invites scientists to work up solutions. Rewards are available if they are effective at addressing the problem. There are more than 200 000 people working to solve problems that are posted on the website. Innocentive has partnered with the Rockefeller Foundation and GlobalGiving to apply this approach to the social context.
- Leveraging the talents of concerned and capable citizens. The many new 'micro-volunteering models' such as Catch-a-Fire, Taproot's pro-bono nation and even social innovation camps can facilitate this. Catch-a-Fire and Taproot have programs to partner corporate talent with NGOs in need of services but without the resources to hire them. Catch-a-Fire[18] focuses on tasks that can be done in 10- to 30-minute increments while Taproot[19] has longer but still short-term engagement opportunities. Another recent model for widening the menu of creative ideas is the Social Innovation Camp.[20] These camps bring together 100 to 200 people, roughly split between web designers and software programmers on one hand and volunteers from the public sector, business and civil society on the other for a weekend innovation cram session.

NOTES

1. Material in this section was adapted from Stephen Goldsmith, *The Power of Social Innovation*, 1st edn (San Francisco, CA: Jossey-Bass, 2010).

2. Stephen Goldsmith, 'Fostering an innovation culture', 20 April 2011, accessed 23 July 2012 at: http://www.governing.com/blogs/bfc/fostering-innovation-culture.html [blog].

3. Norman LaRocque, 'Contracting for the delivery of education services: a typology and international examples', Program on Education Policy and Governance Conference, Harvard University, October 2005, accessed 23 July 2012 at: http://www.innovations. harvard.edu/showdoc.html?id=9189. This paper is a revised version of a background report prepared for the World Bank in December 2004 and draws heavily on World Bank Report No. 31841-CO entitled 'Colombia: contracting education services', 31 March 2005.

4. S. E. Savas, *Privatization and Public-Private Partnerships* (New York: Chatham House Publishers/Seven Bridges Press, 2000).

5. Eduardo Paes, Mayor of Rio de Janeiro, 'How Rio de Janeiro uses tech to solve urban challenges', HBR Blog Network, 8:02 a.m., 27 April 2011, accessed 23 July 2012 at: http://blogs.hbr.org/revitalizing-cities/2011/04/how-rio-de-janeiro-uses-tech-t.html.

6. Stephen Goldsmith, 'Lessons from New York City's innovation efforts', 8:23 a.m. Tuesday 26 April 2011 [blog].

7. 'Ten US cities launch high-impact service plans, joining 11 others in addressing needs through impact volunteerism', 31 March 2011, accessed 23 July 2012 at: http://www. onememphis.org/press/view_post.php?&post_id=158&post_comment_request=y.

8. http://www.ash.harvard.edu.

9. The Harvard Kennedy School of Government's Innovations in American Government Award was created in 1985 by the Ford Foundation in response to widespread pessimism and distrust in government's effectiveness.

10. 'The 21st century challenge: delivering more with less', accessed 23 July 2012 at: http://ash.harvard.edu/Home/Programs/Innovations-in-Government/Municipal.

11. http://www.livingcities.org.

12. Jitinder Kohli and Geoff Mulgan, 'Capital ideas: how to generate innovation in the public sector'. A product of CAP's Doing What Works project in conjunction with The Young Foundation and the Center for American Progress, July 2010.

13. http://www.whitehouse.gov/open/innovations/IdeaFactory.

14. Kohli and Mulgan, July 2010.

15. http://www.mind-lab.dk/en.

16. Kohli and Mulgan, July 2010.

17. Kohli and Mulgan, July 2010, and http://www.innocentive.com.

18. http://catchafire.org.

19. http://www.taprootfoundation.org.

20. http://sicamp.org.

5. Managing the internal and external politics

CHAPTER OBJECTIVES

- To understand the aspects and importance of managing the internal and external politics.
- To understand the most important external political forces.
- To understand the key internal political forces.
- To understand the key external forces.
- To understand how change can occur from the outside.

INTRODUCTION

One of the most significant problems in instituting government entrepreneurship, developing creative new ways of doing things and institutional structures is the presence of internal and external politics. The impact of both of these forces, as well as the source, needs to be clearly identified and a plan for coping with these forces designed before success can be achieved. Care needs to be taken to ensure all parties involved, whether from the inside or outside the government organization, clearly understand that the activity is a win–win situation.

Such was the case confronting Sir Colin Campbell who became vice-chancellor of Nottingham University after establishing and running a number of profitable companies. Sensing some existing negative external and internal forces, he used his entrepreneurial attributes to confront them. Knowing there was internal dissent and that higher education in the UK is very political, one of Campbell's first acts was to establish a formalized university management group comprised of the registrar, the financial officer, four pro-vice chancellors and himself. Through this group and other acts, Campbell provided the university a sense of identity and increased its reputation. To confront the negative external political forces, Campbell's public relations activities corrected the negative views and established the impression that Nottingham was one of the best managed, forward-thinking universities in the UK System.

INTERNAL POLITICS

In order to understand how to manage internal and external politics in the public sector, it is helpful to understand the internal culture of government as well as those external influencing factors. While usually this culture is the opposite of the typical entrepreneurial culture, there are examples of when people have succeeded in bringing an entrepreneurial focus to the government.

The first internal political system is the very culture of government workers. Diane Katz, Senior Research Fellow in Regulatory Policy at the Heritage Foundation, noted in an interview that, 'The lack of competition and risk taking creates a very difficult culture in which entrepreneurial actions can thrive.'[1] Independent research has validated her claim. In 2009, Michael J. Roszkowski and John E. Grable found that, when compared to private sector and self-employed individuals, public sector government employees scored lower on a 51-point financial risk tolerance index.[2]

Government work culture is also affected by the system of motivation and rewards which cannot be matched in the private sector and the nature of decision making. Unlike in private companies, which serve specific target audiences, government has to serve everyone. Therefore, the decision-making process tends to lean toward one of concession, finding a middle path and is slower in process. For example, a typical company can make a decision to launch a new product and create features that would appeal to a certain target audience. Entrepreneurs can make decisions quickly because there are fewer, if any, people to approve a decision. But, in government, even if an agency has the ability to roll out a new service, which must appeal to everyone, it often has many influencing external stakeholders, which will be discussed in greater detail later, that can halt the decision.

For these three reasons, it is evident that government does not naturally attract entrepreneurs and entrepreneurial thinking; it attracts a type of individual who desires a government work culture. But, just because government might attract people with similar behavioral characteristics, this does not mean that changing government to make it more entrepreneurial is impossible. Rather, it depends on how the employees are managed and engaged; three tactics are suggested.

The first tactic to engage successfully in government entrepreneurial actions requires a proper diagnosis of where the roadblock exists and what actions are perpetuating that roadblock. These roadblocks may not exist throughout a government or the agency where an entrepreneurial-minded person works. A second tactic is to understand the hierarchy and where the individuals who need to be influenced are. Just as in any company, it is important to identify those with referent and position power. A final tactic is for the entrepreneur to align with the right type of government employee as part of the guiding team. In the United States, there are typically three types of government employees: civil service, contract and politically appointed. Civil service employees are likely the most difficult to influence and engage in entrepreneurial action. This is because, in many cases, the civil service laws make it very difficult to fire them putting time on their side. This is illustrated in the following example.

In January 2011, New York City Mayor Michael Bloomberg created a Workforce Reform Task Force to prepare a list of recommendations to reform the city's civil service laws, which were created over 120 years earlier. The commission, led by Martha Hirst, a former commissioner for the city's Department of Citywide Administrative Services, prepared a list of 23 recommendations and noted challenges about disciplining and removing employees for poor performance. For example, in New York City, the report noted that, 'The requirement that employers serve employees with formal charges and proceed through an evidentiary hearing simply to issue a reprimand to an employee denies managers the flexibility and opportunity to react in an appropriate manner to misconduct or performance issues that may not warrant suspension, demotion or termination.'[3] Another example was current state law, which notes that, 'layoffs involving other types of permanent civil service employees, must be made in order of reverse seniority, regardless of their performance'.[4]

A second type of government employee is the contract employee. Length of employment contracts can vary from a few weeks to months and, in some situations such as the defense industry, years. The use of contract workers is likely to increase in future years. IDC, a market intelligence company, has estimated that government has led all industries in the growth and desire to outsource functions. Over the last 10 years, outsourcing by federal, state and local government has increased 14.2 percent.[5] Part of the reason is that baby boomers employed by government are rapidly reaching retirement age. Indeed, according to the US Federal Government's Office of Personnel Management, by the year 2016, 60.8 percent of the non-seasonal full-time permanent workforce as of October 2006 will be eligible to retire.[6] While government contractors often do not have final approval authority to make a decision, their role as individuals who pan both the for-profit and government industries afford them to see challenges and be in a position to influence changes. They are also often brought in as consultants who are paid for their advice and recommendations. For this reason, these individuals have a greater ability than traditional civil servants to bring about entrepreneurial change in government.

Similar to the cross-functional role of contract employees, political appointees, a third type of government employee, includes both a government office and external stakeholder who hired them; these individuals are often elected officials. This provides them influence not only within the government office but also with the executive or oversight team as well. A good example of this in the US government is the White House and Congressional liaisons for various cabinet-level agencies.

A cabinet-level agency, such as the Environmental Protection Agency (EPA), has all three types of these employees. The EPA also has many stakeholders including the White House, which they take direction from, lobbyists, lawmakers who fund the agency and external groups such as the World Wildlife Fund. In order to be effective at bringing about change in an agency such as the EPA, one needs to manage effectively all the stakeholders noted earlier. The advantage of working with someone like a White House liaison is that, although they receive a paycheck from the agency, they are also the administration's 'eyes and ears' and typically report directly to the head of the agency or to the White House itself. These individuals, sometimes former campaign workers and volunteers, are often appointed from the private sector, and often have experience in the industry that is regulated by that agency. Therefore, they understand that mindset which is typically more sympathetic to entrepreneurship or they exert influence among elected leadership. This affords them significant referent and position power and access to help bring about entrepreneurial changes quicker if they are so inclined.

Similar to contract workers, but unlike civil servants, a political employee is often employed for a specific duration, typically the term of the elected leader. They are more short term and do not have time on their side, which can be both an asset and a liability. It can be an asset because it may force a political appointee to take action faster in order to produce results that will help their elected official appear more popular. But, it also may hurt them because the civil service realizes a political appointee's time is temporary and entrepreneurial changes often require a longer time horizon. The best course of action for bringing about entrepreneurial change is to align with politically appointed individuals and work to ensure the agenda matches their goals.

Identifying the potential government entrepreneurs is important; failure can still occur if the extensive collection of workplace processes, rules and regulations that are found inside government are not understood. In order to bring more entrepreneurial actions in government, two types of process rules must be understood: procurement and hiring. When you want to initiate an entrepreneurial action in government, it may therefore be helpful to get a briefing from the human resources agent about these key processes.

Understanding the purchasing/procurement process characteristics in a government agency will enable the obtainment of the needed resources to execute effectively the entrepreneurial strategy. It is particularly important to see if there are preferred vendors and the general time period when purchases can be made. For example, in the US federal government, IT spending often occurs most often in September right before the new fiscal year begins. This is because of the 'use it or lose it' rule at many agencies that call for any unspent funds to be returned at the close of the fiscal year. In 2007, the market intelligence firm INPUT noted that, 'Over the last decade, we have seen a consistent move toward agencies spending 30 percent or more of their annual IT budgets in the final quarter of the fiscal year.'[7] In addition to this, one should also be aware of restrictions such as how much can be paid for a certain product or service and the choice of providers. In the United States, this is determined by a General Services Administration (GSA) schedule; companies need to register and become an officially recognized vendor before any business contract can be signed. The GSA is an example of an entity that exerts significant influence on the operations of a government agency, yet exists independently from that agency.

It is also important to be mindful of hiring rules within government. In New York City, for example, the Task Force group chaired by Hirst noted that, 'Inflexible hiring rules require the city to offer most jobs and promotions solely through administering competitive exams, rather than basing these important decisions on a range of assessments, including a candidate's work experience and skills'.[8] Sometimes, however, these rules are not created by the agency themselves but rather an oversight institution. The New York City Task Force efforts to reform its work-force rules noted that, 'Without the approval from the [State Civil Service Commission] currently required by law, the city's efforts to streamline and modernize its system for hiring and managing employees have stalled'.[9] At the US federal government level, there is the Office of Personnel Management (OPM), which administers benefits, workplace rules, collects data and formally hires all workers. In March 2011, it was reported by the OPM that the federal government took an average of 105 days to hire a new employee, which was 17 fewer days than the previous year.[10]

EXTERNAL POLITICS

Having looked at some internal political systems and how to navigate them, it is also important to look at external forces, which can exert significant influence on the ability to bring about entrepreneurial activity in government. Six external forces will be discussed.

The first type of external force is a lobbyist. Lobbyists can be individuals, corporations or collections of individuals acting under the umbrella of a trade association, union or general membership organization. Lobbyists' ability to exert influence and shape the terms of the debate, whether through the voice of its vast membership or its ability to spend money on media advertising, can impact any entrepreneurial initiative. Since this is the case, it is important to know who they are to either seek out their opinion or conduct research on their opinions and the likelihood of their being supportive or disruptive of your intended entrepreneurial activity. For example, the Centers for Medicaid and Medicare Services would never propose a change to Medicare without consulting AARP (American Association of Retired Persons), which claims a membership of 40 million people. Sometimes lobbyists are former government officials who have deep inside knowledge of the governing process. An example is former pro-football Hall of Fame player Steve Largent who was a US Congressman from Oklahoma and is currently President and CEO of CTIA-The Wireless Association. Lobbyists can, in some cases, also be better experts on key issues than internal government employees.

The second external force is the court of public opinion. This category includes professional full-time journalists at credentialed news outlets, part-time bloggers and social media aficionados, and pollsters who develop scientific surveys measuring public sentiment. In 1968, following his return from reporting on the Tet Offensive, journalist Walter Cronkite reported that the American war effort was 'mired in stalemate'. Upon hearing this, then US President, Lyndon B. Johnson, remarked, 'if I've lost Cronkite, I've lost Middle America'.[11] Social media can have a big impact as well. Bloggers and social media can also play a major role in shaping public opinion. In early 2006, conservative US Senator George Allen (R-VA), was well on his way to another 6-year term. Indeed, the prominent conservative magazine, *National Review*, even heralded him as a possible candidate for President of the United States. But, in August of 2006, a mere few months away from his re-election, he was caught on tape uttering a racially insensitive phrase to describe a volunteer of his opponent who was following him around with a video camera. Known as the 'Maccaca Moment', Steve Grove, the head of news and politics for YouTube noted that it 'had a major impact on his campaign, and is heralded by many as the moment that YouTube Politics was born'.[12] Indeed, according to journalist Kyle Trygstad of the political publication Roll Call, the video of Allen uttering the pejorative epithet 'was a major contributing factor to his re-election loss and also upended his 2008 presidential aspirations'.[13]

This external force also includes late night comedians who make jokes about the news such as Jay Leno of *The Tonight Show*, John Stewart of *The Daily Show* or the casts of NBC's *Saturday Night Live* and *MadTV*. In September 2010, the Pew Research Center for People & the Press released a report noting that 7 percent of Americans say they regularly watch *The Daily Show* with John Stewart on Comedy Central. This is significant because the most watched nightly cable news program, *The O'Reilly Factor*, is viewed by just 10 percent of Americans; this has increased from 6 percent since 2002. *The Daily Show* has increased its viewership faster since 2002, having previously been watched by just 2 percent of the population.[14]

The best way to handle the media to ensure entrepreneurial activity in government is to hire or seek the counsel of a trusted press secretary or communications manager. Such an individual can help navigate media relations and ensure that the entrepreneurial story is properly told. It is also valuable to take a course in media and spokesperson training.

The third external force is the executive branch. It is generally understood that the executive branch is the enforcer of the legislative acts voted on by elected leaders. The executive branch in the US political system has a series of measures that allows it to act unilaterally. For example, in 1974, in an effort to curb inflation, US President Richard Nixon impounded between $12 and $13 billion in congressionally appropriated funds, which represented about 4 percent of federal spending. The President of the United States, as well as many governors and other locally elected officials, also have the ability to issue 'executive orders' which are orders directed at federal staff, not citizens, which often have the practical effect of law. Perhaps one of the most famous cases was Executive Order 10340, which US President Harry S. Truman issued in 1952 ordering all US steel mills under the control of the government to prevent a possible strike that might cripple efforts to wage an effective war in Korea. This executive order was litigated all the way to the Supreme Court in the case Youngstown Sheet & Tube Co. v. Sawyer which Truman ultimately lost.[15]

The best way to deal with this external force is to understand the ability for the executive branch to unilaterally make decisions that do not require input or approval from external stakeholders. It is also important, as noted earlier, to find and work closely with a liaison with the executive branch who can help provide an understanding of these issues.

The importance of the Youngstown case indicates a fourth external force, the court system. Court decisions, be they at the state or federal level, can have the impact of law. Some critics describe this as 'legislating from the bench' or 'judicial activism'. Typically, court cases arise from a grieved external party, such as a citizen, corporation, interest group or union official, which files a lawsuit. While court cases can take years to resolve, judges can act immediately and issue a temporary order to address an issue while the facts of the case are gathered and as both sides prepare for a possible trial or hearing. In the Youngstown case, for example, representatives from two steel companies went to the home of Judge Walter Bastian the night the Executive Order was issued and requested a temporary injunction, which was reviewed the following day.[16] The best way to handle this external force is to carefully review the legality of all entrepreneurial government activities with a general counsel to ensure that there is legal standing. Even then, this may not be enough to prevent a lawsuit from being filed. However, there is greater opportunity for long-term success if this is done.

A fifth external force is an elected official. Elected officials have three main ways they can prevent or encourage entrepreneurial activity occurring within government. The first is by inserting an amendment into a bill to defund a specific entrepreneurial initiative at an agency. They can also slow down an entrepreneurial effort by calling for hearings and investigations into the activities. Finally, they can use parliamentary procedures such as not allowing a vote on a specific piece of legislation by keeping it in a committee or, in the United States Senate, using the filibuster. Elected officials can also help increase the pace of change efforts if they recognize that someone is popular and are worried about an upcoming election. In 1996, then US President Bill Clinton vetoed welfare entitlement reform twice before finally signing the measure into law in August, just three months away from his re-election. According to then-Speaker of the House, Newt Gingrich, 'one poll showed that over 90 percent of Americans favored reform, including 88 percent of those on welfare'.[17] Being successful with elected officials requires actively working with, and not ignoring, elected leadership.

A final external force is government employee labor unions. Stewart Liff notes that, 'Labor relations can be very difficult . . . In many cases, management's negative attitude toward the union often becomes a self-fulfilling prophecy'.[18] A union's ability to influence a process can come in the form of collective bargaining rights, which may allow them to strike or file Unfair Labor Practices, which can be a distraction. An entire chapter in Liff's book (*Managing Government Employees*) is devoted to this topic. One example is the failure of US President George W. Bush to reform civil service laws for the Departments of Homeland Security and Defense in the wake of the September 11, 2001, terrorist attacks. Writing in the Review of Public Personnel Administration, authors J. Edwards Kellough, Lloyd G. Negro and Gene A. Brewer argue that the changes failed because it was perceived to be politically and ideologically motivated which met resistance from government unions.[19]

CHANGE FROM THE OUTSIDE

Even though there are a variety of external and internal factors that can inhibit or encourage change in government, there are many examples of government entrepreneurial activity. The following three examples have similar characteristics, which will be explore and analyzed.

Alfred Kahn and Airline Deregulation

From 1938 to 1978, the Civil Aeronautics Board (CAB) regulated rates that airlines could charge and where they landed for domestic-bound air travel in the United States. According to the US General Accounting Office, the regulation was instituted in 1938 to 'alleviate congressional concern over safety, airlines' financial health and perceived inequities between airlines and regulated forms of transportation, such as railroads'.[20] In 1938, there were 16 airlines with scheduled flights between major cities. This number was reduced to 10 by 1974 due to mergers and at the same time, the CAB did not approve the formation of a single new airline, despite 79 requests filed. Existing airlines benefitted from the CAB because it guaranteed them a 12 percent return on flights that were at least 55 percent full.[21]

Concerns over higher ticket prices, in part due to the rising cost of fuel, the ongoing stagflation and advances in aviation technology caused a number of people to re-think the merits of airline regulation. On 3 May 1977, President Jimmy Carter appointed Alfred E. Kahn, a professor of economics at Cornell University and the former chairman of the New York State Public Service Commission, to head the CAB.

While Kahn had no experience with the airline industry, he had a strong vision and an ability to use humor to persuade people about the lack of entrepreneurial thinking in government. In his Senate confirmation hearings, he noted, 'I know less than I plan to know about the airline industry before I make any pronouncements about the things I'm going to do, but I do begin with a clear philosophical economic conviction that in regulated industries generally, more competition is desirable where it's feasible'.[22] During his first month on the job, he immediately focused on the customer by issuing a memo to the entire CAB staff. The memo outlined his disgust with 'bureaucrat speak' and charged his employees to speak 'as though you are talking to or communicating with real people'.[23]

At a speech before the New York Society of Security Analysts, he jokingly recollected that, 'For one thing, I could not possibly have imagined the number and variety of ways in which I was going to be called upon every single day to give my consent before a willing buyer and a willing seller could get together . . . Is it any wonder that I ask myself every day:

is this action necessary?'[24] Given the complexity and sometimes redundancy of government actions today, being successful in government entrepreneurship will likely require an individual to begin by asking that very question: is this even necessary? Stephen Goldsmith, former Deputy Mayor for Operations for the City of New York and former Mayor of Indianapolis, has coined the term the 'yellow pages test'. According to The Manhattan Institute, a New York City think tank, 'If he opened the phone book and found that more than a handful of private companies were providing a service that government also provided, Goldsmith figured that Indianapolis should get out of that particular business'.[25]

Nearly 18 months after Kahn's appointment, on 24 October 1978, President Carter signed Public Law 95-504 that gradually eliminated price controls as well as government authority on airline routes and abolished the CAB altogether by 1984.[26] Kahn was not alone in his efforts. He was able to assemble airline industry leaders, elected officials including then-Senator Ted Kennedy, legal staff including a future Supreme Court Justice, Stephen Breyer and consumer activist Ralph Nader to support his efforts.[27] Two days after the legislation was signed into law, Kahn resigned his position to accept a new position as Chairman of the Council on Wage and Price Stability.[28]

The result of the measure, according to a General Accounting Office report, was that by 1984, average fare prices fell 6 percent and nonstop service offerings expanded.[29] In January 2011, Breyer reflected back on the benefits and added that airline passengers increased from 207.5 million in 1974 to 721.1 million in 2010. 'Airline revenue per passenger mile has declined from an inflation-adjusted 33.3 cents in 1974, to 13 cents in the first half of 2010. In 1974, the cheapest round-trip New York–Los Angeles flight (in inflation-adjusted dollars) that regulators would allow: $1442. Today one can fly that same route for $268. That is why the number of travelers has gone way up.'[30]

Texas State Treasurer Martha Whitehead

In July 1993, the State of Texas found itself with a new State Treasurer, Martha Whitehead. Whitehead was appointed by then-Governor Anne Richards to fill the remaining 16-month term of Kay Bailey Hutchison, who was elected to the US Senate. Richards was also a former State Treasurer and the position was viewed as a political stepping-stone.[31] However, the office was also mired in controversy. At the time of Whitehead's appointment, a district attorney had empanelled a grand jury to investigate 'allegations of tampering with governmental records, tampering with physical evidence, official misconduct and violation of the Open Records Act'.[32]

Critics and some of her political colleagues suggested that the office be eliminated but upon her appointment, Whitehead publically stated that the position still served a purpose. However, just 4 months into her job, Whitehead, like Kahn, asked a similar question and was quoted as saying, 'If it [eliminating the agency] can happen, it should . . . Why maintain unnecessary duplication?'[33]

Whitehead's office was responsible for investing state funds, managing cash, administering the tobacco tax and dealing with unclaimed property. But, she determined all of these functions could be folded into the comptroller's office, which would save over 70 percent of current Treasury expenditures which, at the time, cost the state $11 million.[34]

Whitehead did not have the ability to unilaterally act and close down her office completely. Her office was 'mandated by the Texas State Constitution and could be abolished only by a constitutional amendment approved by two-thirds of the Legislature and a majority of voters'.[35] So, she began crafting her re-election strategy on one of eliminating the office of the State Treasurer.[36]

In addition to inheriting a grand jury investigation, her opponent in the general election had accused her of mismanaging funds when, for the first time ever, her office saw 4 months of consecutive losses totaling $58 million by investing in longer-maturing securities instead of finding the right investments that would be consistent with a longer term vision for the agency.[37]

In November 1994, Whitehead ended up winning her term and, 2 years later, on 31 August 1996, she became the first statewide elected official in the United States to eliminate her own position. As the Associated Press reported, when Whitehead took over in 1993, she had a staff of 255, and by 1996, it was down to 169. Only she and nine other colleagues actually lost their jobs, but it was an exercise in effective entrepreneurial action for two key reasons.[38]

First, she proved her vision could work on a small scale. In February 1994, she was able, through interagency agreement, to transfer the tobacco tax collection division back to the Comptroller's office where it resided until 1989.[39] Second, she was able to get the media on her side. *The Dallas Morning News* had editorialized that the position should be eliminated and called on readers to support her election candidacy.

Nebraska Treasurer's Office

Riding on the success with the elimination of the Texas Treasurer's Office, Nebraska State Senator Dennis Utter had a similar plan to abolish his state's Treasurer's Office. According to published reports, the Nebraska

Treasurer's Office had a budget of $26.5 million, a staff of 49 and, 'receives and disburses state funds, oversees the college savings program, unclaimed property and the long-term care savings plan'.[40] In October 2010, Utter offered a bill in the legislature that was overwhelmingly (35–7) supported by elected leaders to let Nebraskans vote to abolish the Constitutional office.

While legislators strongly supported the bill, there were a few strong detractors. Among them was State Senator LeRoy Louden who, according to published reports, noted, 'When the counties were in charge of handling child support payments, it was in shambles'.[41] Furthermore, according to the out-going State Treasurer, while state government had grown about 5 percent over the preceding years, the office had actually decreased in size.[42] Additionally, State Senator Charlie Janssen noted that eliminating the office would not save any money; rather, 'I think this will expand other areas of government and we'll lose important government transparency'.[43]

This sentiment was echoed by Don Stenberg who, while running for election as State Treasurer, noted, 'Moving those functions to other offices would not increase efficiencies . . . and the checks and balances an elected official provides would be lost'.[44] Instead, Stenberg offered an alternative solution: 'consolidating departments rather than turning away the people's right to choose the State Treasurer . . . elected officials are more responsive to the public than appointed officials'. Additional dissent came from a co-signed letter by the current as well as three former governors of Nebraska. According to published reports, 'the only sure thing was the amount of the Treasurer's salary and benefits: $117 000. Others said state agencies may have had to hire more help to take on those functions, so even the $117 000 couldn't be counted on'.[45]

Is it any wonder then, that the following month voters rejected the ballot initiative by a two-thirds margin and, by a three-fourths margin, elected Stenberg to take over responsibilities?[46]

While the Nebraska effort failed, all three started with the same approach, that entrepreneurial activity must come from the outside and, in Kahn's case, it is not necessarily important that the change agent have deep internal knowledge about the issue. Also, similar to the examples at the CAB and in Texas, Utter started out right by questioning if the office even needs to exist and was able to build a strong coalition of legislative support to send the issue to the voters. Three lessons concerning government entrepreneurship can be learned from why the Nebraska measure failed in contrast to the other successes. This can serve as a guide for those desiring to bring about entrepreneurial initiative in government.

The first has to do with transparency. Voters did not want to approve a measure that would make them less sovereign over fiscal matters. The Association of Government Accountants annually releases surveys indicating voter preference for increased transparency in fiscal matters in government. When desiring to be more entrepreneurial in government, there needs to be an attempt to find a transparency or consumer empowerment angle. Utter was not able to identify that angle, whereas Kahn and Whitehead succeeded.

The second was the issue over savings and efficiency. Kahn and Whitehead could clearly demonstrate how money could be saved and efficiencies could be improved, two natural aspects of any entrepreneurial activity; Utter was not. The third is the sense of urgency. Kahn had rising airline ticket prices and a national recession to support his cause. Whitehead had examples of prior mismanagement in her office. Utter was not able to identify examples where the office had failed people in the past. In fact, it was just the opposite.

There is also the overall issue of coalitions. While Kahn was able to work with a variety of industry and consumer groups, Utter was not able to secure the endorsement of even the current governor. In a post-election interview, he acknowledged that the letter that the current and former governors signed, 'absolutely played a role in the amendment's defeat'.

John Kotter proposed an eight-step framework for leading change and recommended it as a model for perusing entrepreneurial activity in government. In Kotter's model, Phase One is absolutely critical to increase urgency, get the vision right and build a guiding team. It is also important to establish short-term wins like Whitehead did with moving the tobacco tax collection division out from her office.

In light of the sovereign debt crises in Greece, Spain and Ireland and the looming entitlement challenges facing the United States, there will be an increasing need for entrepreneurial leaders willing to enter government and initiate entrepreneurial activities. This will involve overcoming internal and external forces and effectively initiating change and establishing an entrepreneurial government organization.

NOTES

1. David Kralik interview with Diane Katz, Research Fellow in Regulatory Policy at The Heritage Foundation, via telephone, 1 March 2011.
2. Michael J. Roszkowski and John E. Grable, 'Evidence of lower risk tolerance among public sector employees in their personal financial matters', *Journal of Occupational and Organizational Psychology* (2009), **82** (2), 453–463.
3. 'NYC workforce reform task force report and recommendations', 7 January 2011,

accessed 23 July 2012 at: http://www.nyc.gov/html/om/pdf/2011/pr008-11_report.pdf, p. 22.

4. 'NYC workforce reform task force report and recommendations', (2011) p. 24.
5. Stephen Minton, 'Worldwide IT spending 2010–2014 forecast', IDC May 2010.
6. 'An analysis of federal employee retirement data', US Office of Personnel Management, March 2008.
7. 'INPUT expects $20 billion in Q4 GFY 2007 IT spending', Press Release, 22 August 2007, accessed 23 July 2012 at: http://www.input.com/corp/press/detail.cfm?news=1326.
8. 'NYC workforce reform task force report and recommendations', p. 4.
9. 'NYC workforce reform task force report and recommendations', p. 9.
10. Stephen Losey, 'Agencies cut average hiring by to 105 days, OPM says', *Federal Times*, 3 March 2011.
11. Tom Wicker, 'Broadcast news', *The New York Times*, 26 January 1997.
12. David Kralik interview with Steve Grove, Head of News and Politics at YouTube, via e-mail, 1 May 2011.
13. 'Americans spending more time following the news', Pew Research Center for People & the Press, 12 September 2010, p. 24.
14. *The New York Times*, 7 October 1973, p. 63, column 1.
15. William Rehnquist, 'The Supreme Court', *Knopf*, February 2001, 169–192.
16. Alan F. Westin, *The Anatomy of a Constitutional Law Case* (New York: Columbia University Press, 1990), p. 17.
17. Newt Gingrich, 'What is 'reconciliation' and why is it a threat?', *Human Events*, 3 March 2010.
18. Stewart Liff, *Managing Government Employees* (New York: Amacom Press© 2007), p. 161.
19. J. Edward Kellough, Lloyd G. Nigro and Gene A. Brewer, 'Civil service reform under George W. Bush: ideology, politics, and public personnel administration', *Review of Public Personnel Administration* (2010), **30** (4), 404–422.
20. US General Accounting Office, 'Deregulation: increased competition is making airlines more efficient and responsive to consumer', Washington DC, 6 November 1985.
21. Robert D. Hershey Jr., 'Alfred E. Kahn, 93 dies; led airline deregulation', *The New York Times*, 29 December 2010.
22. Carole Shifrin, 'CAB nominee promises increase in competition', *The Washington Post*, 7 June 1977.
23. 'The Writings of Chairman Kahn', *The Washington Post*, 30 June 1977.
24. 'Kahn urging CAB deregulation drive', *Aviation Week & Space Technology*, 6 March 1978.
25. http://www.manhattan-institute.org/html/cci.htm.
26. Carole Shifrin, 'Carter signs airlines deregulation bill', *The Washington Post*, 25 October 1978.
27. Adam Thierer, 'Who'll really benefit from net neutrality regulation?', *CBS News*, 21 December 2010.
28. Carole Shifrin, 'Cohen named CAB head to succeed Alfred Kahn', *The Washington Post*, 26 October 1978.
29. US General Accounting Office, 'Deregulation: increased competition is making airlines more efficient and responsive to consumer', Washington DC, 6 November 1985.
30. Stephen Breyer, 'Airline deregulation, revisited', *Bloomberg BusinessWeek*, 20 January 2011.
31. Sam Attlesey, 'Treasury under scrutiny as Whitehead takes helm', *The Dallas Morning News*, 5 July 1993.
32. Sue Anne Pressley, '15 subpoenaed in probe of Hutchison Campaign', *The Washington Post*, 10 June 1993.
33. Sylvia Moreno, 'Two races anything but ordinary', *The Dallas Morning News*, 20 February 1994.
34. 'Reinventing treasury', *The Dallas Morning News*, 26 October 1994.

35. Sylvia Moreno, 'Two races anything but ordinary'.
36. Sam Attlesey, 'Treasury under scrutiny as Whitehead takes helm'.
37. William Murchison, 'Treasurer battle already is heated', *The Dallas Morning News*, 20 July 1994.
38. 'Texas says goodbye to Treasury', Associated Press, 31 August 1996.
39. Sylvia Moreno, 'Two races anything but ordinary'.
40. JoAnne Young, 'Abolish treasurer post? Voters to decide', *Lincoln Journal Star*, 24 October 2010.
41. JoAnne Young, 'Senators: Let voters decide about treasurer', *Lincoln Journal Star*, 3 March 2010.
42. JoAnne Young, 'Senators: Let voters decide about treasurer'.
43. JoAnne Young, 'Senators: Let voters decide about treasurer'.
44. JoAnne Young, 'Abolish treasurer post? Voters to decide'.
45. JoAnne Young, 'Nebraskans elect Stenberg as treasurer, vote to keep the office', *Lincoln Journal Star*, 2 November 2010.
46. JoAnne Young, 'Nebraskans elect Stenberg as treasurer, vote to keep the office'.

6. Developing the plan and building the coalition

CHAPTER OBJECTIVES

- To understand the aspects of organizational structure and organizational structure in government.
- To understand the aspects of a coalition and its benefits.
- To present the obstacles to forming and operating a coalition.
- To understand how to identify partners for a coalition.
- To understand how to access the risks involved.
- To know how to create a successful coalition.

INTRODUCTION

Why is it so difficult to partner? Why are coalitions so difficult to form? Why do so few coalitions achieve success and endure? The answer to these and other questions surrounding building a coalition are addressed in this chapter. Those who are uncertain about the strength of interactions and coalitions should understand the activities of Admiral Mike Mullen, chairman of the Joint Chiefs of Staff, the top military officer in the United States. Admiral Mullen feels comfortable meeting with US army personnel in Yongsan, Korea; giving a seminar to students at George Washington University; appearing on *The Daily Show* and being interviewed by Jon Stewart; meeting with chief executive officers (CEOs) at the *Wall Street Journal*'s CEO Council Conference; or meeting with Afghanistan President Hamid Korzai. In devoting meaningful time to all these constituencies, Admiral Mullen relies on his low-profile team – the Chairman's Action Group (CAG).

This spirit of cooperation is exemplified in the coalition of Evonik, Taiyo Nippon Sanso Corporation and the city of Yokkaichi, Japan. The two companies invested $200 million in an integrated production facility in the city for the production of monosilane, an industrial gas that is used among other things to form silicon films on thin film solar cells. This partnership enabled Evonik, a German industrial chemical and energy company, to enter the production of electronic-grade monosilane for skin-care and anti-aging products.

Similarly, Estée Lauder has long recognized that Japan is easily the largest skincare market in the world with Japanese women using, on average, seven skincare products 4 to 5 days a week. Estée Lauder teamed up with Kobe City, Japan, to develop a research facility on anti-aging products – the Kobe Skin Research Institute. The Institute partners with the Anti-aging Research Center at nearby Doshisha University sharing data, focusing on how aging spots are formed and learning how to repair damaged cells.

OVERVIEW OF ORGANIZATIONAL STRUCTURE

The organizational structure, most simply put, is a framework within which an organization arranges its lines of authority and communications, and allocates rights and duties. It most often refers to the formal and informal patterns of relationships by which an institution organizes work and distributes power. It is typically hierarchical and determines the manner and extent to which roles and responsibilities are delegated, controlled and coordinated and dictates how information flows between levels of management. The type of structure is tightly linked with the objectives of the organization. In a centralized structure, the decision making power is concentrated in the top layer of management and tight control is exercised over departments and divisions. In a decentralized structure, the decision-making power is distributed and the departments and divisions have varying degrees of autonomy and decision-making authority.

Although the concept of an organizational structure applies to all organizations, it is important to recognize that the organizational realities, goals, constraints and stakeholders differ greatly between the public and private spheres. Organizational structures within government vary significantly depending on the level, function and location.

ORGANIZATIONAL STRUCTURE IN GOVERNMENT

In order for government to have success at fostering entrepreneurship, it will need to create an organizational structure that both identifies and caters to the unique needs and environment of the public sector. A more detailed discussion of public–private partnerships will be given in the following chapter.

An unsettled environment can be conducive to entrepreneurial activity. According to Morris and Jones (1999), the external environment for most of the public sector can be characterized as highly turbulent, which implies an increasingly dynamic, hostile and complex set of environmental conditions. Most government organizations and governments themselves operate in constantly changing and often volatile environments providing tremendous opportunities for entrepreneurship to fit well within the government space. Smaller, more organic structures appear to be more appropriate when faced with high levels of environmental change; the trend should be for the government to shift towards smaller subsets of governmental work.

There is a strong need for strong leadership interaction between the public organization and their entrepreneurial leaders. This leadership style needs to adapt to the changing organizational and environmental needs and, especially in the case of government, be flexible, innovative and conducive to change. According to the Morris and Jones study of fostering entrepreneurship within a public school system, success is dependent on having an effective leader, good planning systems, customer-driven orientation, efficient operations and hands-on management.

Yet, most of the systems within government are, according to The Partnership for Reinventing Government (PRG),[1] 'rigid, hierarchical, and segmented ... [which] dilutes individual responsibility'. PRG's guiding philosophy at changing the US Government was outlined in a White Paper, Transforming Organizational Success.[2] One of their strategies was to 'delay headquarters and streamline field structures' which, at the time of this writing, was costing the government $35 billion a year in salaries and benefits for the more than 660 000 people involved in 34 000 field offices with service delivery patterns that differed by agency. Some may say that PRG was successful in this effort. In their final (1997) Annual Report, they proudly noted that, 'a big reduction in red tape and government bureaucracy – leading to savings of $132 billion for the taxpayer'.[3]

Simply changing the organizational structure of government may not be enough to foster true entrepreneurship, nor would it be enough to treat entrepreneurship within the public sector the same as in the private sector. The motivations of public versus private entrepreneurs differ. Most notably public sector employees – and potential entrepreneurs – are not driven by profit and are most likely not able to continuously create a venture and then move on to another as is the case within the more traditional private entrepreneurial sector. It is important to consider the motivations, reward systems and culture when designing an organizational structure and subsequent change of strategy in order for the new mindset and structure to occur.

The imbedded culture and systems of government do not inherently foster collaboration within or across different sectors or departments; this means building a support group or coalition is one key.

WHAT IS A COALITION?

A coalition is a diverse group of individuals or organizations that come together to work for a common goal. Strong coalitions often leverage the different backgrounds, experiences, skill sets and influences of their members to tackle complex problems. They come in a variety of forms including permanent or temporary, single or multi-issue.

Coalitions are the cornerstones of transformational change within any community, organization or industry and can be the necessary catalyst for governments to foster entrepreneurship, break through bureaucratic red tape and create sustainable solutions. They have the ability to bring together organizations and individuals to build a power base that works to influence social change, create efficiencies and leverage synergies within the public and private sectors.

One of the most important aspects of a coalition is the partners involved. The process of identifying partners is succinctly described in Figure 6.1

BENEFITS TO A COALITION

Ros Tennyson (2003) contends that partnering is easy to talk about but invariably somewhat harder to undertake. It requires courage, patience and determination, and above all else time. In her 'Partnering Toolkit' developed for the International Business Leaders Forum (IBLF), Tennyson presents a slightly different view. She explores a number of partnership initiatives in different parts of the world that illustrate how cross-sector collaboration can be highly effective and sustainable. The keys are to assure it is designed, developed and managed in a systematic way. 'Single sector approaches have been tried and have proved disappointing. Working separately, different sectors have developed activities in isolation – sometimes competing with each other and/or duplicating efforts and wasting valuable resources (Tennyson)'. Working separately has all too often led to the development of what Tennyson refers to as a 'blame culture' in which chaos or neglect is always regarded as someone else's fault.

Coalitions that span across sectors and industries provide a new opportunity to recognize the qualities and competencies of each sector and find new ways of leveraging these for mutual benefit and sustainable solutions.

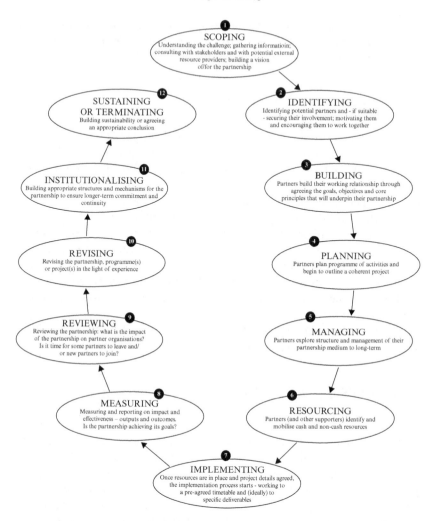

Source: Tennyson, R. (2003), The Partnering Initiative/International Business Leaders Forum and Global Alliance for Improved Nutrition. Barbara Torggler (ed.). Available from: thepartneringinitiative.org.

Figure 6.1   Identifying partners for the coalition

The International Business Leaders Forum (IBLF) is a not-for-profit organization established in 1990 to promote responsible business leadership and partnerships for sustainable international development. The Partnering Initiative is a global program of the IBLF in association with the University of Cambridge Program for Industry. The Partnering

Initiative focuses on advancing and disseminating cutting-edge knowledge and methodologies for effective cross-sector collaboration.

An analysis of the survey of the Partnering Initiative suggests that partnering experiences, perceptions and challenges tend to be common across all sectors, cultures and roles.

When respondents were asked what they saw as significant achievement in their partnering work, their responses included:

- Individual Level Achievements
  - Personal and professional growth
  - Recognition
  - Job satisfaction
  - Increasingly being seen as 'change agents'
  - Making important contributions to society
  - Gaining relationship-building skills
  - Being better equipped to facilitate complex interactions between very different players
  - Increased access to significant resources from new sources
- Management Level Achievements
  - Increased confidence in developing appropriate processes for more effective partnering
  - Better able to build more robust partnerships capable of overcoming challenges
  - Improved ability to develop a learning culture among partners and within partner organizations
  - The ability to keep up the momentum beyond the initial 'honeymoon' period themselves and as a staff.

Coalitions can also lead to significant changes in the systems and policy areas. The survey highlighted how coalitions were able to transform opinions and institutional practices; successfully promote a partnering approach to other key policy makers, donors and leaders; and contribute to creating an enabling environment for more effective partnering and resource sharing.

OBSTACLES TO A COALITION

Forming a coalition can bring about great support, momentum and change, but there are many barriers that need to be overcome in order to create and sustain a successful coalition. It can be helpful to organize the potential, perceived and actual challenges into categories in order to better prepare for and handle them when they arrive. Common challenges will fall within their own organizations, with the partnerships and within the bigger environment in which the coalitions are operating. Some common pitfalls are indicated in Table 6.1.

Not all coalitions or partnerships are going to succeed. When there are too many obstacles or when initial attempts to work through the obstacles fail, sometimes it is best to abandon the idea of a coalition and wait for a better time, a change in environment or an election. One such example of this occurred in 2002 when a Commission to study the long-term financial sustainability of the US Social Security system reported back with a recommendation to move to private accounts but advised to delay any such vote on the measure until the following year.[4]

However, most obstacles can be overcome with the right blend of patience, commitment and effort. Sometimes major obstacles or crises may actually be good for the coalition and may provide a key turning point.

There is significant research on the concept of coalition building in a variety of spaces – ranging from public to private, small to big and internal versus external. There are many models that can be used to go about forming a coalition often with the same underlying themes on the variety of names given to the steps. Much of the research also indicates that the steps are not necessarily linear and some may need to be cyclical or revisited in order to move forward.

The Tennyson Partnership Toolkit identifies the following steps to building a coalition:

- Scoping
- Identifying
- Building
- Planning
- Managing
- Resourcing
- Implementing
- Measuring
- Reviewing
- Revising
- Institutionalizing
- Sustaining or terminating.

Table 6.2 indicates aspects of a strong partnership; these aspects have attracted the best set of partner organizations. At an early stage, it is critical to:

- Identify what types of partner organizations would add value
- Explore the range of options available either by building on existing and proven contacts or by seeking new ones
- Select the most appropriate partners and secure their active involvement.

Table 6.1 Obstacles to forming a coalition

Challenges at the Individual Level within the Partnership
- Limited partnering skills or competencies needed
- Uncertainty about how to create and maintain partnership structures
- Lack of personal empowerment
- Difficulties in juggling different priorities
- Potential for personnel burn-out
- Inadequate partnering skills
- Restricted internal or external authority
- Job or role is too narrowly defined
- Lack of belief in or buy in for the partnership

Challenges within the Partner Organizations
- A lack of understanding about partnering and partnership potential
- Leadership shortcomings
- Low level of management 'buy in' to the partnership
- Human resource challenges
- Competing organizational priorities
- Inability to capture and communicate the benefits of partnering
- Sector characteristics (actual or perceived)
  - Public sector: bureaucratic and intransigent
  - Business sector: single-minded and competitive
  - Civil society: combative and territorial

Challenges within the Coalitions
- Time constraints
- Partnership politics and hidden agendas
- Lack of commitment from partners
- Relationship and behavioral issues
- Too few colleagues with partnering skills
- Flawed decision-making processes
- Lack of clarity within the partnership structures and procedures
- Conflicting priorities
- Competitiveness (within sector)
- Intolerance (of other sectors)

Challenges with the External Environment
- General misunderstanding and misuse of the term 'partnership'
- Lack of dialogue with key external players
- Financial and other resource constraints

Table 6.1 (continued)

- Unexpected external factors that impact the partnership
- Inadequacies in the public sector in its approach to partnering – whether in terms of active engagement or in creating a more enabling environment
- Local social, political and economic climate
- Scale of challenge(s) and speed of change
- Inability to access external resources

Challenges within the Coalitions
- Attitude of skepticism
- Rigid preconceived attitudes about specific sectors, partners, or ways of doing things
- Inflated expectations of what is possible

Additional Challenges Specific to Governments
- Governmental policies, procedures, bureaucracy and red tape
- Personnel restrictions (hiring/firing)
- Limitations to amount or type of rewards
- Limited managerial autonomy
- Autocratic management
- Changing nature of governments, especially in volatile states or when parties are not consistent
- Long history of non-innovative 'play by the rules' culture
- Typical government organizational structure does not foster collaboration across sectors or with external partners.

Table 6.2   Continual process of sense-making

- Defining identity in a constantly uncertain environment;
- Retrospectively creating meaning – current and past meanings reciprocally influence each other;
- Shaping the environment in which meaning is created;
- Interacting through dialogue and discourse to share (and mutually create) subjective meanings;
- Extracting a momentary sense out of continuous, complex, ongoing situations;
- Selecting and amplifying single clues to represent the meaning of larger data sets, and;
- Embellishing and elaborating a single piece of information to create plausible (although not necessarily accurate) meanings.

It may be necessary to explain the idea of a partnership and to make a sound case for why the particular organization would have something to contribute and how the government organization would be able to benefit. It usually takes time to persuade enough people in the prospective partner organization that this partnership will be worth the time and effort involved. There may also be some value in organizing special activities such as workshops, site visits and exchanges between several potential partner organizations to explore the idea of partnering more fully and collaboratively before any firm commitments are agreed.

In some instances, there may be little or no choice about the partners in the coalition because membership may be stipulated by statute and oftentimes divided equally in terms of ideology. For example in February 2010, President Obama appointed an 18-member panel with eight Republicans and ten Democrats to study how to reduce the federal deficit. The organizational charter called for six Republican and six Democrat members from both the House and Senate with four being named by the President with the requirement that 14 votes would be required for implementation.[5]

If it is important to work with a local government department, for example, then effort will need to be dedicated to persuading them to become actively involved by showing how they can benefit by having their own goals and objectives achieved through the partnership and by working in constructive collaboration with other sectors. In each coalition situation, it is important to be realistic about what is likely to be achieved and to be open about the challenges involved.

CREATING THE COALITION'S IDENTITY: APPLYING SENSE-MAKING TO A COALITION

The difficulty of coalition building mainly occurs in bringing together organizations that may have significant cultural differences and widely varying identities, meanings and 'senses' or that may even be (and can remain) competitors in one manner or another. Sense-making refers to a specific process of literally creating meaning or sense in a social context to explain a cue or event. The central premise of sense-making is that meaning is not discovered or revealed – meaning is constructed by the sense-maker. Since coalitions are usually composed of participants who come from different organizational cultures with different experiences and senses of identity, this concept can be valuable for coalition leaders as they approach simple questions of organizational design.[6] The theory of sense-making presents a useful framework for the government entrepreneur to address gaps in meaning between coalition members on key issues.

Sense-making emphasizes the gap that exists in the meaning attached to an event by one person (or organization) and the meaning attached by another. The implication for the governmental entrepreneur is that there may be organizational design features that accommodate the idea that coalition participants do not require consistent meanings, no matter how much material, documentation, argument, history, logic or persuasion is presented. The first lesson of sense-making is that more evidence does not necessarily alter the meaning participants have already constructed. The assumption is that individuals see what they believe – not what they are told or taught.

The importance of identity construction for sense-making by coalition members may have significant implications for the initial design of the organization, as well as the importance of continued monitoring of changes in that identity – if the answer to 'Who are we?' changes. Changes can also be expected in the meaning that members attach to previously positive information.

The process of sense-making, outlined in Table 6.2, involves several aspects. These include defining the identity; creating meaning; shaping the environment; interacting; extracting sense from the situations; selecting clues that represent meaning; and elaborating to create plausible meanings.

ASSESSING RISKS

The Partnering Toolkit indicates that each partner needs to assess the risks that may arise from being involved in a cross-sector initiative. Risk assessment is important and sometimes easily ignored in the enthusiasm for potential benefits from collaboration in a coalition. Partners should encourage each other to undertake such assessments at an early stage of their collaboration and find opportunities for addressing any concerns together as a partner group in an objective atmosphere. Organizational risk for each of the sectors may arise in any of the following areas:

- Reputational impact: All organizations and institutions value their reputation and are concerned about whether that reputation can be damaged either by the fact of the coalition itself or by any fall-out in the future should the partnership fail. One example of reputational impact by joining a coalition was the US Senate's 'Gang of 14' moderate Senators who joined together to stop the stymied Judicial confirmation process. One member, Senator Lindsey Graham from South Carolina, particularly felt pressure from his most loyal constituents because, as former 'Gang of 14' member and Louisiana Democratic Senator John Breaux noted, 'The bases of both parties don't like anyone who looks like they've helped the other side'.[7]
- Loss of autonomy: Working in collaboration inevitably means less independence for each organization in the areas of joint work.
- Conflicts of interest: Whether at strategic or operational levels, coa-

Table 6.3   Goals of a successful coalition

- Believable: beware of the 'pie in the sky goals' that may undermine your realistic goals.
- Attainable: it should be possible to complete the goals in a determined amount of time.
- Tangible: the goals should be capable of being understood or realized and it should be clear who will do what and when it will be completed.
- Developed jointly: input and acceptance are vital ingredients to successfully accomplishing the group's goals and therefore all members need to be present for their formation.
- On a timetable: a completion date should be included in the goal statement and mini-deadlines can often provide good checkpoints along the way.
- Win–win: the goals must allow all members of the coalition to be successful.

---

lition commitments can give rise to split loyalties and/or to feeling pushed to settle for uncomfortable compromise. In proposing solutions to pay down the US debt, the Simpson-Bowles commission recommended $1 trillion in new taxes which was not acceptable to some members of Congress who had signed a pledge not to raise taxes.[8]

- Drain on resources: Coalitions typically require a heavy 'front end' investment (especially of time), in advance of any appropriate level of 'return'.
- Implementation challenges: Once a coalition is established and resources procured, there will be a fresh set of commitments and other challenges for each partner organization as the partnership moves into project implementation.

GOAL SETTING AS A COALITION

The Ohio Center for Action on Coalition Development for Family and High Risk Youth[9] has done significant research on what makes coalitions effective. They have found two key components to successful coalitions: (1) the creation of a needs assessment, and (2) targeted goal setting. The needs assessment, done prior to goal setting, allows members or organizations to: (1) develop a list of priorities; (2) share what problems or needs are being addressed by the coalition; (3) identify group goals; (4) find new problems to address; and (5) enhance present problems. The needs assessment provides the natural platform for effective goal setting.

Table 6.3 presents some of the goals of successful coalitions. These goals include believable, attainable, tangible, jointly developed, having a succinct timetable and win–win obtainment. To be successful, each member of the coalition must have each of these goals being obtained for themselves and their organization.

CREATING A COALITION-FRIENDLY ENVIRONMENT

The public sector is increasingly affected by the dynamic environment in which it operates. This environment includes the political system, in which political authorities operate as principals of bureaucratic agents, as well as society as a whole, in which individual citizens and the organizations operate as the consumers of the services and products.

The responses to the Partnership Initiative Survey revealed a number of recommendations on how to create the best environment for building coalitions. Coalitions can be much more effective if there are sufficient capacity-building opportunities focused on developing individual and organizational collaborative skills. It is also necessary to focus on how best to articulate the added value that can be obtained in order to attain the most from the coalition. In order to ensure that the coalition is responsible, rigorous and effective, it is imperative to create a full understanding by donors, managers and leaders of the need for a proper investment of time that is required for the coalition. Senior managers in all sectors need to provide collaborative and innovative leadership. The government needs to understand and be committed to its role and work to develop national policy frameworks to support coalitions and partnering. Time needs to be spent on building comprehensive communication strategies that incorporate the role of the media in the coalition's success.

The survey also identified the changes participants recommended in order to enable partnership practitioners to achieve their partnering goals more effectively. The results of the survey led to The Partnership Declaration, a challenge to sector leaders, policy makers and donors to create the most effective environment for successful partnerships.

ELEMENTS OF SUCCESS

It is important for the coalition to leverage the strengths of its individuals and organizations. Time should be taken to identify individual strengths when forming goals helping to ensure: (1) that time is not wasted; (2) key resources are brought to the table; and (3) work is not duplicated.

It is especially important to be transparent at all stages of coalition work, but especially during the goal setting. In the last 20 years, at least two major US Presidential commissions faced a backlash in the political system and failed to get their recommendations implemented in part because the process was not transparent. Current US Secretary of State, Hillary Clinton, when she was serving as First Lady under President Bill Clinton, was appointed to head up the Task Force on National Health Care Reform. She was appointed on 22 September 1993 and by 29 October 1994, the outlook was very grim with analysis pinning its failure on 'the closed-door negotiating posture'.[10] Similarly, in 2001, Vice President Dick Cheney's National Energy Policy Development Group (NEPDG) also faced challenges with transparency. The *International Herald Tribune* described NEPDG's work as the product of, 'writing energy policy behind closed doors with oil executives'.[11]

Members should not allow hidden agendas to jeopardize the work of the coalition and should commit to an honest conversation and transparency. Each member or organization may have its own priorities and may struggle to accept the different priorities of others, but a transparent discussion explaining why a particular principle matters may go a long way to reconciling apparent differences and to achieving compromise.[12]

In the University of Florida's adaptation of Ohio State University's series on coalition building,[13] a number of other key success factors are developed for forming and maintaining strong coalitions including:

- Common goals: What is the expressed need the group agrees is a priority? What is the desired change? These need to be understood and agreed on by all involved.
- Communication: Use common language that everyone can understand. Avoid professional jargon. Each member needs to know what is expected.
- Opportunity to participate: Each member should have input into goals, methods and decisions, as well as discussion.
- Ownership: Feeling a part of the coalition and responsibility for some action is an important result of participating in the decision-making process.
- Delegation: Delegate to each entity a part they can control. That provides an opportunity for individual accomplishments as well as contributes to the overall success of the coalition.
- Efficient, effective meetings: Keep the meetings moving toward the agreed goals. Each should show progress toward the overall target(s) and participants should recognize this progress when they leave.
- Process and pattern: Establish a format for conduct of meetings and decision making early in the development of the coalition.

BROKERING THE PARTNERSHIP IDEA: AN EXAMPLE OF COALITION BUILDING IN KRAKOW

As Poland began its move to market economy and democracy following 50 years of communism in the early 1990s, the IBLF and the Krakow-based Progress and Business Foundation (PBF) joined forces to broker a new way of engaging businesses in helping the City of Krakow and its people to take full advantage of newly won economic and political freedoms.[14] The initiative brought together leaders from all sectors in a damaged and unconfident Krakow in 1993, including the newly elected Mayor of Krakow. A variety of ideas and projects were discussed at the meeting, and the Krakow Development Forum was born. It was established as a non-profit organization, responding to opportunities and problems within Krakow. By 1996, the coalition organization had 88 members representing key sectors in the city. An original aim of the KDF was to be a temporary partnership. By 1998, a number of projects initiated through the KDF had gathered their own momentum, and partnering had become an accepted way of working between sectors, hence the organization was disbanded. The process of cross sector collaboration remains common practice in Krakow today.

PUBLIC–PRIVATE PARTNERSHIPS

Any collaboration between public bodies, such as local authorities or central government, and private companies tends to be referred to as a public–private partnership. It is not a donation by a private firm or a mandate by a governmental body, but rather a joint collaboration with mutual benefits. These will be discussed in terms of benefits and examples.

Benefits of Public–Private Partnerships

There are many benefits of public–private partnerships. These include:

- Provides checks and balances to the non-profit seeking angle
- Offers differing perspectives
- May provide ability to circumvent some of the red tape
- Provides collaboration and training opportunities
- Taps into bigger networks and more contacts
- Can streamline initiatives; bigger impact

Klijn and Teisman (July 2003), articulate some of the tensions that may exist when public and private sector parties collaborate.

The relationships between core businesses, values and strategies of the public and private sectors are indicated in Table 6.4. Particularly noteworthy are the tensions that can result. For example, in terms of the difference in the core business of the two types of organizations can result in different problems that each organization is trying to solve particularly in terms of political risks versus market risks. Similarly, there can be tension between the public sector organization and private sector organization if the creation of added value is not realized.

Examples of Public–Private Partnerships

For the past two decades, a large number of countries have been investigating and promoting public–private partnerships. These partnerships have initiated various projects in a number of arenas.

Netherlands
The Dutch Knowledge Centre on Public–Private Partnerships, set up in the late 1990s by the Dutch Ministry of Finance, has stated that, 'International experiences demonstrate that a faster and more efficient implementation of infrastructure projects is possible through public–private partnership'. Both public and private sectors in the Netherlands have displayed an interest and willingness for public–private partnerships.[15]

The Utrecht Central Station Project (UCP) involves redeveloping the area around the railway station, including the Hoog Catharijne shopping center in which the station is situated. The project was designed to: (1) improve public space; (2) improve internal traffic facilities so that passengers have quick, efficient and easy travel using public transport and achieve good connections to other types of transport; and (3) to strengthen economic opportunities. The Dutch government, the Dutch national railways (NS), the owners of the Jaarbeurs Complex and the owner of the Hoog Catharijne shopping center drew up plans to redevelop the area. A memorandum of understanding was published in 1988 when the four bodies agreed to develop a master plan for the area. Taking into account the differences of opinion between the municipality and the three landowners, a new initiative was launched after realization of the master plan in 1993. This involved the creation of a development corporation owned by the municipality and by three large project developers.

United Kingdom
Public–private partnerships are at the heart of the government's attempts to revive Britain's public services. Tony Blair was excited to expand the range of private–public partnerships because he believed it was the best

Table 6.4   *Relations between the core businesses, values and strategies of public and private sectors*

	Public actors	Private actors	Tension
Core business	Objectives: (sectoral) public objectives Continuity: political conditions	Objectives: realizing profits Continuity: financial conditions	Different problem definitions: political risks in expectations versus market risks in annual figures
Values	Loyalty Devoted to a self-defined public cause Controllability of process and approach (political/social) Emphasis on risk avoidance and preventing expectations	Competitive Devoted to consumer preferences Controlled by shareholders on the basis of results Emphasis on market opportunities and risks and innovations	Government reluctant in process versus private party reluctant with knowledge Government reluctant in result versus private parties reluctant with their own effort
Strategies	Search for ways to guarantee substantive influence (primacy of the public sector) Minimizing expectations and in security of implementation costs	Search for certainties to produce and/or obtain a contract Minimizing political risks and organizational costs as a consequence of public 'viscosity'	Confrontation leads to a mutual 'locking-up' of agreements and thus to tried and tested types of co-operation (contracts)
Consequences for public–private partnerships	Emphasis on a limitation of risks and on agreements that lead to agreed procedures and public sector dominance	Emphasis on certainty of market share and profit, which leads to an expectant attitude and limited investments until the moment when the contract is acquired	The creation of added value through cross-border interaction is not realized

Source: Klijn, E.-H. and G. R. Teisman. Institutional and strategic barriers to public–private partnership: an analysis of Dutch cases. First published in *Public Money & Management*, Vol. 23, No. 3, 2003. Reproduced with the authors' and copyright holder's permission.

way to secure improvements in public services. According to the BBC, he thought private companies are often more efficient and better run than bureaucratic public bodies. In trying to bring the public and private sectors together, the government hopes that the management skills and financial acumen of the business community will create better value for the money for taxpayers.[16]

United States

The Biomarkers Consortium is a public–private partnership including the National Institutes of Health; the US Food and Drug Administration (FDA) as part of FDA's Critical Path Initiative; the Centers for Medicare & Medicaid Services; the pharmaceutical, biotechnology, diagnostics and medical device industries; non-profit organizations and associations; and advocacy groups. It is managed by the Foundation for the National Institutes of Health. Its purpose is to promote the discovery, qualification, development and regulatory acceptance of biological markers in order to accelerate the delivery of successful new technologies, medicines and therapies for prevention, early detection, diagnosis and treatment of disease.

It has an Executive Committee, representing founding partners and stakeholders that sets the policy and makes decisions regarding projects. A Subject Matter Steering Committee oversees the development and implementation of projects by dedicated project teams. Policies have been developed through a multi-sector process of discussion and negotiation, and apply to all activities.[17]

NOTES

1. The National Partnership for Reinventing Government http://govinfo.library.unt.edu/npr/library/reports/tosexe.html.
2. http://govinfo.library.unt.edu/npr/library/reports/tosexe.html.
3. 'Businesslike government: lessons learned from America's best companies', National Performance Review, 1997.
4. Sean Higgins, 'Is reform of Social Security no longer politically taboo?' *Investor's Business Daily*, 27 February 2002.
5. Mark Trumbull, 'Can Obama's deficit commission work as partisanship rages?' *The Christian Science Monitor*, 18 February 2010.
6. Craig Christiansen, 'Sense-making and entrepreneurial coalition building: a case of competing interests, cultural barriers, and interorganizational relations in a nonprofit health plan', *International Journal of Public Administration* (2006), **29** (7), 501–515.
7. Jonathan Darman and Holly Bailey, 'Squeezed in the middle', *Newsweek*, 14 August 2006.
8. Jed Graham, 'Deficit panel's proposal to hike taxes, slash spending struggles for support; ObamaCare a deal breaker?' *Investor's Business Daily*, 2 December 2010.
9. The Ohio Center for Action on Coalition Development for Family and High Risk

Youth's Building a Coalition, Series, accessed 23 July 2012 at http://edis.ifas.ufl.edu/fy493.

10.   J. Jennings Moss, 'Clinton faces grim prospects in 104th Congress', *The Washington Times*, 29 October 1994.
11.   'Dick Cheney's Imperial Presidency', *International Herald Tribune*, 24 December 2005.
12.   Ros Tennyson, *The Brokering Guidebook* (London: IBLF, 2005).
13.   'Building Coalitions: Coalition Function'. This series on Coalition Building was developed by The Ohio Center for Action on Coalition Development for Family and High Risk Youth, Richard Clark, PhD, Director. It has been adapted for County Extension Faculty in Florida to facilitate work with local and regional organizations and groups such as non-profits, cooperatives, county extension associations and others that might benefit from a plan for working together to achieve support for mutual goals. This document is FY495, Part 3 of the 16-part series adapted for use in Florida by Elizabeth B. Bolton, Professor, Community Development, and Lisa Guion, Assistant Professor, Program Planning and Evaluation; Department of Family, Youth and Community Sciences, Florida Cooperative Extension Service, Institute of Food and Agricultural Sciences, University of Florida, Gainesville, 32611-0310. Reprinted with permission March 1997. Revised April 2002.
14.   The Partnership Initiative, accessed 23 July 2012 at: http://thepartneringinitiative.org/what_is_partnering/When_to_partner.jsp.
15.   Kenniscentrum [Knowledge Centre] (1999), 'PPP Progress Report', The Hague.
16.   'What are public–private partnerships?' BBC News: World Edition, 12 February 2003, accessed 23 July 2012 at: http://news.bbc.co.uk/2/hi/uk/1518523.stm.
17.   NIH Public–Private Partnership Program, accessed 23 July 2012 at: http://ppp.od.nih.gov/pppinfo/examples.asp.

BIBLIOGRAPHY

Klijn, Erik-Hans and Geert R. Teisman (July 2003), 'Institutional and strategic barriers to public–private partnership: an analysis of Dutch cases', *Public Money & Management*, **23** (3), 137–146.

Morris, Michael H. and Foard F. Jones (Fall 1999), 'Entrepreneurship in established organizations: the case of the public sector', *Entrepreneurship: Theory and Practice*, **24**, 71–91.

Tennyson, Ros (2003), 'Partnering ToolKit', International Business Leaders Forum, Shambhala Publications, Inc. Phoenix.

7. Funding the venture

CHAPTER OBJECTIVES

- To understand new ways of financing government entrepreneurship.
- To understand public–private partnerships as a funding mechanism.
- To learn how venture capital can be used to fund government entrepreneurship.
- To learn about several innovative ways to fund government entrepreneurship.

INTRODUCTION

The recent financial crisis and economic recession has forced everyone to reevaluate current practices and strategies. The historical method of taxation as revenue generation is common in some countries, such as the United States, and the taxation runs the gamut from income to various taxes on many diverse goods and services.

Citizens often cringe at the thought of governments raising taxes. This is often an easy solution, especially for non-essential and luxury goods. However, governments are looking to diversify their revenue streams – or at least spend the money they have more judiciously in order to free it up for other ventures or programs.

Following the economic crisis the world has been through for the past few years, there are many who believe that 'business as usual' will never be the same again. This provides an opportunity for all types of businesses, whether not-for-profit, public sector or private sector.

NEW WAYS OF FINANCING

Research indicates that there is more focus on a global scale on innovation and new ways of structuring activities and financing than ever before. Governments want to be more efficient in their programs and to create more value for their investments, wanting to do things in a more business-like manner. There are similarities between this situation with the government and that faced by social entrepreneurs in their partnership efforts; the following may be very applicable for government:

> This relationship supports entrepreneurial patterns in that the more innovative strategies a venture employs, the more able they are to attract funding and partners. The reverse is also true, the more resources a venture has access to, the more innovative their strategies can become (e.g., offering new technology, products, ways of doing things). Thus, if the venture is able to respond with an innovative strategy and effectively manage the stream of diversified resources, these three components will work together in favor of the venture.[1]

The government is unique in many ways, which can both impede and facilitate this progress. In the end, though, regardless of a new structure, focus or business model, an evaluation of the results from the investment is necessary. Research indicates that through smarter business, a return on investment can be made through cost savings and actually generating revenue through activities in a government or governmental activity.

As Posner (2011) points out, the fiscal problems facing all levels of government are daunting. New data has shown that the federal, state and local sectors in the United States as well as other countries are facing not only short-term fiscal deficits, but also decades-long fiscal challenges stemming from three common forces: aging, growing healthcare costs and a slower growing economy and revenue base.

As governments all over the world try to tackle these challenges, the following choices emerge:

- Go-it-alone: each level of government pursues their own policies.
- Fiscal offloading: each level of government offloads their fiscal problems by passing them off to other levels of government.
- Fiscal collaboration: governments can join together in developing win–win solutions to common problems.

Posner contends that, 'Go-it-alone and fiscal offloading strategies reflect a general lack of regard for the effects of policy on other government entities, resulting in higher costs as well as public confusion and skepticism over the effectiveness of government. The effects on state and local officials are underscored by their struggle to meet higher costs induced by the federal government at a time of historic budget cutbacks.'

Posner also suggests an example of how fiscal collaboration might produce a win–win outcome when he discusses the consideration of a consumption tax or a value-added tax (VAT). The United States is the only major advanced nation without a value-added tax on consumption. When compared with state sales taxes, a VAT has several advantages, including a national and international reach into the service economy, and revenue potential that could go a long way toward filling fiscal gaps at all levels of government.

COST-SAVING ACTIVITIES

Several cost-savings activities are also a way to free up money for such activities as government entrepreneurship and innovation. These include automation and business incubators.

Automation

For many governments, taxation as a revenue-generating activity will not decrease any time soon, despite the desire for diversification. Governments can, however, try to simplify and make activities as efficient as possible. Automating and centralizing processes and using the internet (such as for filing taxes and direct deposit of refunds) speeds up processes, requiring less paperwork and fewer staff labor hours. Costs can be cut significantly using methods such as these. As infrastructure and reliable internet access grow, what is now a rather common practice in the developed world will be extending its reach exponentially.

Business Incubators

The business incubator and accelerator concepts are relatively new to some governments, but projects are found internationally. The incubator model is one in which funding from various sources is used to help entrepreneurs transform ideas into viable businesses by giving them the support and resources necessary to innovate and to create new jobs for the economy. Studies commissioned by the US Department of Commerce Economic Development Administration have shown that business incubators can produce jobs at lower cost to the government than other infrastructure projects.

According to the 2006 State of the Business Incubation Industry report,[2] North American incubators are financed in the following ways:

- About 31 percent of North American business incubators are sponsored by economic development organizations
- 21 percent are sponsored by government entities
- 20 percent are sponsored by academic institutions

- 8 percent are sponsored by other types of organizations
- 8 percent of business incubators are 'hybrids' with more than one sponsor
- 4 percent are sponsored by for-profit entities
- 8 percent of incubators have no sponsor or host organization.

During down economic times, this model is particularly attractive because the value for the investment is great and the investment required is less for an equal return. The result from the investment is a source for continued economic growth (the jobs created/entrepreneurial efforts funded). North American incubators assisted more than 27 000 start-up companies that provided full-time employment for more than 100 000 workers and generated annual revenue of more than $17 billion.[3]

PUBLIC–PRIVATE PARTNERSHIPS

In many ways, public–private partnerships are a combination of a procurement process with a business-operating model. Public–private partnerships are now being viewed through the innovation lens and are gaining in popularity, especially for infrastructure projects. Many models exist, but the Design–Build–Finance–Operate (DBFO) is the one most commonly used.

In the DBFO public–private partnership, the private sector brings the expertise and the willingness to take on the risk, while the government provides up-front funding so projects can be completed without the delays often experienced when the private sector is responsible for securing the financing independently. By specifically using a PPP, the government establishes the regulations and requirements the private company must meet (and can be fined for violation), but does not have to manage the project itself.

Through a PPP structure, a 'user' fee structure takes the burden of repayment of principle and interest off the taxpayer (which is typical under a non-PPP structure). Infrastructure projects are particularly good for this arrangement as they can typically be a drain on society because of the large capital costs and slow payback (from taxpayers). They are often delayed running up additional costs such as in labor and incurring opportunity costs of not being able to be used sooner. They can easily apply the 'user pay' fee model to take the burden off taxpayers (a win–win for government and voters).[4] A private company is also potentially more likely to look for solutions to upcoming problems, whether that be in technical innovation or organizational (or management).

If a PPP is structured in such a way that the private sector has to put up a large capital investment, the lender then also becomes a player in the partnership. This puts the public sector on one side as the regulator and the lender on the other side demanding reimbursement. Both the lender and the government should want the same objective – a good quality product or service.

PUBLIC–PRIVATE PARTNERSHIP EXAMPLES

To better understand the funding behind public–private partnerships, four examples will be discussed. These are from several different geographic areas and include: Private Finance Initiative, the SEED School, Harlem's Children's Zone and (PRODUCT)RED™.

The PFI in the United Kingdom

A specific type of public–private partnership is illustrated through the Private Finance Initiative (PFI) of the UK. This model has been used in various industries since the 1990s, and had relatively good success under Tony Blair's leadership in the healthcare industry. As stated by Her Majesty's Treasury, 'By requiring the private sector to put its own capital at risk and to deliver clear levels of service to the public over the long term, PFI helps to deliver high quality public services and ensure that public assets are delivered on time and to budget'.[5]

The SEED School and the SEED Foundation

The SEED Foundation partners with urban communities to provide innovative educational opportunities that prepare underserved students for success in college and beyond.[6] The SEED Foundation opens and supports college-preparatory, public boarding schools that provide a 24-hour-a-day nurturing environment designed specifically for children not receiving the needed support at home. Their model includes academic, residential, mental health, physical health and social and enrichment programs.

Although SEED is a public – free – school, it is really the result of a public–private partnership.[7] The SEED Foundation secures private money to build the school and the state provides the operating costs. SEED receives 85 percent of the state per-pupil funding the student would receive had he/she stayed in his home county, plus an additional $2 million per year for transportation support and program administration. In

Maryland, $30 million was privately raised to fund the $60 million project
and the rest was financed through traditional means.

The Harlem Children's Zone

The Harlem Children's Zone (HCZ) has been called one of the most
ambitious social-service experiments of our time by *The New York Times*,
President Obama and a number of education and community experts. It is
a unique, holistic approach to rebuilding a community so that its children
can stay on track through college and obtain employment. The goal is to
create a 'tipping point' in the neighborhood so children are surrounded by
an enriching environment of college-oriented peers and supportive adults,
a counterweight to 'the street' and a toxic popular culture that glorifies
misogyny and anti-social behavior.[8] The HCZ Project launched its Phase
3 expanding its comprehensive system of programs to nearly 100 blocks of
Central Harlem in 2007. Many communities have begun to emulate these
'Promise Neighborhoods' across the country based on the comprehensive,
data-driven approach used.

The main source of funding for the HCZ is through leveraging the
public–private partnerships. The HCZ Board of Trustees has a strategy to
raise a substantial amount of public and private dollars in collaboration
with its core supporters. The agency's $67 million FY09 budget came from
a mix of 33.3 percent public funding and 66.7 percent private funding from
foundations, corporations and individuals.[9] This money enables HCZ to
create new programs where no public funding stream exists. The Harlem
Children's Zone realizes that not all communities are able to garner as
much private funding as they have. They recommend that every effort be
made to ensure that a budget never exceeds two-thirds public dollars. They
remind us that public dollars are often the first ones lost in an economic
downturn.

The bulk of HCZ's private funding is unrestricted and provided through
large, flexible, multiyear grants. Flexible dollars linked to mutually agreed
upon outcomes enable HCZ to respond to new arising needs with innovative strategies in a timely manner rather than being tied down with strict
guidelines for how and when money can be spent. In short, this flexibility
enables HCZ to function more like a private corporation and less like a
bureaucracy.

Mayor Michael R. Bloomberg, the US Department of Housing and
Urban Development, the Goldman Sachs Group, Inc. and the New York
City Housing Authority joined forces with the Harlem Children's Zone
to build the new home of the Promise Academy Charter School and a
new community center, the newest example of their use of public–private

partnerships to work around funding and resource restrictions.[10] Funding for the school building was made possible in part by a $60 million grant from the New York City Department of Education's Charter Facilities Matching Grant Program, a $20 million gift from Goldman Sachs Gives and a $6 million gift from Google, Inc. The building's developer, Civic Builders, donated its $5 million development fee and the law firm Shearman & Sterling LLP provided pro bono legal services.

(RED)

(RED) is a simple idea that transforms the collective power of consumers into a financial force that helps those affected by AIDS in Africa.[11] (RED) empowers the consumer to choose products – that they would buy anyway – to generate money for the Global Fund to help eliminate AIDS in Africa. (RED) has teamed up with the world's most iconic brands to produce (PRODUCT)RED™ branded products. A portion of profits from each (PRODUCT)RED™ item sold goes directly to the Global Fund to invest in African AIDS programs. To date, more than $170 million has been generated and over 7.5 million people have been helped through the Global Fund programs that (RED) supports.

(RED) is not a charity. It is a business model designed to create awareness and a sustainable flow of money from the private sector into the Global Fund. Consumers buy (PRODUCT)RED™ items and, at no cost to them, a portion of the profits is sent directly to the Global Fund. When brands partner with (RED), they license the (PRODUCT)RED™ mark to create and market items and services. Each brand pays a licensing fee that funds the management and marketing of the (RED) brand. This licensing fee does not infringe on the amount of money sent to the Global Fund via sales of (PRODUCT)RED™ items, nor does it affect the cost of the (PRODUCT)RED™ items. (RED) does not pay for any marketing campaigns associated with the products. (RED) works with partner companies to direct some of their overall marketing budget to market not only the (RED) products but also the issues. These are funds from their existing marketing budgets that, if not used to market (RED), would be spent to market other products that do not contribute at all to the fight against AIDS in Africa.

The process is simple and straightforward; funds generated by (RED) partners are contributed directly to the Global Fund. The Global Fund then transfers those funds to (RED) grants in line with the achievement of their respective performance targets. The money is used for awareness building, education and life-skills, nutrition, HIV testing and counseling,

ARV treatment and the prevention of mother to child transmission in Rwanda, Lesotho, Swaziland, Ghana, Zambia and South Africa. Each country determines their needs and how the money will be used. All programs are reviewed and measured for success.

VENTURE CAPITAL

Another source of funding for innovation and government entrepreneurship is venture capital. This is not the typical venture capital industry that operates throughout the world but rather a very specific niche in the industry. Several examples are presented including: T2Venture Capital, the Chicago Public Education Fund and Pre-Seed Government Venture Capital Funds in Australia.

T2 Venture Capital

T2VC is an early-stage venture firm that invests money and time in start-ups spinning out of academia and government.[12] Their mission is to find the best technologies in the world and help jump-start young companies by connecting entrepreneurs and their companies to a global network of top-tier investors, partners and talent. The personnel at T2 Venture Capital are well versed in the intersection of venture capital and public policy; the core competencies of the company rest in connecting startups, governments and the venture community. They affiliate with nonprofit organizations at the heart of the innovation ecosystem. T2VC has had early access to over 1000 cutting-edge technology startups moving into the market including collaborations with the National Institutes of Health, the Department of Agriculture, the Technology Innovation Program, the National Science Foundation and over 50 universities.

The Chicago Public Education Fund

The Chicago Public Education Fund is the only firm of its kind dedicated to one urban school system – Chicago, America's third largest district.[13] The Fund applies principles of venture capital to make systemic improvements in education, with a focus on talent and leadership in public schools. Every 4 years, a series of funds are raised and invested in high-impact programs and outstanding management teams focused on improving the quality and performance of principals and teachers. Their success is rooted in a strict adherence to the typical venture capital model, investments that meet critical needs of the school system and a strong alignment across all strategic partners. The Fund's investors represent a broad cross section of Chicago's business, civic and philanthropic leaders who have thus far committed nearly $50 million. Their investments combined with state and federal money allow America's third largest school district to stay afloat.

Pre-Seed Government Venture Capital Funds in Australia

An understanding of effective public policy towards entrepreneurial finance is increased through Douglas Cumming's research on a pre-seed fund (PSF) government venture capital program in Australia. The program is a public-private partnership started in 2002 for fostering more investment in nascent high-tech entrepreneurial companies in Australia. Data from Venture Economics indicate these funds are the primary provider of seed stage enterprise capital in Australia; the funds are equally likely to invest in high-tech companies as other types of VC funds.[14] They tend to have smaller portfolios per manager than other types of VC funds, and are more likely to invest in companies resident in the same state; they do not stage and syndicate more frequently than other types of VC funds. The structure of the program has resulted in mixed performance in terms of finance and governance provided to nascent high-tech entrepreneurial companies. Cumming suggests that the program lessens the incentives for Innovation Investment Funds (a previously existing Australian government VC fund program) to invest in seed stage ventures. He contends that these competing government initiatives appear to be crowding one another. Another important lesson from the research is that the impact of government sponsored VC funds depends not only on the design of the program but also on the selection of the VC managers carrying out the investments. One PSF outperformed the other PSFs with respect to the investee company patents and financial statement performance, even though this fund invested less money and charged lower management fees than its counterparts.

LESSONS FROM THE EU

EU financial support is available for European businesses, directly or indirectly. The EU supplements mechanisms of member nations and widens their scope.[15]

While the EU recognizes that establishing a business and developing its activity requires considerable financing, they also recognize the importance of helping cultivate these new businesses, especially when they have innovative ideas that benefit the country, the region and the union. Some feel they are leading the way in spurring entrepreneurial activity within and around their government agencies.

The European Regional Development Fund (ERDF) supports development and structural adjustment in regional economies by helping small businesses and promoting entrepreneurship. The initiative provides a loan guarantee system as well as equity financing. The purpose of the Joint European Resources for Micro- to-Medium Enterprises initiative (JEREMIE), that became operational in 2007, is to improve access for small- and medium-sized businesses to financing in the less developed regions. The result is the creation of new businesses, particularly in innovative sectors.

Financing under the Structural Funds is made available through the national or regional authorities. Under the JEREMIE initiative, financing can be accessed through financial intermediaries, banks and investment funds, and in particular through the European Investment Fund (EIF) and the European Investment Bank (EIB).

Businesses can also have direct access to European financial support when it is to be used for the achievement of specific objectives. These community programs offer the possibility of direct financing in the fields of research and innovation (the Sixth and Seventh European Community Framework Programs for Research), environment and energy, education and training and health and safety. If they meet the criteria established by the specific program, businesses can apply directly for financial support to the European Commission department responsible for the program.

In addition to supporting these programs directly, the European Union supplements and widens the scope of national structures by offering European businesses financial support indirectly through financial instruments. These indirect methods are perhaps more pervasive than the direct financing, and have a more sustainable impact.

The financial instruments fall within the scope of the Framework Program for Innovation and Competitiveness (2007–2013), which has allocated 3.6 billion euros to qualifying initiatives. More specifically, the Entrepreneurship and Innovation Program, which is a subset of the Framework program, ensures the continuity of the multi-annual program for businesses and entrepreneurship, has allocated 510 million euros to entrepreneurial innovations.

The financial instruments provide indirect financial support to European businesses. The European Investment Fund covers the management side on behalf of the Commission. It works through financial intermediaries, banks and investment funds, thereby guaranteeing proximity financing.

The seed capital provided by the Multiannual Program and the capacity-building instrument of the Enterprise and Innovation Program supports investment funds by improving their technical and technological potential and helping with the recruitment of specialized staff. The collaboration is mutually beneficial.

INNOVATIVE PROGRAMS OF FUNDING

In addition to the government sources of funding previously discussed, there are several new initiatives to support government entrepreneurship and innovation. These innovative programs include: Arizona Department of Transportation's *Arizona Highways* magazine, credit card revenues, Pay for Success Bonds and dedicated budgets. Each of these is discussed below.

Arizona's Department of Transportation's *Arizona Highways* Magazine

Arizona Highways magazine is owned by the State of Arizona and is managed by the Department of Transportation.[16] The magazine is not appropriated, but operates out of an 'Enterprise Fund'. The fund itself is not subject to budget cuts but is subject to 'fund sweeps'. The mission is to promote travel, not to generate a profit. However, through travel-related activities and businesses highlighted, the magazine is responsible for boosting the state's economy by $35 million a year.

Credit Card Revenues to Government Working Capital Funds

Governments' working capital funds (WCF) are often used to fund worthy projects such as those of the US Agency for International Development (USAID).[17] The USAID WCF finances authorized missions with other partnership organizations with the expectation that the fund will be reimbursed. In order to grow the fund, though, the USAID has been authorized to deposit the rebates it earns from the use of US government credit cards into the WCF thereby making the credit cards a revenue-generating activity and an innovative dual use of an existing technology.

Pay for Success Bonds

Massachusetts was the first state in the nation to implement so-called 'pay for success' bonds. These innovative financing tools enable governments to fund programs that produce results rather than simply promising them.[18] In a pay-for-success bond (also known as a social impact bond), a government agency decides what outcomes it wants to accomplish (such as keeping people drug-free or out of jail), and then it brokers a deal with a nongovernmental intermediary – but it pays only if the outcome is achieved. The intermediary raises money from private investors and uses it to hire service providers to achieve the desired outcome. The intermediary carefully manages the performance of its service providers to ensure the outcome is achieved in order to receive payment. If the approach fails to accomplish the outcomes agreed on with the government, the intermediary receives nothing, its investors lose their money, and taxpayers are off the hook.

The Massachusetts experiment resembles the first pay-for-success trial currently under way in Peterborough, England, where government funding is contingent on reducing the rate of recidivism by at least 10 percent. If the approach works, the British government will release up to $20 million. If the approach does not work, government keeps its money.

Dedicated Percentage of Budgets to Innovation and Entrepreneurship

The Young Foundation proposed a broad target that at least 1 percent of all agency budgets should be used to develop, test and scale up new and better ways of doing things in the public sector. There is a wide range of ways that the government can use financing to spur innovation, from very small grants for ideas from frontline staff to stage-gate investment models.[19]

Diverting a small proportion of your budget to harnessing innovation would be very impactful as about 2.7 percent of US GDP is spent on research and development activities – one of the highest proportions in the developed world. About half of this comes from public sources, but it largely funds high-tech research at universities or in the defense field. Only a small proportion of these funds are used to ensure that there is sufficient innovation across government agencies in issues such as education, housing or small-business policies and programs. Diverting a small amount of federal agencies' budgets to innovative practices creates an amazing potential to really invest in generating innovative ideas and scaling up those that are proven to be most effective.

Recently dubbed the 'i3 Fund', the program represents a portion of the $100 billion set aside for education in the American Recovery and Reinvestment Act.[20] As opposed to the highly publicized Race to the Top Fund, which is operating on the state level, the i3 Fund will accept applications from local education agencies (LEAs) and nonprofit organizations working with LEAs or a consortium of schools. The purpose of the fund is to:

- Improve Kindergarten through twelve, or K–12, achievement and close achievement gaps;
- Decrease dropout rates;
- Increase high school graduation rates; and
- Improve teacher and school leader effectiveness.

The grants are given out in three tiers, and local coalitions are most likely eligible for the Fund's $5 million 'Development' grants. These awards will be given to local programs that have 'reasonable research-based findings or theories', and are aimed at further developing and scaling up the efforts.

NOTES

1. Colleen Post and Moriah Meyskens, 'Social venture strategy from a resource-based perspective: an exploratory study assessing Askoka fellows', Working paper, 27 May 2008.
2. http://www.nbia.org/resource_library/faq/#5.
3. http://www.nbia.org/resource_library/faq/#5.
4. http://www.oregon.gov/ODOT/HWY/OIPP/docs/PowerofPublicPrivate050806. pdf?ga=t.
5. http://www.hm-treasury.gov.uk/ppp_index.htm.
6. http://www.seedfoundation.com/index.php/about-seed.
7. 'Planting a seed in Baltimore', *Baltimore Magazine*, July 2008, online version accessed 23 July 2012 at: http://www.baltimoremagazine.net/this-month/2008/07/ planting-a-seed-in-baltimore.
8. http://www.hcz.org/about-us/the-hcz-project.
9. Harlem Children's Zone, 'Whatever it takes: a white paper on the Harlem Children's Zone'. http://www.hcz.org/images/stories/HCZ%20White%20Paper.pdf.
10. NYC Government Press Release: PR 110-11, 6 April 2011, accessed 23 July 2012 at: www.nyc.gov/html/om/html/2011a/pr110-11.htm.
11. www.joinred.com/.
12. http://www.t2vc.com/.
13. http://www.thefundchicago.org.
14. Douglas Cumming and Sofia Johan, 'Pre-Seed Government Venture Capital Funds', *Journal of International Entrepreneurship* (2009), 7 (1), 26–56.
15. 'Access to financing for business', http://europa.eu/legislation_summaries/enterprise/ business_environment/n26110_en.htm.
16. http://www.arizonahighways.com.
17. USAID, 'ADS Chapter 635 Working Capital Fund', http://transition.usaid.gov/policy/ ads/600/635.pdf, p. 4.
18. 'Bay State takes lead in innovation finance: Massachusetts aims to be first state with "Pay for Success" bonds', accessed 23 July 2012 at: http://www.americanprogress.org/ issues/2011/05/pay_for_success.html.
19. Jitinder Kohli and Geoff Mulgan, 'Capital ideas: how to generate innovation in the public sector', A product of CAP's Doing What Works project in conjunction with The Young Foundation and the Center for American Progress, July 2010, accessed 23 July 2012 at: http://www.innocentive.com/.
20. 'Building neighborhoods: coverage of federal urban policy from United Neighborhood Centers of America', accessed 23 July 2012 at: http://unca-acf.org/?p=476.

BIBLIOGRAPHY

Posner, Paul (10 May 2011), 'Can't we all get along? collaboration in crisis', accessed 20 July 2012 at: http://www.governing.com/blogs/bfc/collaboration-in-crisis.html.

Appendices: case histories

Appendix 1   The Irish Celtic Tiger

Patricia Kavanagh

Ireland, also referred to as the Emerald Isle or the Land of Saints and Scholars, is a small well-developed trade-dependent country, which is ranked high worldwide for its press and economic freedoms. Ireland is a member of the EU, the OECD, the WTO and the UN with a population of approximately 6.2 million people. Around 4.5 million people live in the Republic of Ireland and 1.8 million people live in Northern Ireland. Its location and the other EU countries are indicated in Figure A1.1.

Ireland is famous for its contribution to the world of literature and the arts; for its traditional style of Irish music and dance; its unique sense of humor, style of theatre and modern rock music. Ireland is also well known for its lush green land, its food, its excellent educational system, political freedom and democracy. More recently, Ireland has become famous for its legendary so-called 'economic miracle' the 'Celtic Tiger'. At the height of the Celtic Tiger, the Irish people were showered with wealth and affluence for over a 10-year period as the economy grew by 5 to 6 percent annually.

DEFINITION OF THE TERM 'CELTIC TIGER'

The Celtic Tiger is a moniker for the Republic of Ireland during its period of rapid economic growth. The colloquial term Celtic Tiger is used for both the years associated with the booming economy (as in *Celtic Tiger years*) and the country during that period. The first recorded use of the phrase is in a 1994 Morgan Stanley report by Kevin Gardiner, head of global equity strategy at the investment banking unit of global bank HSBC, comparing Ireland's unexpected economic take-off to the East Asian *tiger* economies of South Korea, Singapore, Hong Kong and Taiwan during their periods of rapid growth in the late 1980s and early 1990s (Gardiner, 1994). There is a general agreement that the Irish Celtic Tiger's gestation period was from 1987 to 1992 and that it was born in 1993 and lasted until the global financial crisis of 2007–2010.

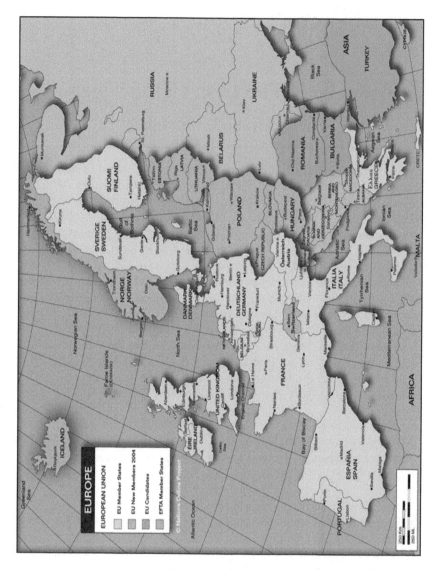

Notes: A map of the 27 EU countries. About 493 million people live in the EU.

Source: europa.eu

Figure A1.1
The EU countries

IRELAND'S ECONOMIC EVOLUTION

In the 1700s, Ireland boasted a rich history in several major industries: clothing, milling, equine, cabinetry, farming, dairy and cheese making. Throughout its history, the island of Ireland has been regarded as a single national unit. Prior to the Norman invasion from England in 1169, the Irish had their own system of law, culture and language, and their own political and social structures. Following the invasion, the island continued to be governed as a single political unit, as a colony of Britain, until 1921. During the occupation of Ireland by the British, nearly all Irish industries were removed and the British used Irish resources to build its empire. Ireland as a State was founded in 1922. At this stage, Ireland did not have any significant industrial history or an industrial revolution.

THE EARLY YEARS

The first three years of the Irish Free State's existence were among the most crucial in the Republic of Ireland's history and can be equated with a management team taking over a failing business drained of all its resources. The new and inexperienced government began to show their entrepreneurial flair as William T. Cosgrave and his Cumann na nGaedheal (Party of the Irish) government managed to suppress an internal revolt, overcame an acute scarcity of finance, enacted a constitution, and defined how the state would be governed. They established an Irish civil service, army, courts service, police force and diplomatic corps; passed legislation to purchase agricultural land held by absentee English landlords; commenced exploitation of the natural resources, extended the use of Irish in schools, and began the task of increasing the state's sovereignty. The administration of the Irish Free State was quickly changed from the British system of loosely coordinated boards and departments to a centralized Irish system (Corcoran, 2009).

Although Ireland was one of Western Europe's most disadvantaged countries suffering high levels of unemployment and emigration, the government displayed a distinct level of entrepreneurship within the public sphere with their goal to expand the market share for Irish products by adopting a free trade strategy. This strategy was favored by the farmers and large companies such as Guinness and Jacobs. The government also improved the quality of Irish produce by regulating the breeding of livestock with the introduction of minimum standards for dairy produce.

Following the signing of the Anglo-Irish Treaty of 1922, one of the most significant entrepreneurial actions undertaken by the Irish government was the development of a sugar beet industry. Ireland was still very much an agriculture-based society, and therefore the development of industry based around agriculture was important. The Sugar Company existed for over 60 years and during that time almost 1000 people were directly employed in the industry. In a host of downstream and supply industries over 25 000 jobs were also created. In 1991, the Sugar Company was privatized and became a part of the Greencore Plc. Group, which is listed on both the Irish Stock Exchange and London Stock Exchange. While starting out in the sugar industry, Greencore is today the world's largest sandwich manufacturer.[1]

In 1926, the Irish government made attendance at school compulsory for all children aged 6 to 14 years. It built the Shannon hydro-electrical power station to supply energy for industry and placed taxes on a limited range of imported goods like clothes, footwear and margarine to boost employment in the manufacturing industry. By 1930, Irish industry employed 13 000 more workers than in 1922. In 1927, the government set up the Agricultural Credit Corporation Bank for farmers to obtain cheap loans. However, this government kept income tax down favoring the wealthier in society, which resulted in its defeat in the 1932 election when Eamon DeValera's Fianna Fail government took over.

THE DEVALERA ERA

The Wall Street crash of 1929 created a worldwide economic recession, and governments everywhere responded by putting protectionist policies in place. In 1932, the Irish government under Eamon DeValera drafted a new constitution, and put an industrial policy together which involved heavy protectionism and self-sufficiency with the imposition of high tariffs on imports. The behavior of Eamon DeValera as a public sector entrepreneur reflects how a government leader can behave like a private sector entrepreneur who was responsible for running a country in a very inappropriate way for personal gain and power. DeValera's policies remained unchallenged for 30 years and while the country did well with his industrial policy during World War II, it subsequently had a devastating effect on the Irish economy and indigenous industry for more than 40 years.

Throughout DeValera's 50–year rule (the longest reign of a twentieth-century leader), he tailored Ireland to fit his own ideals and created a cult of personality. DeValera's government deformed the economy by wholesale subsidization of economic activities, rather than letting entrepreneurial activity discover the correct product for the correct market. However, the co-operative movement, which had originated in the 1920s, attempted to keep the entrepreneurial spark alive (Johnston, 1999).

THE CO-OPERATIVE MOVEMENT

The seeds of private entrepreneurship in Ireland were sewn with the start and development of the co-operative movement by Horace Plunkett. He and his associates had observed how co-operative creameries had raised farming standards in Denmark since 1882 and believed that it could also be an effective remedy for the problems faced by Irish farmers. Plunkett devoted himself to the development of the movement with the assistance of Robert Anderson whom he had chosen as the first co-operative organizer in 1889. Anderson would become a central figure in the movement as secretary of the Irish Agricultural Organization Society (IAOS).

Following independence, the government increasingly recognized that the economic wealth of Ireland resided in its dairy industry and milk wars were waged between co-operative and private creameries as they fought for market share. The Irish government decided, however, that dairying could be developed more efficiently through co-operation than through internecine wars, and intervened in 1928 to form the Dairy Disposal Board Company, the aim of which was to take over private creameries and bring about some rationalization of their activities. The co-ops were funded with equity from farmers and dedicated banks like the Agricultural Credit Corporation and the Industrial Credit Corporation. Industry was now starting to occur and, as demand was being created more entrepreneurs came in to fill the gaps.

At the turn of the century, rural Ireland was a landscape of peasant farmers producing primarily for local consumption. Today, rural business produces mainly for export and is dominated by a small group of entrepreneurial billion-euro exporters like Kerrygold and Glan Bia. The co-operative movement has played a major role in this transformation representing a major source of Ireland's indigenous industry.

THE IRISH SWEEPSTAKE

During the 1930s and 1940s, Ireland continued to face economic difficulties reflected in the lack of finance, the absence of indigenous industry, lack of entrepreneurship and low employment. To raise finance for hospitals, DeValera's government created a lottery called the Irish Hospitals' Sweepstake in 1930. Although the creation of the Irish Sweepstake might be seen as an enterprising move by the government to raise much needed funds for its run down hospitals, it was in fact another ploy to enable the members of a golden circle to make money at the expense of the Irish people. Of the millions that poured in, it has been estimated that less than one tenth went to hospitals. The Sweepstake was promoted as a public charitable lottery, with nurses and the police force featuring heavily in the promotion and drawings. In reality, it turned out to be a private for-profit lottery company, which tainted Ireland's reputation around the world.

The directors were paid huge dividends from the profits, which they invested in new enterprises. *Fortune* magazine described the Irish Sweepstake as 'a private company run for profit and it's handful of stockholders have used their earnings from the sweepstake to build a group of industrial enterprises that loom quite large in the modest Irish economy. Waterford Glass, Irish Glass Bottle Company and many other new Irish companies were financed by money from this enterprise and up to 5000 people were employed' (*Fortune* magazine, 1966).

THE FIANNA FAIL ERA

The Fianna Fail government responded to Ireland's chronic economic problems by formulating, developing and managing effective public policies, the most innovative of which led to the establishment of the State sector. Among the companies created were Aer Rianta and the Irish Life Assurance company. Public policy innovation was also instrumental in setting up the Industrial Credit Corporation in 1933 to encourage investment in industry. The government's Keynesian[2] approach to and management of public policy produced excellent results as the number of people employed in industrial jobs increased from 100000 in 1931 to 166000 in 1938. A house-building program also created thousands of jobs in the construction industry between 1932 and 1942 and house building in turn impacted the manufacture of concrete, furniture and carpets.

On the negative side, the government's lingering protectionist policy was damaging economic growth following World War II as it restricted competitiveness through importation and it controlled businesses to trading internally within the state, thereby restraining the development of export markets (Garvin, 2004). These policies also resulted in creating a trade war with Britain and as a result farmers went bankrupt and Irish exports declined even further.

In 1935, the British and Irish governments agreed to a coal for cattle pact. Ireland would buy British coal and Britain would increase the number of cattle imported from Ireland. The Irish economy was heavily dependent on imports of coal, oil, wheat, tea and fertilizers, which remained scarce until after the war. In 1941, the Irish government set up Irish Shipping and by 1945, it boasted a fleet of 15 ships, which transported vital supplies in and out of Ireland. However, income from exports was not enough to pay for imported products leading to a significant trade deficit.

THE INTER-PARTY GOVERNMENT ERA

After 16 years in office, the Fianna Fail party was deemed to be out of touch and was replaced by a new inter-party government led by John A. Costello (1948–51) whose behavior as a public sector entrepreneur was in stark contrast to that of DeValera. Costello acted in a more positive entrepreneurial manner with the establishment of the first duty-free zone in the world at Shannon Airport in 1947. In 1951, a duty-free liquor shop was opened together with a training school for hotel management. During the 1950s, further airport shopping opportunities were added. This duty-free shopping was a first in the history of world aviation. By 1954 there were 500 people employed in sales and catering with a £1.5 million annual turnover, and they introduced another world's first, a mail order service (Shannon Development, 2011).

The Irish government showed its ability to manage public policy innovation with the formal declaration of Ireland as a 'Republic' in 1949. The Irish economy was opened with the establishment of the Industrial Development Authority (IDA), an independent state agency to attract foreign direct investment (FDI).

Coras Tractala (The Irish Export Board) was created to market Irish products abroad and the Central Statistics Office was set up to compile the necessary information for working in a developing industrial economy. The IDA was not viable until after 1965 when it was effectively promoted by Sean Lemass, a proactive and revolutionary politician.[3]

The Irish government unsuccessfully attempted to boost agricultural exports by forcing Irish customers to pay more for Irish produce than that being paid by British consumers. The vast bulk of Irish exports were to Britain and it remained in deep economic recession until the late 1950s. However, in 1954, Fianna Fail was returned to power and in 1956, Sean Lemass took over as leader. During this period the behavioral aspects of Sean Lemass as a courageous public sector entrepreneur resulted in Ireland becoming one of the most open economies in Europe, with imports and exports together much greater than GNP, and with FDI playing an important role.

This is the first real example of Ireland being 'outward' looking and entrepreneurial in its approach to economic growth. Sean Lemass's innovative economic policies set Ireland on a totally different growth trajectory starting with a free trade agreement with Britain and then with membership of the European Union.

In 1957, Sean Lemass promoted a new generation of politicians and pursued a shift in economic policy from agricultural subsidies and tariffs protection towards free trade, an expansion of exports and incentives for inward investment. Pursuant to the influx of industrial enquiries in the late 1950s, Lemass established Shannon Free Airport Company (SFADCO) in 1959 as a limited liability company. Its main objectives included promoting all types of air transport business, assisting tourism and transport, and encouraging enterprise at Shannon Airport. This was the background for SFADCO, now Shannon Development, to emerge.

Lemass appointed Brendan O'Regan, the controller of sales and catering at Shannon Airport to develop traffic, tourism, investment and airfreight at Shannon and O'Regan's behavior as a public sector entrepreneur was instrumental in the development of Bunratty Castle Co. Clare, Knappogue Castle near Quin in Co. Clare and Dunguaire Castle near Kinvara in Co. Galway. In 1959, the then minister for Transport and Power, Erskine Childers, requested exchequer funds be made available to SFADCO for factory construction (share capital) and operating expenses (annual grant in aid). He pointed out that two incentives were already in place – customs freedom for import/export and exemption from corporation taxation for 25 years.

PLANS FOR ECONOMIC EXPANSION

The first economic expansion for Ireland was developed by DeValera and it was a typical autocratic plan of an independent entrepreneur who ran the country like it was a private company. There was no evidence of any coalition being created.

The second plan was developed in 1958 by Sean Lemass and Kenneth Whitaker, a celebrated civil servant and the chief architect behind the ending of protectionism and the promotion of economic liberalization. Their vision for economic expansion was opening up the decision making process in collaboration with the private sector rather than ramming it through without consensus. They created a coalition with business leaders who had been operating under the old protectionist policies and many of whom went out of business following the Free Trade Agreement with Britain. Many other entrepreneurs went out of business when Ireland joined the EU.

The third plan for economic expansion was developed post European Union membership. A new coalition had to be formed with EU member states, as the EU became a major investor in Ireland. Ireland's agriculture and tourism policies together with its roads program were all funded by the EU.

DEVELOPING THE PLAN AND CREATING A COALITION

Sean Lemass's plan for economic expansion in 1958 was the first to include the creation of a coalition with the private sector and the opening of the economy by entering into trade agreements with outside governments. The plan reflects how successful the behavioral aspects of a public sector entrepreneur can be, in particular the way Lemass positioned Ireland to create a climate for the country to prosper. This plan comprised a series of innovative public policies, which included major funding and a range of incentives to help attract foreign direct investment. For example, companies would be exempt from paying tax on profits made on the products they exported. The multinational corporations (MNCs) attracted to Ireland brought 70 percent of funding with them creating a multiplier affect.

In 1960, the Irish government signed the General Agreement on Tariffs and Trade (GATT), a worldwide agreement to reduce tariffs. Sean Lemass also signed the Anglo Irish Free Trade Agreement in 1965, which abolished all tariffs between Ireland and England. Lemass's encouragement of FDI resulted in a substantial increase in enterprise and employment and this in turn ultimately changed Ireland from being a rural-based economy to an industrial-based economy. Developing a world-class education system was a radical part of the plan as was the application for membership of the European Economic Council now the European Union.

Industrial estates were created to provide the type of infrastructure required by modern industry and in 1961, Ireland's first television station RTE was established. The new media was responsible for creating thousands of jobs and introduced a new platform for foreign and Irish companies to market a wide range of new products and services. It also provided a much-needed forum for debate with politicians and church leaders.

The implementation of Lemass's economic plan resulted in the expansion of the construction industry with the building of new roads and

industrial estates. Also between 1960 and 1968, 656 foreign-owned manufacturing companies were established in Ireland creating thousands of new
jobs and promoting entrepreneurship. Towns, cities and housing estates
were built to accommodate the increasing population. For the first time
in almost 120 years, the pattern of emigration and decline, which had
plagued Ireland, was beginning to reverse. Under Lemass's leadership, the
Irish population gained a new energy and sense of self-worth.

As the demand for luxury goods, cars, televisions and modern house-
hold goods surged, the need to develop an infrastructure to support indigenous industry and entrepreneurship became imperative. Manufacturing
industries, entertainment, dance halls, cinema and theatres began to
sustain continuous growth, as did the sales and services of new technologies such as television and hi-fi. This resulted in attracting new high-tech
industries and increased entrepreneurial activity (Sweeny, 1999; Garvin,
2004). The introduction of small fashion boutiques also created a host of
new enterprises and more employment in the textile industry.

DEVELOPING A WELL-EDUCATED WORKFORCE

A key ingredient of Lemass's plan for economic expansion was the development of a well-educated workforce. Having access to a young educated English-speaking, professional workforce is a major requirement
for attracting foreign-owned companies. Investing heavily in education
displayed a high level of entrepreneurial thinking and leadership by the
government.

- Educational grants to build new schools were introduced, and from
  the 1950s onwards, the government made a determined effort to
  increase educational participation rates.
- Policies were developed to create programs that were aimed at aligning the abilities of students with the needs of the global economy.
  To assist students to complete more advanced educational programs
  successfully, free education was introduced.
- Regional technical colleges (RTCs) were created to address the need
  for technical competence, and also to create links between emerging
  high-technological industries and education.
- Two National Institutes of Higher Education (NIHE), now the
  University of Limerick and Dublin City University, were established.

The growth in tertiary education in Ireland has been extraordinary with
the age participation rate rising from 11 percent in 1965 to an estimated

57 percent in 2003, and in numbers from about 21000 in 1965 to over 137000 by 2003. Ireland was one of the first European countries to grasp the economic importance of education, and economists suggest that this up-skilling of the labor force accounts for almost 1 percent per annum of additional national output over the last decade or so (Department of Education and Skills Ireland, 2001).

THE EVOLUTION OF IRISH CURRENCY AND ENTRY INTO THE EURO

The first Irish pound was introduced in 1928, although monetary union with sterling was maintained. As with sterling, the £.s.d. system was used. Distinctive coins and notes were introduced. From 1938, the means of tender was referred to as the Irish pound, after the Constitution of Ireland changed the state's name.

When the British government decided to decimalize its currency in the 1960s, the Irish government followed suit. The legislative basis for decimalization in the Republic was the Decimal Currency Act, 1969. The pound itself was not revalued by this act and therefore pound banknotes were unaffected, although the 10 shilling note was replaced by the 50 pence coin.

In the 1970s, the European Monetary System was introduced and Ireland, following significant Parliamentary debate, decided to join in 1978, while the United Kingdom did not. The European Exchange Rate Mechanism finally broke the one-for-one link that existed between the Irish pound and the pound sterling. By 30 March 1979, the parity link between the two currencies was broken and an exchange rate was introduced (Donnelly, 2002).

Although the euro became the currency of the euro-zone countries including Ireland on 1 January 1999, it was not until 1 January 2002 that the state began to withdraw Irish pound coins and notes, replacing them with euro.

MANAGING INTERNAL AND EXTERNAL POLITICS

From 1960 to the present, managing the 'internal' politics has not been an issue as the Irish government has predominantly been led by the Fianna Fail party and there is usually a general consensus of opinion. However, during the late 1970s, the government faced an urgent problem with the onslaught of social unrest and industrial strikes. They provided an entrepreneurial solution to the problem by establishing the Social Partnership, a neo-corporatist set of voluntary 'pay pacts' between the government, employers and trade unions. The implementation of the Social Partnership took the threat of strikes out of the equation and offered wage rate certainty to workers. This meant that companies located in Ireland could plan in advance, a critical factor for attracting and sustaining FDI industries.

Managing the 'external' politics has not always been handled by the Irish government with skill and expertise. The protectionist policies of the 1930s, which led to a trade war with Britain, were managed badly by the DeValera government; the first break-through happened with the signing of the Anglo Irish Free Trade Agreement in 1965.

The second breakthrough came when Ireland broke its links with sterling. Between 1973 and 1977, the Irish government faced two crises. First, the war in the Middle East in 1973 resulted in an increase in oil prices that plunged the global economy into a recession and sparked massive inflation. The government tried to solve the problem by borrowing that resulted in deep recession and unemployment soared.

The second crisis occurred when violence erupted in Northern Ireland heralding the start of the 'Troubles'; this became the most important external political issue faced by the Irish government. The other external political issues were in relation to its membership in the EU and its close ties to the United States.

MEMBERSHIP IN THE EUROPEAN UNION

Thirty years of EU membership radically transformed Ireland's perception of itself and how it is perceived by others. Ireland's membership facilitated a greater openness to the external world in trade, ideas, mobility of workers and strengthening of national capacity in terms of long-term planning. Ireland became full partners in one of the most innovative and successful exercises in political and economic cooperation between states ever undertaken.

While membership in the European Union did not automatically guarantee success, it did, however, offer a range of opportunities for Ireland. Entry into the European Union marked a new level of political engagement for the Irish and its membership had a positive impact on Ireland's trading environment. For Ireland to operate as a viable member of the European single market system, the EU invested heavily in building the country's infrastructure. Since joining the EU in 1973, Ireland has received over €17 billion in EU Structural and Cohesion Funds. The

Funds contributed by increasing the net capital inflow into the economy and, more importantly, by co-financing structural measures for regional development, infrastructure and human resource development (Irish Regions Office, 2011).

Although this transformation made Ireland a desirable location for foreign direct investment, Ireland's membership of the EU has not been a painless operation. As with any major restructuring and repositioning exercise, many of Ireland's traditional industries closed in the initial stages of its membership and the transition from the relative security of the old economic order to the entrepreneurial challenges of the new one was painful. EU membership expanded the 'domestic' market for Irish goods and services from a population (consumer) base of 3 million within the 26 counties to over 400 million (Roche cited in OECD, 2003).

Ireland's cultural ties with the United States factored heavily in making Ireland an attractive destination for several major US enterprises and Ireland's strong relationship with the United States over the years has been important in its ability to manage its external politics. First, post-World War II, the United States signed an agreement for Ireland to export its beef to the States creating a very important market for the industry.

Second, Ireland's very close political ties with the United States have been pivotal to attracting foreign direct investment, which accounts for the biggest contribution to Ireland's business development.

Third, America's diplomatic intervention and negotiations with Northern Ireland assisted the Irish and English governments to broker the Good Friday Peace Agreement in 1998. This crucial breakthrough was significant in making Ireland a more attractive place to invest in.

THE ENTREPRENEURIAL CHALLENGE DURING THE GESTATION OF THE CELTIC TIGER (1987–92)

The Irish economy stalled in the 1980s and early 1990s with almost 19 percent unemployed during 1992–95. Fianna Fail, the opposition party since 1982, won the general election in 1987. When Charles J. Haughey was elected to power, his government surprised many, including its supporters, with a program of severe cuts in expenditure accompanied by some novel consensus-building and developmental measures. Within a few years, these steps began to show dividends helped by a coincidence of other factors (Dorgan, 2006). For example, the promotion of competition by the government provided an incentive for the creation of Ryanair in 1985.

The Irish low-cost airline adopted a groundbreaking business model originally developed by Southwest Airlines in the United States. Ryanair gained access to the Dublin–London air route, which had been controlled by a duopoly of state-owned airlines, Aer Lingus and British Airways. Ryanair's cut-price fares expanded the market by 65 percent within a couple of years. This led to an unprecedented growth in employment, tourism and wealth generation. The success of Ryanair paved the way for competition to be extended to other highly regulated sectors. Today Ryanair continues on its high growth trajectory despite the downturn in the economy, and it claims the largest passenger numbers of all the European airlines.

As soon as people started buying again, the overseas companies who had invested in Ireland were there to supply the demand – the start of the Celtic Tiger.

FUNDING THE ENTREPRENEURIAL ACTIVITIES: ADOPTING EARNED INCOME MODELS

Post-independence the country had virtually no private enterprise so the Irish State provided funding for the development of an industrial infrastructure. As these early companies traded successfully, many diversified into other areas of activity. When the co-operatives began to emerge, they played an important role in Ireland's economic development. The co-ops, in turn, were funded by farmers with private equity and bank loans from the Agricultural Credit Corporation (ACC) and the Industrial Credit Corporation (ICC) and other banks. The EU funding played a fundamental role in Ireland's economic growth and during the 1990s when Ireland started to create wealth, many entrepreneurs financed their own businesses leading to the property boom.

Ireland, in general, has made prudent use of the funds available from Europe. Successive Irish administrations have been skillful in behaving entrepreneurially and in adapting domestic strategies to maximize benefits available from European funding.

In 1985, an important entrepreneurial strategy was implemented by the Irish government with the introduction of the Urban Renewal Act. The core objectives of the scheme were to promote urban renewal and redevelopment by supporting investment and reconstruction of buildings in designated areas. The act was introduced by the government to stimulate urban renewal through FDI and entrepreneurship; this led to the creation of the International Financial Services Centre (IFSC) in the old, derelict Spencer docklands area of Dublin.

The new act also provided for the designation of six Enterprise Areas situated in Dublin, Cork and Galway, which attracted double rent relief, rates remission and capital allowances. This part of the act was aimed at attracting high technology industries to the various locations. Another three Enterprise Areas were designated in 1997. Arrangements were also put in place for the designation of Enterprise Areas immediately adjacent to seven regional airports.

INTERNATIONAL FINANCIAL SERVICES CENTRE

The development of the IFSC was the idea of Dermot Desmond, a highly successful Irish financier and entrepreneur. Desmond's proposal was approved and supported by the then Taoiseach Charles Haughey whose insightful behavior as a public sector entrepreneur made it a reality with the approval of the EU in 1987. The creation of the IFSC reflected the responsiveness of the Irish government to the promotion and support of entrepreneurship.

By 2004, Ireland's financial services industry was employing some 50 000 people involving, for example, the management of about €300 billion in assets. Late entry into and heavy investment in this sector ultimately served Ireland well in that it provided the most advanced and comprehensive digital network in Europe.

The National Development Plan also led to improvements in roads and new transport services were developed, such as the Luas light rail lines, the Dublin Port Tunnel and the extension of the Cork Suburban Rail. Local authorities enhanced city streets and built monuments like the Spire of Dublin. In the 1990s, Ireland created a good trade economy exporting much of its agricultural and manufacturing produce giving it a competitive status in a global free trade economy. Its favorable conditions for international investment attracted large corporations, such as Intel, IBM, Dell Computers, Microsoft, GlaxoSmithKline and Bristol Myers Squibb, to locate in Ireland, and ensured high employment.

IRELAND'S LOW CORPORATION TAX RATE

Ireland's low corporation tax system was introduced by the Irish government in the 1950s for the manufacturing sector and was extended to the business and financial services sector in 1989 with the establishment of the IFSC. This move by the Irish government was visionary and entrepreneurial due to the increase in the importance of the market services sector within the Irish economy.

The reduction of corporation tax fell from 40 percent in 1994 to 32 percent by 1998, and finally to 12.5 percent in 2003 for all sectors. Ireland's low tax rate succeeded in attracting much higher levels of FDI and this in turn played an important role in stimulating economic growth.

FDI provided a platform for a flexible, innovative Irish economy to flourish and thrive in the 1970s. Since its establishment, the Industrial Development Authority (IDA) has been successful in identifying, pursuing and securing FDI. Throughout the 1990s, foreign direct investment was one of the most significant contributors to high growth in gross domestic product in Ireland. The OECD estimates that over the period 1993–2002, Ireland attracted net inflows of US$70.8 billion.

In 1989, Intel Corporation decided to build its first European manufacturing center in Ireland after years of negotiations with the IDA. The availability of well-educated Irish engineering talent, working with leading global electronics organizations both sourced and made available to Intel by the IDA, was a key factor. The investment was notable for its size, the leading-edge technology involved and the credibility that it gave Ireland in advanced manufacturing.

Emphasis has been on the use of fiscal policy to attract industries that play to Ireland's strengths. Specifically, in an effort to retain and utilize valuable human capital, Ireland lowered corporate taxes on software firms to encourage high-tech, high-growth job-creating industries. Organizations such as Microsoft, Dell, Gateway, Hewlett-Packard and IBM were attracted to Ireland due to its European Union membership and because it was an attractive location to serve their European markets. Improved economic management and favorable economic conditions generally created a suitable backdrop for attracting further foreign investment to Ireland.

However, during this time some questioned Ireland's overdependency on FDI (O'Hearn, 1998; O'Sullivan, 2000). Many politicians expressed concern that the IDA overly focused on attracting foreign multinationals to the detriment of local Irish Industry. These concerns were addressed with the passing of the Industrial Development Act of 1993.

Not only was the quantity of Foreign Direct Investment in Ireland significant in terms of Ireland's growth and development, but also the quality of investment was highly important. More than other countries, Foreign Direct Investment in Ireland has been relatively concentrated, not by accident, in high-tech and high-skilled sectors. These sectors have been specifically targeted by Irish job creation agencies.

DUBLIN BUSINESS INNOVATION CENTRE

In 1987, the Dublin Business Innovation Centre was set up to promote indigenous industry. The EC Business and Innovation Centres (BICs) are regionally and locally based organizations involved in identification, selection and specialist support for new and existing enterprises.

BICs typically operate as public–private partnerships, combining government funding and private cash or in-kind contributions. The strategy is to foster businesses that are market led and business and innovation led. BICs are pan European with 200 BIC partnerships and networks across the EU and the Dublin BIC is partnered with Maryland in the United States.

MANAGING THE PROCESS

Ireland has always had structures and processes in place to monitor and control the development of its economy. Since the State of the Central Statistics Office was established in 1949, its work greatly increased in the coming decades, particularly from 1973 with Ireland joining the European Community; good, timely, statistical information has been available. The Economic and Social Research Institute (ESRI), an independent evaluation organization, was established in 1960, the date on which the Institute – then known as the Economic Research Institute (ERI) – was first legally incorporated. A Social Research Institute was established and then amalgamated with the Economic Research Institute to form the Economic and Social Research Institute, supported by the establishment of a field survey unit within the Institute. Post Ireland's entry into the European Union has been monitored very closely by the Industrial Development Authority (IDA). Where Ireland has been lax in its management and control is in the regulation and proper implementation of financial controls.

THE BIRTH OF THE CELTIC TIGER IN 1993

Against a background of growing unemployment and intense lobbying by local politicians for the support of entrepreneurship, specifically new start-ups, and with the closure of large multinationals like Digital Equipment in the west of Ireland, the Irish government embarked on a major turnaround regarding industrial policy.

The Industrial Development Act of 1993 was established to restructure the IDA. Three separate agencies were generated to promote and support entrepreneurship: Forfas (the agency responsible for creating enterprise policy), Forbairt (now known as Enterprise Ireland, was responsible for implementing the policies for indigenous enterprise) and the IDA (with responsibility for attracting industrial undertakings from outside the state). Another significant government intervention to boost indigenous industry in the early 1990s was the creation of the City and County Enterprise Boards (CEBs). For the first time in Irish economic history, policy moved towards a nurturing of the micro sector (ventures with less than ten employees) and embraced the services sector (Hanley and O'Gorman, 2004).

THE LEVEL OF ENTREPRENEURIAL ACTIVITY DURING THE CELTIC TIGER YEARS

In 1997, Forbairt (Enterprise Ireland) reported that in the period 1978 to 1995 indigenous industry had flourished with the aid of their innovative 'Enterprise Development Program'. Four hundred and thirty companies had been set up at an average rate of 25 per year. At this time, the Irish software industry was also beginning to flourish with 483 companies employing 11 784 people.

Forbairt also ran three programs for new start-up companies: Small Business Program, Enterprise Development Program and the Irish International Services Program. Feasibility grants of 50 percent of £30 000 expenditure were also available to new startups.

Other financial support/benefits available for entrepreneurs included BES – Business Expansion Schemes Equity, at a rate of £1.0 million per company; Seed Capital Schemes – tax rebates for entrepreneurs from the previous 5 years of employment prior to setting up a new business; and specialist venture funds including access to business angels and subsidized loans at a rate of 6.5 percent funding from Enterprise support units, Bank of Ireland and Allied Irish Bank. Forbairt also offered access to venture capital and tax-free royalties and assistance with intellectual property and patents (Forbairt, 1997).

Other support for entrepreneurs included: The Forbairt Business Partnership Programs; an invention service and assistance from the Irish Trade Board to export, complete market research; and access to FAS-Training schemes and access to over 400 mentors. The Celtic Tiger was beginning to roar and the government was actively promoting Ireland's success. In 1998, Bertie Ahern the then Taoiseach (Prime Minister) told the European Union Heads of Mission, 'We have carved out a presence in the EU and in the world which far exceeds the normal expectation of a country our size.'[4]

From 1990 to 2003, Ireland's gross domestic product (GDP) more than tripled, from €36 billion to €138 billion, as did its GDP per capita, which rose from €10 400 to €35 200. During the same period, merchandise exports grew 4.5 times, from €18 billion to €81 billion. Meanwhile, Ireland's debt as a percentage of GDP fell from 96 percent to 33 percent; the total labor force rose nearly 50 percent, to 1.9 million; and the rate of unemployment dropped from 12.9 percent to 4.8 percent. Inflation barely changed, from 3.4 percent to 3.5 percent (Dorgan, 2006). The growing success of Ireland's economy encouraged entrepreneurship and risk-taking, qualities that had been dormant. This reflected Ireland's pro-market strategies, the availability of finance and the constant supply of high quality labor. However, while a culture of entrepreneurship was being fostered by the government, foreign-owned companies still accounted for 93 percent of all Ireland's exports.

The Irish government's success in promoting entrepreneurship and an entrepreneurial culture highlighted another indisputable factor, the management skills, ambition and global orientation of Irish managers in multinational organizations. This was especially valuable when many information technology businesses stalled in 2001, sparing many Irish subsidiaries from retrenchment because of their performance and strategic importance (Dorgan, 2006).

A TEMPORARY DOWNTURN IN 2001–03

Economies globally experienced a downturn and the Celtic Tiger's trajectory slowed significantly in 2002 after numerous years of high growth. The economic downturn in Ireland was not a recession but a reduction in the rate of economic expansion. The economy was impacted by a large reduction in investment in the worldwide information technology industry in which Ireland was a major player. The industry had over-expanded in the late 1990s, and its stock market equity declined sharply.

In 2002, Ireland exported US$10.4 billion worth of computer services, compared to $6.9 billion from the United States. Ireland accounted for approximately 50 percent of all mass-market packaged software sold in Europe in 2002 (OECD, 2002, 2004). Irish economic growth began to accelerate again in late 2003 and 2004 (see Figure A1.2). There was a renewed investment by multinational firms. For example, Intel expanded its operations in Ireland; Google created an office in Dublin in 2004 and expanded to a second location in 2011. Abbott Laboratories and Bell Labs also built new Irish facilities during 2004.

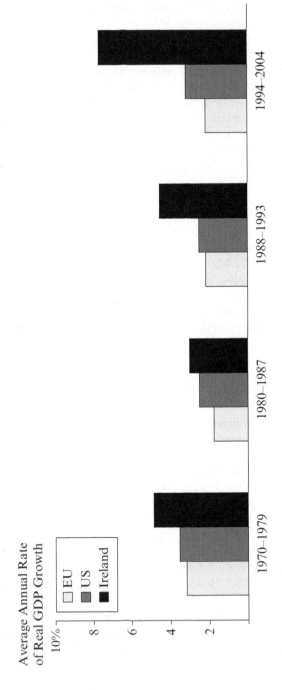

Source: Ireland Central Statistics Office and Organisation for Economic Co-operation and Development, Economic Outlook.

Figure A1.2   Ireland's economic growth, 1970–2004

ESTABLISHMENT OF ENTERPRISE IRELAND AND THE HPSU

As previously mentioned, in July 1998, the Irish government continued to show its commitment to entrepreneurship with the establishment of Enterprise Ireland (previously known as Forbairt). The new enterprise development agency had a clear strategic mandate to concentrate on enterprises that had innovative potential and the drive to deliver products and services that customers were willing to buy.

In 2000, Enterprise Ireland set up its High Potential Start-up Unit (HPSU) to focus on helping high growth indigenous enterprises with significant ability to export their products and services. It offered a comprehensive development package for marketing, technology, enterprise development, business training, science and innovation. With the support of Enterprise Ireland, Irish indigenous enterprises began emerging as major strategic players in the successful performance of the economy, and were looked at as the best solution to securing Ireland's future.

During the Celtic Tiger years, Ireland created 800 software companies employing 15 000 people. For instance, Iona Technologies created by Chris Horn and Trintech are prime examples. Trintech, which was founded in Dublin in the 1990s by brothers Cyril and John McGuire as an online payments system developer, had been mainly operating from Dallas, Texas, and was sold for a price of $93 million (Hennigan, 2010).

Iona, on the other hand, had a slow, steady growth fuelled by bootstrapping, winning EU research grants and coping with being turned down by local venture capitalists before an investment by Sun Microsystems, as well as a landmark technology deal with Boeing, propelled the company. At its peak in 2000, Iona, which was leading the world in the development of middleware for large enterprises, was worth US$1.75 billion and had an annual turnover in excess of US$100 million. While Horn stepped down to pursue other interests, he returned 3 years later to take the reins while a search for a new CEO was under way. Although Iona was sold in 2008 for US$162 million to US firm Progress Software, valuing the company at US$4.05 a share – a long way from the peak price of US$98 a share – it showed Irish business people, especially those in the technology business, what was possible (bizstartup.ie, 2011).

It is worth noting that at this time all government departments displayed a commitment to policies, programs and investments designed to make Ireland an enduring knowledge society. These initiatives included: investment support for research and development in engineering and scientific disciplines that would promote a strong educational system;

uncompromising economic strategies; partnerships with countries rich in knowledge-based businesses and, above all, developing highly skilled professionals. While economic success during the Celtic Tiger years can be attributed to a range of domestic and international factors, it was not accidental. Ireland has long had, and intends to sustain, low tax rates to attract investment (Dorgan, 2006).

THE SCIENCE FOUNDATION OF IRELAND

In 2000, the Irish government established the Science Foundation Ireland (SFI) as part of the National Development Plan 2000–2006 (NDP). The SFI's main role was to dedicate itself to world-class research and to Ireland's standing in the world rankings in key areas of the scientific world, particularly in the areas of nanotechnology, therapeutics bio-technology and information and communications technology (ICT). Its permanence was confirmed in 2002, as part of an agreement with unions on the development of the economy (Partnership Agreement). The SFI is a government initiative set up to improve Ireland's long-term com-petitiveness and growth objectives by underpinning MNC involvement in Ireland.

The SFI invests in academic researchers and research teams who are most likely to generate new knowledge, leading edge technologies and competitive enterprises in the fields of science and engineering, support-ing three broad areas: biotechnology, information and communications technology and sustainable energy and energy-efficient technologies.

During 2002, US academic Dr Bill Harris was appointed director general of the SFI with a fund of €675 million aimed at reforming Irish universities into world-class scientific research institutes and to attract leading researchers and scientists into Ireland. The SFI also channeled €125 million into research projects in a diverse range of biotech and ICT fields. This amount was increased to €200 million to financially support centers for science, engineering and technology grants. Commenting on the establishment of the SFI, Harris said that it marked a milestone in the ongoing development and growth of first-rate scientific research in Ireland. By establishing SFI on a statutory basis, the Irish govern-ment committed to building an ecosystem of world-class research in the country. Since its creation, the SFI has advanced co-operative efforts among education, government, and industry that support its fields of emphasis, and promotes Ireland's ensuing achievements around the world.

SCIENCE FOUNDATION IRELAND AND ENTREPRENEURSHIP

The SFI strongly encouraged research collaboration between SFI funded scientists and engineers and industry. Such interactions allowed SFI scientists and engineers to be more informed about industrial priorities and research needs, which in turn led to industrial collaborators being informed about important new science and engineering research developments in Ireland. For example, over 30 percent of SFI funded researchers have established collaborations with industry. A dramatic increase in collaborative research was seen in 2009 with a 53 percent increase in the number of small–medium enterprises (SMEs) collaborating with SFI funded researchers (compared to 2008). Industry–academic collaborations also contributed to the Industrial Development Authority's profile shift towards research and development investments, from less than 10 percent 5 years ago to almost 50 percent in 2009.

The Irish government's capital allocation in 2011 of €161 million to SFI represents an €11 million increase over 2010 funding. During this period of economic difficulty, this investment highlights the government's commitment to investing in high quality scientific and engineering research to support long-term, sustainable economic growth and development. The SFI research community continues to enhance Ireland's international reputation in science and engineering, enabling increasing levels of high-tech foreign direct investment and indigenous innovation.

The SFI Starter Investigator Research Grant program was reopened in 2011. SFI has leveraged significant funding from Europe's Marie Curie scheme and will co-fund a program designed to support high-performing young researchers to make the transition and develop their own independent research teams and program. SFI will treble the investment in its Conference and Workshops program, which supports international scientific conferences that attract thousands of delegates to Ireland each year. In addition to the significant economic dividend, they realize for Ireland that they are an essential mechanism by which Ireland's improved scientific reputation is communicated internationally. With this financial provision and selected investment in programs, SFI anticipates maintaining its cohort of approximately 3000 researchers, led by a team of approximately 350 Principal Investigators across a range of research areas (Science Foundation Ireland, 2011).

IRELAND'S COMPETITIVENESS

As a direct result of supporting and encouraging entrepreneurship, Ireland was successful in creating a new knowledge intensive indigenous industry for the first time in its economic history. Computer equipment and software has become particularly dominant in Ireland. The fact that Ireland has, in recent years, vied with the United States for the top position in terms of software exports, attests to this. There is of course a relationship between Ireland's success and other high tech industries and educational investment (Dick Roche, 2004).

The Global Entrepreneurship Monitor (GEM) reported that in 2002 Ireland ranked twelfth overall and the highest of the EU countries as being the most entrepreneurial. The report stated that: (1) 5 percent of the adult population (110 000 people) of Ireland were actively planning to start a business; (2) 4 percent of the adult population partly or fully owned a business started in the previous 3.5 years; (3) 13 percent of the adult population expected to start a business in the next 3 years; (4) 2 percent believed their businesses would employ over 20 people within 5 years; (5) 40 percent believed there were good opportunities; (6) 50 percent believed they had the skills to start a business; (7) 33 percent would be put off by the fear of failure; and (8) 30 percent of entrepreneurs were women (GEM, 2003).

The GEM Report for 2008 confirmed that Ireland was at heart an entrepreneurial nation at the forefront of the EU in the rate of established entrepreneurs (9 percent) among the adult population. It indicated that entrepreneurial activity remained high with an average of 2800 individuals setting up new businesses every month. The findings of the 2008 report confirmed that the culture and social norms remain broadly positive towards entrepreneurship and that the aspiration among people to become entrepreneurs remained strong (GEM, 2008). Overall, the Irish government's positive investment in infrastructure and its dedicated strategy for supporting entrepreneurship and indigenous industry had a marked effect on employment as indicated in Figure A1.3.

THE IRISH GOVERNMENT'S ENTREPRENEURIAL STRATEGIES FOLLOWING THE DEMISE OF THE CELTIC TIGER

Since joining the EU in 1973, the European Union's directives have provided Ireland with an overall framework for entrepreneurial activity and support. This framework assisted Irish policy makers to shift their focus

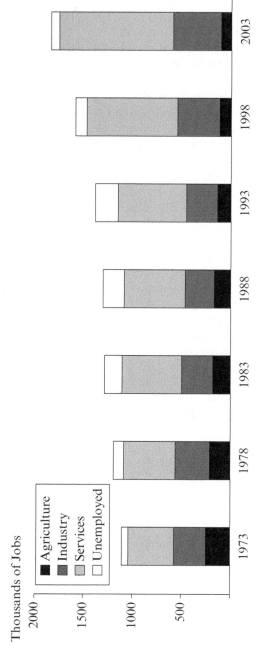

Source: Ireland Central Statistics Office.

Figure A1.3 Employment by sector and unemployment, 1973–2003

away from foreign direct investment to emphasis on SMEs and micro-enterprises. The IDA and Enterprise Ireland are two very effective bodies funded by the State to assist indigenous enterprises to be effective and flexible in operating in a very dynamic situation.

In 2009, the Irish government continued to act entrepreneurially focusing on innovation and offering tax breaks and grants to companies who innovate. Ireland's low-tax regime has been a proven winning formula for attracting foreign direct investment (FDI) as evidenced by many of the new EU member states from Central and Eastern Europe copying the low-tax regime emulating Ireland's economic performance. For example, 15 of the 16 leading pharmaceutical companies are located in Ireland. The Irish government provided over €4 billion for universities to carry out basic research for commercialization. MNCs and indigenous industry are enjoying international success.

In parallel with the focus on the commercialization of research and development, there are a number of initiatives launched to support innovation in the workplace. These include: (1) provision of financial incentives and training to companies to create capability for employees to become innovative in their area; (2) leadership development which has delivered greater results in innovation; (3) taxation policy to stimulate innovation and research and development; and (4) tax benefits to companies losing money as a credit against payroll taxes. As a result, many US and Australian companies have located in Ireland since the United States is better at commercializing research than the EU, which is very good at developing research.

THE GLOBAL IRISH NETWORK

The Irish government's dedication to creating an entrepreneurial culture was evident in the establishment of the Global Irish Network in 2009. This network is comprised of over 300 highly influential individuals from 37 countries. Network meetings have been hosted in a number of key markets including London, Paris, Abu Dhabi and Shanghai. The Network provides Ireland with an invaluable resource of international expertise to draw from as it works towards economic recovery. The last meeting was held in New York during November 2010 (Department of Foreign Affairs, 2010).

The Irish Technology Leadership Group (ITLG) is an independent organization composed of a number of high-level technology leaders in Silicon Valley who are Irish or Irish-American. The group includes senior executives from some of the Valley's leading corporations who are committed to helping Ireland address the challenges of embracing new technology opportunities (Irish Technology Leadership Group, 2010).

On 14 March 2010, the Taoiseach, Brian Cowen, formally opened a newly created Irish Innovation Center (IIC) in San Jose, California during his official visit to the United States. The IIC in Silicon Valley was established to provide Irish technology start-up companies a base to develop partnerships, markets and funding in the United States.

The Farmleigh Fellowship was founded in Singapore in 2009 following the Global Irish Economic Forum. While Ireland had opportunities to grow business interests in Asia, the country lacked sufficient numbers of qualified professionals on the ground. The Fellowship was established by a group of Irish-based business people in Singapore as a not-for-profit charity organization. The Fellowship's goal is to develop a critical mass of highly skilled professionals with a profound understanding and first-hand experience of business in Asia who will spearhead greater business engagement between Ireland and the Asian region. This year's graduate scheme commenced in January 2011 and provided 23 Irish participants with the opportunity to work and study in Asia and Ireland for the year.

A UNIQUE INTERNET PLATFORM FOR IRELAND

Gateway Ireland, another private sector initiative aimed at creating a new high-quality Irish portal website, is being developed by John McColgan in cooperation with a number of prominent private sector partners. Gateway Ireland is a unique internet platform for a country and its people worldwide. It is a national online initiative built by the private sector, endorsed by government and in the public interest. The opportunity now exists to connect the Irish Diaspora in ways previously not possible. This global economic portal can impact the economy and culture of Ireland, reinforcing Brand Ireland in countries where Ireland has an established presence as well as penetrating new markets such as China, Brazil, India, Russia, South Africa and South America (Gateway Ireland website, 2010).

Other activities of the Irish government include: an investment of €500 million Innovation Fund-Ireland to develop a vibrant venture capital community in Ireland; a new €90 million National Energy Retrofit Program; and the Trading and Investing in a Smart Economy, which provides a framework to ensure the integrated and coordinated promotion of overseas trade, tourism and investment in established key high growth markets. Former Taoiseach John Bruton was appointed as chairman of IFSC Ireland to promote Ireland's international financial services industry.

AFTERMATH OF THE CELTIC TIGER

Former Taoiseach Garret FitzGerald has blamed the fall of the Celtic Tiger on a series of 'calamitous' government policy errors. According to the former Taoiseach, the first mistake was committed in the years 2000 and 2003 by then Finance Minister Charlie McCreevy when he boosted public spending by 48 percent while cutting income tax. The second mistake occurred when government policies encouraged a housing bubble to develop. This bubble was accompanied by a bubble in asset-related tax, which helped to fuel further cuts in income tax. He went on to point out that revenue from asset-related tax is expected to fall in 2012 to less than half its 2007 level. Also, initial government reactions to the crisis were slow, according to Dr Fitzgerald. However, all was not lost; positive public attitude and decisive action from the government made it possible for Ireland to start to come back from the brink of financial ruin (Cody, 2009).

It would seem appropriate at this stage to recall the visionary entrepreneurial strategies Sean Lemass employed in the late 1950s to show the need for a new visionary who would be capable of driving Ireland out of its current economic difficulties. Ireland needs new entrepreneurial visionaries who are prepared to implement strategies that will put Ireland and the Irish people ahead of political power and personal gain and wisely employ the €85 billion bailout from the IMF and the EU.

Ireland's glittering Celtic Tiger ended in economic disaster similar to the way of the East Asian economic tigers. Several factors contributed to the demise of the Irish Celtic Tiger including the global banking crisis and a succession of ineffectual and corrupt politicians who ignored the warnings of their own financial advisors in favor of political power and personal gain.

In an interview with the Irish *News of the World*, Eamon Gilmore of the Labor Party blamed the lack of accountability for much of the present crisis. He argued that politicians were hiding behind the rules, which govern how the political system works. What the government did was transfer the powers ministers used to have over to state agencies like the Health Service Executive (HSE) and the National Roads Authority (NRA). This action meant that ministers could not be questioned in the Dail (Irish Parliament) about their activities and expenditures (*News of the World*, 2011).

The Irish government's insightful and enterprising tax incentive schemes introduced to promote investment in property and attract foreign direct investment should have been slowly eliminated by 2003. For example in 2004, 80 000 new houses were built compared to the UK's 160 000 – a nation that has 15 times Ireland's population. It is estimated that home completions in 2006 reached 90 000. During this time, the Irish housing market was priced significantly above the market level and yet the Irish government decided to invest in several properties at over-inflated prices. When the property bubble burst, there were empty properties everywhere and property developers were left owing billions to the Irish banks.

THE PROPERTY BUBBLE

There are claims that the return to growth in 2004 was principally the result of the construction sector catching up with the demand caused by the first boom. The construction sector represented 12 percent of the country's GDP and a large proportion of employment among young unskilled men. At one point, a fifth of the labor force increased by tens of thousands of immigrants who worked in construction. The total stock of dwellings, which had stood at 1.2 million in 1991 increased to 1.9 million by 2008 (Whelan, 2010). The property bubble of 2000 to 2006 was the result of a combination of increased speculative construction and rapidly rising prices. As elsewhere, prices stabilized in 2007 and the bubble burst during 2008. By the second quarter of 2010, house prices had fallen by 35 percent compared with the second quarter of 2007, and the number of housing loans approved fell by 73 percent (Davy Stockbrokers, 2006). The fall in domestic and commercial property prices contributed to the Irish banking crisis. The Central Bank admitted in November 2005 that they had estimates of overvaluation of zero percent to 60 percent in the Irish residential property market.

Brendan Keenan of the *Irish Times* revealed the minutes of a meeting with the OECD where they indicated that property was overvalued, but was fearful of precipitating a crash by 'putting a number on it'. Their 2009 Annual Report had virtually nothing to say about how and why the Irish banking system was brought to the brink of collapse. There were four Central Bank directors on the board of the Financial Regulator, yet the Central Bank maintains it had no powers to intervene in the market (Keenan, 2009).

THE NATIONAL ASSET MANAGEMENT AGENCY

The National Asset Management Agency (NAMA) was set up in 2009 by the Irish government in response to the financial crisis and the deflation of the property bubble. NAMA's main function was to act as a 'bad bank', acquiring property development loans from Irish banks in return for government bonds, primarily to improve the availability of credit in the Irish economy. Nobel Prize-winning economist Joseph Stiglitz was one of many experts who were highly critical of the NAMA. Speaking at a conference in Dublin, he argued that the Irish government was 'squandering' large amounts of public money with its plan to bail out the banks. 'There's a sort of a view that there's no alternative.' That view is 'nonsense', Stiglitz said, adding, 'The rule of capitalism says that when firms can't pay what they owe, they go bankrupt.' Stiglitz told RTE that overpaying for the loans was 'criminal' (Fahy and Meier, 2009). Since the creation of NAMA and the bail out of the banks, the Irish government has significant property, which may have to be given away or torn down.

THE POOR MANAGEMENT OF IRELAND'S CELTIC TIGER

The comment 'if I have it I will spend it' made famous by then Minister for Finance, Charlie McGreevy, summed up the period of the Celtic Tiger and the Irish government's approach to economic and social management under Taoiseach Bertie Ahern. The speed of the fall-out for social spending from the spendthrift government, banking sector and property elites has been spectacular (Moran, 2009) The health service did not receive fundamental reform during the period, as funding, waiting lists, bed shortages and short-staffing remained widespread. Ireland's poverty rate in the developed world remained second only to the United States. The Irish government's own statistics reveal that 17 percent of the population lives at the poverty level. The new found wealth of the Irish middle class was critically dependent on the value of property as national house prices rose at a rate of 270 percent from 1998 to 2008 (Fitzgerald, 2008). When the property bubble burst in 2007, Irish families who had been encouraged by the banks to borrow heavily or cash in their pensions to invest in property were now in negative equity. As a result, Ireland now has approximately 350 000 empty houses.

The government of Ireland is guilty of mismanaging and ruining the economy with a property Ponzi scheme that was legitimized by junk banks like Anglo Irish Bank. These banks were fed funds from Germany and France without proper regulation. Despite its mandate for stricter oversight, the financial regulator never imposed major sanctions on any Irish institutions, even though Ireland had experienced several major banking scandals in the form of overcharging customers. Ireland was the home to unchecked financial frauds. In December 2008, revelation of irregularities in director's loans that were kept off a bank's balance sheet for eight years, forced the resignation of the financial regulator.

The Irish economic crisis is a twin crisis of: (1) the day-to-day spending deficit of the government, and (2) a hole in the balance sheets of the banks. The former is akin to the profit and loss account of a private company being out of skew and the latter, its balance sheet. Because of the former not being resolved quickly enough, the latter could not continue to be propped up with the guarantee that was possible and effective in 2008. One imploded on the other when the markets perceived this, and the IMF had to be called in. The fatal delays in fiscal reform and the fact that the government allowed its own finances to remain unstable, and eventually de-stabilize, meant that the banking system could not be fixed, which in turn, fed back into the instability of the economy and the government's own finances (Finance Dublin, 2011).

In February 2010, a report by Davy Research in the *Irish Times* concluded that Ireland had 'largely wasted' its years of high income during the boom, with private enterprise investing its wealth 'in the wrong places', comparing Ireland's growth to other small Eurozone countries such as Finland and Belgium. The physical wealth of those countries exceeded that of Ireland, because of their 'vastly superior' transport infrastructure, telecommunications network and public services (White, 2010).

In response to the Lehman Brother's collapse in the United States, the Irish government did the right thing by guaranteeing the deposits of the banking system. The head of the IMF mission in Dublin, Ajai Chopra, writing (in October 2010) about the Swedish banking crisis of the early 1990s emphasized the value of the Swedish decision to issue an explicit guarantee of all bank deposits at the outset, 'to calm matters, while diagnosis and policy preparations proceeded . . . Among the benefits was a clear exit strategy, because the crisis could be formally declared over once the guarantee was withdrawn.'

However, the effectiveness of the 2-year Irish guarantee began to decrease from the day it was introduced. Eventually, it fatally collapsed around August 2010 amidst a maelstrom of confusion, haircuts, defaults and NAMA strategies with the two Irish banks in the Euribor system – AIB and Bank of Ireland – under stress. The extension of the guarantee to June 2010 was too little, too late. It was too timid and limited to just 9 months, and was accompanied by growing credibility problems about the sovereign's stability (Hennigan, 2011).

THE ENTREPRENEURIAL CHALLENGES FACING IRELAND'S FUTURE

Like other advanced economies, Ireland faces new entrepreneurial challenges in conserving natural resources, protecting the environment and planning for longer life expectancies. Ireland has provided an attractive gateway for international investment to access European and wider markets, and has provided a link between cultures and continents. One key objective for Ireland is building new sources of competitive advantage.

Overall, the United Kingdom will remain Ireland's biggest single market particularly for Irish-owned firms and first time exporters. The new Irish government needs to make increased penetration into other EU markets a priority. There also needs to be selective development of other growth markets such as the United States and Asian countries. The Irish government needs to be proactive in increasing competitiveness by being innovation driven, fostering an entrepreneurial culture, increasing the levels of productivity, focusing on gaining a leadership position in telecommunications with enlightened regulation and excellent administration systems, being environmentally conscious, and supporting a high level of education. This can pave the way for the return of the Celtic Tiger.

NOTES

1. For more information see Irish Economic History, www.generalmichaelcollins.com.
2. John Maynard Keynes' theory for economic recovery states that the economy is not self-correcting and can languish for years in what is termed 'underemployment equilibrium'. The economy can be 'in equilibrium' with high levels of unemployment. As such, a government stimulus is required to jump-start the economy.
3. Sean Lemass was a legendary figure in Ireland's political history. He was a founding member of the Fianna Fail political party, a long-serving minister and Taoiseach (Prime Minister from 1959–66) following the retirement of Eamon DeValera.
4. Bertie Ahern, 'Address to European Union heads of Mission', 30 April 1998.

BIBLIOGRAPHY

bizstartup.ie (2011), www.bizstartup.ie.

Chopra, Ajai (2009), 'Sweden's approach to bank resolution: Have we learned the right lessons?', *iMFdirect*, 11 August, accessed 20 July 2012 at: http://blog-imfdirect.imf.org/2009/08/11/sweden%e2%80%99s-approach-to-bank-resolution-have-we-learned-the-right-lessons/.

Cody, Caitrina (2009), 'Fitzgerald says Crisis Started with McCreevy', Independent. ie.

Cooper, Matt (2009), *Where it All Went Wrong, Who Really Runs Ireland? The Story of the Elite who Led Ireland from Bust to Boom – and Back Again*. Dublin, Ireland: Penguin Ireland.

Corcoran, Donal (2009), 'Public policy in an emerging state: the Irish free state', *Irish Journal of Public Policy*, **1** (1): 1022–1025.

Culliton Report (1992), 'A time for change industrial policy for the 1990s', Report, Dublin Stationery Office: Industrial Review Group.

Davy Stockbrokers (2006), 'The Irish economy – An Assessment of Risks and Forecasts 2008–2010', report, Davy Stockbrokers, Ireland.

Department of Education and Skills Ireland (2001), Report accessed 23 July 2012 at: www.education.ie.

Department of Foreign Affairs (2010), accessed 23 July 2012 at: http://www.for eignaffairs.gov.ie/home/index.

Donnelly, James (ed.) (2002), *Encyclopedia of Irish History and Culture* Vol.1, Detroit, MI: Macmillan Thomson Gale.

Donnelly, Judi (2007), Irish history synopsis: troubles to Tiger 1990–2007, accessed 20 July 2012 at: http://www. irishhistorysynopsis.blogspot.com.

Dorgan, Sean (2006), 'How Ireland became the Celtic Tiger', The Heritage Foundation, accessed 20 July 2012 at: http://www.heritage.org/research/ reports/2006/06/how-ireland-became-the-celtic-tiger.

Dunphy, Richard (1995), *The Making of Fianna Fail Power in Ireland 1923–48.* Oxford: Oxford University Press.

Fahy, Louisa and Meier, Simone (2009), 'Government "squandering" money in bank bailout', Independent.ie, accessed 20 July 2012 at: http://www. independent.ie/business/irish/government-squandering-money-in-bank-bailout-plan-1906787.html.

Finance Dublin (2011), *The Irish Constitution and the Banking Crisis.* Dublin, Ireland: Finance Dublin.

Fitzgerald, M. (2008), The Celtic Tiger's underbelly, *Prospect Magazine,* **142**, accessed 20 July 2012 at: http://www.prospectmagazine.co.uk/magazine/ theceltictigersunderbelly/.

Forbairt (1997), 'Transforming Irish industry: lead innovate grow', accessed 20 July 2012 at: http://www.enterprise-ireland.com.

Fortune Magazine, (1966), 'The Irish Sweep – A History of the Irish Hospitals Sweepstake', 1930–87, November 1966.

Gardiner, Kevin (1994), 'The Irish Economy: a Celtic tiger', *MS Euroletter,* August 1994.

Garvin, T. (2004) *Preventing the Future: Why Was Ireland so Poor for so Long?* Dublin, Ireland: Gill and McMillan.

Gateway Ireland (2011), accessed 20 July 2012 at: http://www.gateway-ireland. com.

GEM (2003) Report accessed 20 July 2012 at: http://www.gemconsortium.org.

GEM (2008) Report accessed 20 July 2012 at: http://www.gemconsortium.org.

Gorman, W. and Cooney, T. (2007), 'An anthology of enterprise policy in Ireland', *Irish Journal of Management,* **28** (2), 1–27.

Hanley, M. and O'Gorman, B. (2004), 'Local interpretation of national micro enterprise policy, to what extent has it impacted on local enterprise development'. *International Journal of Entrepreneurial Behaviour and Research,* **10** (5), 305–324.

Hennigan, Michael (2010), 'Trintech sold to US for a knockdown price', Finfacts Ireland's Business and Finance Portal, accessed 23 July 2012 at: www.finfacts.com.

Hennigan, Michael (2006), 'Comment: Irish Economy 2006 and future of the Celtic Tiger: putting a brass knocker on a barn door', Business and Finance Portal, accessed 20 July 2012 at: http://www.finfacts.com.

Hennigan, Michael (2011), 'Irish Economy 2011: Two tiered jobless recovery expected this year', 8 February, accessed 20 July 2012 at: http://www.finfacts.ie/ irishfinancenews/article_1021585.shtml.

Ireland Central Statistics Office: Employment by Sector & Unemployment 1973–2003, accessed 20 July 2012 at: http://www.cso.ie/en/index.html.

Irish Agricultural Organisation Society (IAOS) Annual Report (1994), Dublin: Irish Agricultural Organisation Society.

Irish Regions Office (2011), 'Impact of the structural funds in Ireland (1998–2006)', accessed 20 July 2012 at: http://www.irishregionsoffice.ie.

Irish Technology Leadership Group (2010), accessed 20 July 2012 at: http://www.itlg.org/about-itlg.php.

Keenan, Brendan (2009), 'Fixing the government is now more important than fixing our banks', *Irish Independent*, 23 July, accessed 20 July 2012 at: http://www.independent.ie/opinion/columnists/brendan-keenan/fixing-the-government-is-now-more-important-than-fixing-our-banks-1835596.html.

Moran, Joe (2009), 'Catholic Church dominance to social partnership promise and now economic crisis, little changes in Irish social policy', *Irish Journal of Public Policy*.

News of the World (2011), 'News', 9 January 2011, p. 15.

OECD Report (2002), (cited in OECD report on education 2003), Speech by Minister of State Dick Roche UNESCO Education Seminar, Brasilia: The Irish Economy – the analysis of a success (Department of An Taoiseach), accessed 20 July 2012 at: http://www.taoiseach.gov.ie/eng/News/Archived_Speeches_and_Press_Releases/2003/Government_Press_Releases_2003/Speech_by_Minister_of_State_Dick_Roche_UNESCO_Education_Seminar,_Brasilia_The_Irish_Economy_-_The_Analysis_of_a_Success.html.

OECD (2003), Speech by Minister of State Dick Roche UNESCO Education Seminar, Brasilia: The Irish Economy – the analysis of a success (Department of An Taoiseach), accessed 20 July 2012 at: http://www.taoiseach.gov.ie/eng/News/Archived_Speeches_and_Press_Releases/2003/Governent_Press_Releases_2003/Speech_by_Minister_of_State_Dick_Roche_UNESCO_Education_Seminar,_Brasilia_The_Irish_Economy_-_The_Analysis_of_a_Success.html.

OECD (2004), Directorate for Education/Education committee, Review of National Policies for Education: Review of Higher Education in Ireland, Examiners Report, 13th September 2004.

O'Hearn, D. (1998), *Inside the Celtic Tiger: the Irish economy and the Asian model*, London: Pluto Press.

O'Sullivan, M., (2000), 'Industrial development: a new beginning?', in John O'Hagan (ed.), *The Economy of Ireland: Policy and Performance of a European Region*, Dublin: Gill & MacMillan.

Science Foundation Ireland (SFI) (2011), accessed 20 July 2012 at http:// www sfi. ie.

Shannon Development, accessed 23 February 2011 at: http://www.shannondevelopment 2009 'Early days the birth of Shannon Development'.

Sweeny, P. (1999), *The Celtic Tiger: Ireland's Continuing Economic Miracle*, 2nd edn., Dublin: Oak Tree Press.

Whelan, Karl (2010), 'Policy lessons from Ireland's latest depression', *The Economic and Social Review*, **41** (2), 225–254.

White, Rossa (2010), 'Fruits of boom largely wasted, says Davy report', *Irish Times*, 2 October 2010.

Appendix 2   Singapore: The Lion City

Katie Nehlsen

Since its independence in 1965, Singapore has been studied from numerous economic, political and sociological perspectives attempting to understand its unexpected economic success. Singapore's British colonial rule left a political impression on the people who are now governed by more of a unicameral parliamentary system. This decidedly authoritarian slant is, in some ways, contradictory to the cultural heritage of the natives. Critics of big government have been waiting for nearly five decades for Singapore to collapse or at least have substantial economic and social difficulties. The economy was impacted when China and other Asian tigers emerged as serious competition in the global market in the 1990s, and significant problems arose during the currency crisis in Asia in 1997. However, Singapore adapted to the changing environment, as other autocratic countries failed to do, and flourished. Despite the Western notion that democratic capitalism is the only formula for success, Singapore continues to prosper as one of the strongest and most fascinating economies in the world.

HISTORY

In order to understand Singapore's present situation, it is necessary to understand the city-state's history. Lying to the south of the Malay Peninsula, present-day Singapore is a chain of islands strategically located in the midst of Southeast Asia (see Figure A2.1). Largely unadulterated for much of early history, it was inhabited mostly by Chinese immigrants and controlled by Malay rulers until the Portuguese invaded and burnt the settlement to the ground in the sixteenth century.[1] The islands remained rural jungle with locals living in palm-roofed huts for the next two centuries. It was colonized by the British in 1824 after the sultan and Temenggung signed a treaty handing the land over to the British East India Company.[2] British rule persisted essentially until 1959, except for a span of 3 years from 1942–45 when the Imperial Japanese Army invaded Malaya during World War II, and the British were defeated for a brief period.[3]

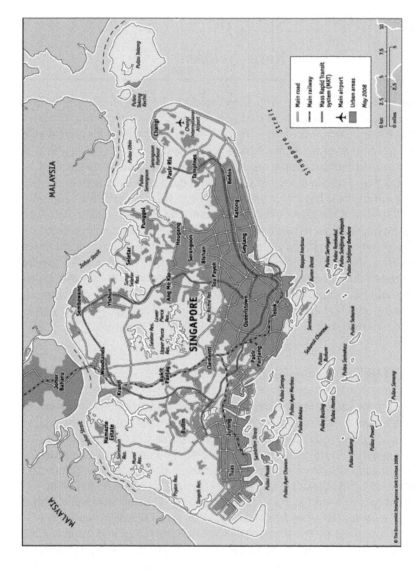

Figure A2.1   Geographic location of Singapore

As an important hub for the British East India Company, Singapore's economy grew as an entrepôt and primary port for refueling and refitting ships traveling between the east and west. Development was stifled by the Japanese invasion as the natives suffered from malnutrition, disease and persecution at the hands of their aggressors.[4] After the war ended and the British reclaimed the land, civil unrest ran rampant. Over the next decade or so, Britain slowly eased their control of the territory until it became entirely self-governing in 1959 under elected Prime Minister Lee Kuan Yew, the founder of the People's Action Party (PAP). The PAP worked closely with the Communist Party to completely sever British colonial rule, and sovereignty was granted in 1963. A brief attempt at unification with other former British territories to form the Federation of Malaysia that same year was futile, and Singapore seceded in 1965 due to ideological and cultural differences between the ruling parties of Malaya and Singapore.[5] In the end, Singapore became an independent nation on 9 August 1965 (see Figure A2.2).

Present-day Singapore is a multi-cultural fusion of people from around the world. In 2006, A. T. Kearney identified Singapore as the most globalized country in the world on their Globalization Index.[6] Singapore currently has approximately 5.1 million residents, a substantial 40 percent of whom are foreigners compared to about 60 percent born in-country. Of the Singaporean natives, roughly 75 percent are of Chinese descent, about 15 percent are Malay and 10 percent are Indian, leading to four official languages: English, Malay, Chinese and Tamil.[7] Although it is difficult to identify a single unique Singaporean culture due to the diversity of its inhabitants, the common threads throughout the country are education as first priority, then quality of life and a general respect for others.

Although Singapore is theoretically a parliamentary republic with a free-enterprise economy, the economic role of government is pervasive. The parliamentary legislative system is a legacy from over 100 years of British colonization, but the influence of Communism in the region has also played a major part in the governance structure. From the outset, the government took control and responsibility for the welfare of the people, arranging and accounting for everything from international relations to trash collection. A far cry from pure capitalism, the government has set wages and prices, allocated land and resources, regulated capital and controlled labor. There are very few issues in which the government is not involved in one way or another. Singapore is ranked 83rd out of 169 countries in the Economist Intelligence Unit's Democracy index (one being the most democratic).[8] Singapore is truly unique in its ability to run on democratic values with communistic efficiency.

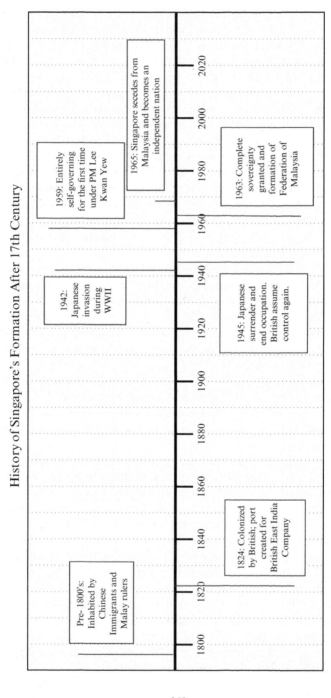

History of Singapore's Formation After 17th Century

Pre-1800's: Inhabited by Chinese Immigrants and Malay rulers

1824: Colonized by British; port created for British East India Company

1942: Japanese invasion during WWII

1945: Japanese surrender and end occupation. British assume control again.

1959: Entirely self-governing for the first time under PM Lee Kwan Yew

1963: Complete sovereignty granted and formation of Federation of Malaysia

1965: Singapore secedes from Malaysia and becomes an independent nation

1800 1820 1840 1860 1880 1900 1920 1940 1960 1980 2000 2020

Figure A2.2 Historical timeline

EARLY CHALLENGES

As the first Prime Minister of a newly established nation, Lee Kuan Yew faced a great deal of uncertainty in his new role. Although the land had been partially developed during the British East India Company's occupation, the residual pollution from centuries of poverty lingered. The waterways were full of garbage and sewage, there was little infrastructure and many people were still living in huts. Beyond that, racial clashes and political unrest were causing chaos in the streets. With hardly any natural resources and land only about the size of Manhattan, it seemed questionable that the little city-state would become an independent nation. Lee describes his despair at the outset, 'We faced tremendous odds with an improbable chance of survival . . . Singapore was not a natural country but rather man-made, a trading post the British had developed into a nodal point in their worldwide maritime empire. We inherited the island without its hinterland, a heart without a body.'[9]

Despite the hardship, Lee made it his first priority to establish civil order by creating both an internal and external defense system with police and army forces.[10] He recognized that all other attempts for growth would be futile if fighting continued. Once peace was established, he could focus on how to create an economy with few identifiable resources. After much debate and many failed attempts, Lee and his government found Singapore's greatest asset to be its people. The solution was clear: rather than trying to create wealth internally (without natural resources), they would focus on attracting foreign wealth into the country. Foreign direct investment (FDI) became the backbone of Singapore's economy (see Figure A2.3). In 2006, Singapore's former US Ambassador, Frank Lavin, put the importance of foreign investment into perspective when he noted that, '[in 2005] India had received $45 billion in foreign direct investment (FDI) in total, with $8 billion of that from the United States. Compare that to one of your neighbors, tiny Singapore, which at the same time had received more than $186 billion in total and $48 billion from the United States'.[11]

INITIAL DEVELOPMENT STRATEGY

The main initiative in their quest for FDI was to attract US- and European-based companies to set up manufacturing sites in Singapore for direct re-export back to the west. In order to accomplish this, the government took an unconventional approach in bypassing neighboring countries as trading partners. Relying more heavily on multinational corporations

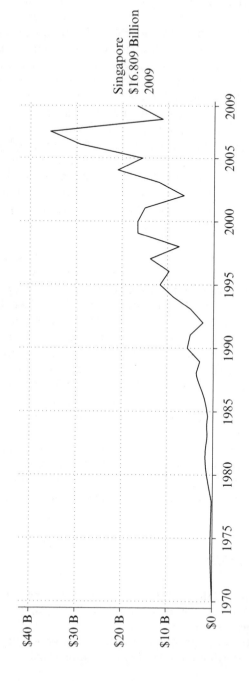

Source: The World Bank.

Figure A2.3 Foreign direct investment, net inflows (*BoP, current US$*)

(MNCs) would allow Singapore to reduce dependence on Southeast Asian countries.[12] Lee also saw the necessity of making Singapore an attractive place to do business for the MNCs with which he wanted to partner. His goal was to reposition Singapore as a 'first-world oasis in a third-world region'.[13] Lee's repositioning approach emphasized the importance of Singapore as a strategic gateway for the west to broader Asia. Indeed, as Lavin noted in a speech before the US–SEEAN Business Council,

> Singapore is a strategic market. It's not a strategic market because of its size; it's actually rather smallish, but it's a strategic market for Americans because of ease of entry. So if you're starting to think about Asia, Southeast Asia, getting in there, start to grab at the low-hanging fruits that's in Singapore because it's predominantly English speaking, because it's highly educated population, because it's a very transactional, commercial society. Anything that you have to sell or do, you'll find distributors, you'll find bankers, you'll find a real estate. You can just look at a phonebook the same way you would look in any American city, and you can be up in business by the end of the day.[14]

Five major factors helped attract foreign direct investment:

- Sound infrastructure
- Labor peace
- Internal savings and investment at extraordinary levels
- Noninflationary currency with stable exchange rates
- Sufficient government control to drive necessary reforms and regulations.

Lee and the rest of the government made significant capital expenditures to create a working, modern infrastructure in an environment that would be comfortable for Westerners. To encourage labor peace, almost all labor unions (especially those in opposition to new governmental regulations) were abolished and replaced with the state-run National Trade Union Congress (NTUC). The National Wage Council was also established to regulate wages in order to dissuade disputes over money. Likewise, the government created the Central Provident Fund (CPF) as a mandatory savings program for all Singaporeans. Much like Social Security in the United States, this fund is given to people after retirement as well as other public loan programs. Mandatory contributions by both employees and employers are set by the government and have fluctuated over the years. The one constant is that Singaporeans consistently over-save, leading to a gross domestic savings of between 45–50 percent annually. Excess funds were used to continuously improve infrastructure and to build one of the most modern cities in the world. Currency stability was handled soundly, with exemplary macroeconomic management to the extent that Singapore had a deficit only occasionally since 1965.[15]

Among the countless sound measures put into place to facilitate FDI, a few made the biggest impact including the elimination of trade and investment barriers, the creation of the Housing Development Board (HDB) that generated thousands of jobs and eventually housed more than 85 percent of the population, and the creation of the Economic Development Board (EDB) as an extension of the Ministry of Trade and Industry. Rather than passively awaiting recognition from MNCs, the EDB proactively met with potential customers to convince them to invest in Singapore. Their strategic mission was to nurture relationships with corporations in certain industry clusters including petrochemicals, ship refitting and repair, metal engineering and electronics. Lee quickly understood that it was not simply manufacturing that he wanted to attract, but more specifically value-added and high-technology manufacturing, where the lion's share of the money is, and where his skilled labor force would be put to good use (see Figure A2.4).

SINGAPORE, INC.

Another notable measure the government employed to increase FDI was through the purchase of minority stakes in various local companies, while also acquiring and establishing others. The Ministry of Finance was responsible for the care and growth of these companies until the incorporation of Temasek Holdings in 1974. At inception, Temasek started with a portfolio of around US$100 million which they have grown to an estimated US$159.2 billion.[16] The Ministry of Finance remains the sole shareholder of this sovereign wealth fund today. The government also has a second investing arm, the Government of Singapore Investment Corporation Private Limited (GIC), established in 1981 to manage the country's foreign reserves. With an estimated portfolio worth US$330 billion, both institutions are in the world's top ten largest sovereign wealth funds.

Through vehicles such as these as well as the EDB, some have valued the government's commercial assets upwards of 60 percent of GDP. However, Temasek responded by claiming that it contributed closer to 10 percent citing the following statistics: foreign owned companies = 42 percent, non-government related Singapore owned companies = 33 percent, government-linked companies = 13 percent, majority owned government-linked companies = 9 percent and companies with minority government related ownership of 20–50 percent = 4 percent.[17] Temasek has a stake in many of the largest local companies including SingTel, DBS Bank,

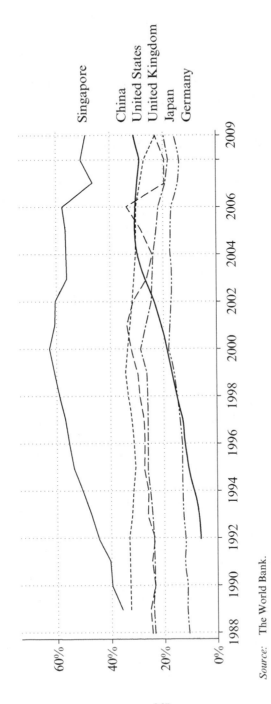

Source: The World Bank.

Figure A2.4 High-technology exports (% of manufactured exports)

Singapore Airlines, PSA International, SMRT Corporation, Singapore Power, Neptune Orient Lines and Mediacorp, as well as large foreign companies such as Standard Chartered, Bank of China, China Construction Bank, ICICI Bank and Global Crossing. Although some companies have later gone public, Temasek continues to maintain a majority stake in many of them, especially the historical monopolies.

NEW DEVELOPMENT STRATEGY

With constant development, reassessment and realignment, Singapore's FDI strategy had great success for many decades, even enduring a grave recession in 1985. However, the simultaneous emergence of the other Asian tiger economies, as well as China opening its doors to foreign markets, created significant competition for Singapore by the 1990s. China emerged as the world leader in cheap-labor manufacturing, and Western countries were no longer reliant on Singapore as a gateway to the east. Furthermore, China's entry into the World Trade Organization (WTO) as well as free trade agreements between China and the ASEAN-5 left Singapore's industrial model outdated.[18]

INNOVATION AND ENTREPRENEURSHIP

Having come so far in less than 30 years, the government looked inward for a solution. The country had become a trading powerhouse, growing from a seeker of foreign investment to an investor in lower-wage regions. In comparison to the world's most developed economies, such as the United States, Europe and Japan, an obvious difference was the lack of entrepreneurship in Singapore, a key driver in the larger economies. Although Lee Kuan Yew is no longer Prime Minister (his son, Lee Hsien Loong, is the nation's third Prime Minister), Lee Kuan Yew's own viewpoint on Singapore's economic strategy has evolved over time, 'The greatest challenge to Singapore today is to get our people to move away from the old model. Just being clean, green, efficient, and cost-effective is not enough. You've also got to be innovative, creative, and entrepreneurial.'[19] By definition, traditional entrepreneurial activity is bottom-up, starting with very little and resulting in prosperity via growth. However, Singapore's approach to entrepreneurship, as everything else, is decidedly top-down, involving big investments and intervention by the government and state-owned enterprises (SOEs). Bypassing the lean years of 'startup' for traditional nascent companies provides the potential to expedite growth.

WHY IS THERE SO LITTLE ENTREPRENEURSHIP IN SINGAPORE?

Singapore's first step in its new development strategy was to assess why there was such little entrepreneurial activity in the country compared to the rest of the world. If its leaders could find the underlying reason, then they could plausibly find a solution. Numerous theories surfaced, among which four seem to carry the most weight:

- Too much government-run business overcrowding the private sector
- The educational system traditionally steered the most talented individuals towards careers in the public sector
- Overarching culture of risk avoidance
- Economic prosperity has created an environment where entrepreneurship is not needed.

At its inception in 1965, flailing companies needed the resources and guidance of government intervention in order to survive. Since then, the ventures have become wildly successful, but the government has not stopped supporting them. As late as 2002, six out of ten of Singapore's top listed companies by market capitalization were largely or wholly owned by the government.[20] With such large SOEs congesting the small market, there is little room for small- to medium-sized companies to grow. If there is no growth potential, the environment will not attract would-be entrepreneurs.

Likewise, the traditional education system was built around the principles of Singapore's early development strategy, thereby using the majority of resources to mold the most talented students into highly talented bureaucrats. Even though it is one of the most successful economies in the world, the Singaporean education system continues to push the best and brightest towards civil service or management of SOEs through high salaries, job security and scholarships for higher education.[21] This not only leaves a talent gap in the private sector, but it also reaffirms a culture of bureaucracy which squelches independent thinking and entrepreneurship.

Beyond an affinity for bureaucracy, culture also has a great deal to do with Singapore's lack of entrepreneurs. With a large Chinese population, the cultural tradition of valuing academics above all else has prevailed. Therefore, being a scholar by profession is still the ultimate goal. The second most valued occupation is a farmer, third is a worker and fourth is a merchant or entrepreneur. Unlike the Western mentality that prizes original thought and individuality, the Singaporean ethos

frowns upon selfish independence. It is widely accepted that the greatest achievement is a perfect replication of the master. Unfortunately,
this type of thinking leaves little room for innovation. Having built the
country on a doctrine of discipline and conformity, even Lee Kuan Yew
understands the need for a change in mindset, 'The easy things – just
getting a blank mind to take in knowledge and become trainable – we
have done. Now comes the difficult part. To get literate and numerate
minds to be more innovative, to be more productive, that's not easy.'[22]
Changing the mindset of an entire society is difficult, if not impossible;
however, Lee's admission of the need to do so is an important step in
the right direction.

Finally, many feel that the lack of entrepreneurship in Singapore
is merely a response to the country's economic prosperity. The lack
of an entrepreneurial culture may partially be attributed to the country's restrictions on political speech. As Lavin has noted, 'prosperity
has come at the cost of political freedom, and without such freedom
Singapore will find it hard to compete in the twenty-first century'[23]
and that the country will 'pay an increasing price for not allowing full
participation of its citizens'.[24] Dubbed a 'crisis of affluence', perhaps
the complacency that has settled over the Singaporean people is one
of contentedness in the way things are.[25] In an entrepreneurial society,
people are willing to take risks because there is little to lose. Failure
is commonplace, and therefore nothing to fear or to be ashamed of.
Most importantly, a true entrepreneurial culture is built by people
who are trying to make a better life for themselves or their children. In
Singapore, the unemployment rate is about 2 percent, and 15.5 percent
of all households surpass the million dollar threshold making for the
highest percentage of millionaire households in the world.[26, 27] In other
words, life is good in Singapore, so necessity-based entrepreneurship
is simply non-existent. Lavin held a particularly high profile position
during his tenure as Ambassador by overseeing negotiation for a US–
Singapore Free Trade Agreement and helping assure businesses that
Singapore was a safe country in which to conduct business, especially
after the 9/11 terrorist attacks and attacks in nearby Bali, Indonesia.
In a 2002 interview with Channel NewsAsia, Lavin echoed the quality
of life sentiments by saying, 'Singapore is a great place for people to
do business and to raise families'.[28] In 2004, Lavin expanded on his
thoughts on Singapore life by noting that, 'It's a great place. It's not so
much of a holiday destination for Americans because it's so far away
... Singapore is an environment that is sufficiently different and that
can grow on Americans. But it is also sufficiently similar, so that it's not
so exotic that it becomes challenging.'[29]

MEASURES AND REFORMS TO BOOST ENTREPRENEURIAL VENTURES

True to form, the Singapore government acted quickly on measures to support its new strategic goals to transform the city-state into a knowledge-based economy, encourage innovation and move up the value chain. In the 1990s, they embarked on numerous efforts to offer direct subsidies to spark an otherwise absent venture capital industry. Their US$1 billion investment proved their sincerity in encouraging the start-up of new companies.[30] However, they quickly found that financial assistance was not enough inspiration to change the risk-averse mindset of the people, and the government could not afford to throw money at every problem it encountered forever. Specifically, the environment in which people operated would need to change in order for attitudes toward entrepreneurship to evolve within society. Although changing a climate takes time, energy and a great deal of resources, Lee had done it before and was actively encouraging it again. 'We cannot create entrepreneurs,' Lee stated in 2003, 'we can only facilitate their emergence.'[31] As such, Singapore focused on building a favorable climate in which entrepreneurs could thrive. Josh Lerner broadly summarized Singapore's most worthwhile efforts in his book *Boulevard of Broken Dreams* as:

- The provision of public funds for venture investors seeking to locate in the city-state
- Subsidies for firms in targeted technologies
- Encouragement of potential entrepreneurs and mentoring for fledgling ventures
- Subsidies for leading biotechnology researchers to move their laboratories to Singapore
- Awards for failed entrepreneurs (with a hope of encouraging risk-taking).

POLICIES, LAWS AND DEREGULATIONS

In response to the need to create an environment that would appeal to entrepreneurs, both foreign and domestic, the government enacted legal reforms. Domestically, bankruptcy laws were drastically relaxed and tax deductions were given to those who invested in new companies in an attempt to encourage risk-taking behavior in Singaporean nationals.[32] To attract foreign entrepreneurs, already liberal immigration policies opened up even further. Another step in their proactive recruitment of talented individuals to lead their new economy was to remove almost all barriers for skilled and educated people who want to immigrate into Singapore. The Ministry of Manpower will even expedite the paperwork of foreign entrepreneurs who are interested in starting a company in Singapore, if the company is in a high-growth industry. Likewise, Singapore adheres to strict intellectual property (IP) laws, unlike many of their neighbors who are notorious IP lawbreakers. The IP protection provided is especially helpful in attracting information-sensitive businesses, such as those in the high-tech and biomedical industries that Singapore has openly targeted. IP protection was strengthened after the passage of the US–Singapore Free Trade Agreement. As Lavin noted in an interview shortly after the FTA was signed, 'With the FTA, Singapore will offer protection comparable to that in the United States, and probably the best in Asia. This is a tremendous selling point for Singapore.'[33]

Financial policies have also been put into place to encourage new ventures. Beyond the US$1 billion venture capital fund provided by the government for startups, the EDB also partially subsidizes research expenses for new innovation initiatives.[34] Deregulation has been noteworthy as well. It previously was illegal to run a business out of one's home, a law that obviously dissuades entrepreneurial activity.[35] That regulation was removed once the politicians realized how many companies such as Apple, Inc and Facebook were created in the comfort of a person's garage or college dorm room. Also, corporate taxes were cut and a Minister for Entrepreneurship was appointed to oversee such measures[36] (see Figure A2.5).

In an effort to address the concerns posed by the SOEs crowding out the private marketplace, Singapore has even begun to consider shedding some of its corporate control. In a 2002 interview, the current Prime Minister Lee Hsien Loong explained the government's reasoning for considering privatization of currently government-controlled firms:

> We own certain significant industries and companies – SingTel, the Development Bank of Singapore, Singapore International Airlines, the power industry, the port, the shipyards – because of historical circumstances. We built them into world-call companies. Now, as we look forward, the question is which should we hold and which no longer make sense? We're looking for opportunities to sell those enterprises that no longer make sense for us to keep.[37]

TRAINING AND DEVELOPING POTENTIAL ENTREPRENEURS

To address issues concerning educational misdirection and the talent gap in the private sector, the government made several educational reforms. The government now encourages academic institutions to promote creative thinking and to put greater weight on the importance of liberal arts

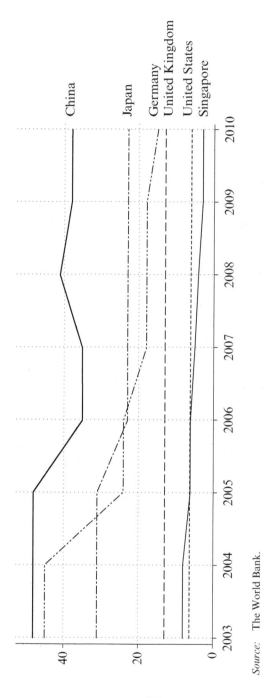

China
Japan
Germany
United Kingdom
United States
Singapore

40

20

0

2003   2004   2005   2006   2007   2008   2009   2010

Source: The World Bank.

Figure A2.5   Time required to start a business (days)

and sports, as opposed to the rote learning of the past. At one time, 250 of the top 300 students graduating from secondary school received scholarships from government agencies. The scholarship recipients were required to work for the government for 6 years after graduation, which led to nearly all of them continuing their career in the public sector. A new proposal states that these scholarship recipients should only have to serve the government for 'several' years, after which they would be free to choose a career in the private sector if desired.[38]

At the university level, the government increased spending for academic research threefold from 1996 to 2001. Additionally, top ranking universities were given support to create various entrepreneur-development activities, such as incubators and classes where students could work with faculty to cultivate new ideas.[39] Singapore believes that it is easier to breed a new generation of entrepreneurs through educational support, rather than try to change the ways of the older bureaucrats who are set in their ways.

In addition to the new liberal immigration laws, Singapore actively recruits entrepreneurial talent from foreign countries via TV and print ads, especially targeting India, Malaysia, China and the west coast of the United States.[40] The idea behind this investment is not to attract and pay consistently for foreign talent, but for Singaporeans to learn from the first generation of immigrants who can inspire domestic talent thereafter. Essentially tapping the cultural tradition of learning from the master, Singapore hopes that its youth will emulate the professionals they recruit for future business ventures. Net migration has more than doubled between 2005 and 2010 (see Figure A2.6); while this suggests that Singapore has been successful in attracting new professionals, it is too early to determine if this influx of foreign workers will be successful in influencing the entrepreneurial mindset of the next generation.

In addition to attracting entrepreneurial professionals into the country, Singapore has engaged in other developmental efforts such as events, competitions and awards to encourage innovation and entrepreneurship. For instance, the Bluesky Festival, Enterprise Day and the Phoenix Award all commend those who try to create new growth enterprises. The Phoenix Award is given to an entrepreneur who has failed in the past but was able to recover and ultimately achieve success, or as the name suggests someone who is born again like a phoenix from the ashes.

SPRING

In an effort to boost overall productivity, the government created SPRING, a board dedicated to improving Standards, Productivity and Innovation

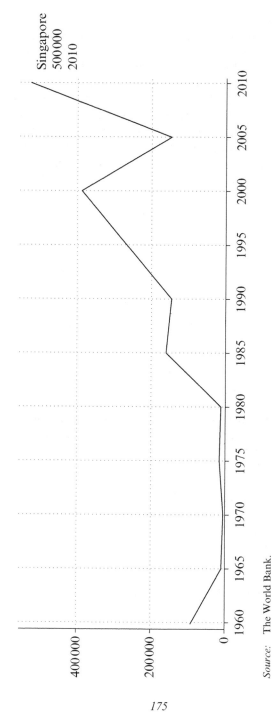

Source: The World Bank.

Figure A2.6   Net migration

in Singapore. Originally created to push productivity in more than 2000 firms via productivity training, lean operating, quality improvements, retailer networking and wellness promotion, the board also focused on incentivizing small- and medium-sized enterprises (SMEs). By encouraging relationships between SMEs to help promote training, research, and other capital-intensive activities that small companies alone would not be capable of funding, SPRING also provides grants to startups that need help from consultants in order to boost success rates. As SPRING chairman Lim Boon Heng, who also serves as the secretary of the National Trade Union Congress, explained, 'We believe in promoting productivity, because if we increase this, we can negotiate sustainable increases in wages. Instead of just concentrating on sharing the cake, we concentrate on making a bigger cake.'[41] These innovative and forward-thinking organizations are the impetus for growth and success in Singapore.

BIOPOLIS

Perhaps Singapore's largest investment and greatest triumph in their quest for innovation is Biopolis, a $500 million corporate park consisting of seven buildings each complete with state-of-the-art laboratories. Home to the country's top research institutes, it was built to attract the biomedical industry, one of Singapore's most highly sought-after engines of growth. Their aggressive recruitment strategy worked as world-class researchers from some of world's most prestigious research universities (MIT, University of California, Kyoto University) as well as corporate giants such as Merck & Co. and Pfizer Inc. now call Biopolis home. In addition to the facilities, Singapore also lured in top researchers with outlandishly high salaries (purportedly up to $1 million annually), research funding and little political restriction on types of research, setting it apart from regulated research in the United States.[42] A few of the many notable researchers who relocated to Singapore to continue their work include Sydney Brenner, 2002 Nobel Prize winner for medicine, Alan Colman who helped clone the sheep Dolly and cancer geneticists Neal Copland and Nancy Jenkins.[43]

THE BIGGEST CHALLENGE: CHANGING THE MINDSET OF A PEOPLE

Although not an exhaustive list, the previously discussed measures taken by the Singaporean government have certainly improved the economic sustainability of the city-state. However, the question still remains as to whether or not the Singaporean people have truly changed, or if the efforts made by the government have been little more than a Band-Aid for the problem. Changing an entire society's values is an obstacle not easily overcome. Lee Hsien Loong said, 'We can change the incentives, the social expectations and norms, but then finally the person has to want to go and do it.'[44]

Jeffrey Goh, one of the few Singaporean national entrepreneurs, is skeptical that the government's efforts will produce the results they want. He blames the educational system for removing the ability to think independently. However, he does admit that at least the word 'entrepreneur' is now in the people's vocabulary, unlike 10 years ago.[45] He, like many other entrepreneurs in Singapore, have become frustrated by the lack of human resources willing to take the risk of even being a part of a startup, as they struggle to find employees. The risk-averse culture is pervasive, and no amount of subsidies or tax incentives can remedy that. However, others remain more optimistic in that even if it takes a generation, the Singaporean people will adapt to survive, as they have in the past.

HAS IT WORKED?

The future will determine whether or not the government's efforts to produce internal entrepreneurs have been successful. Singapore's economic growth in the past 50 years provides a strong foundation for continued sustainable entrepreneurial activity within the public and private sector. Current economic data suggests that the nation is well positioned to facilitate the growth of entrepreneurship. According to the World Bank (Figure A2.7), Singapore's GDP per capita growth has continually surpassed the global average since the 1970s. Furthermore, in 2009, Singapore was rated the world's most open economy on the Globalization Index compiled by the EIU and Ernst & Young. The 2009–10 Global Competitiveness Index produced by the World Economic Forum listed Singapore as the third most competitive economy in the world, trailing only Switzerland and the United States. Additionally, the 2011 Global Innovation Index produced by INSEAD Business School ranked Singapore third in the world behind Switzerland and Sweden. The World Bank consistently ranks Singapore the number one country in the world for ease of doing business. According to the 2010 *CIA World Factbook*, Singapore ranked 41st in the world for purchase power parity (Figure A2.8) and third in the world for real growth rate of GDP. While solid economic growth is an important ingredient for entrepreneurship, it is by no means the only indicator for future success. In addition to access to capital, the government needs to provide its citizens with a strong political

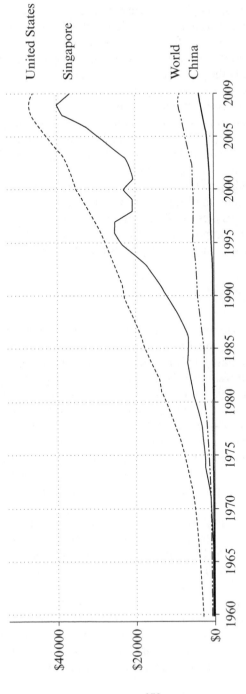

Source: The World Bank.

Figure A2.7   GDP per capita (current US$)

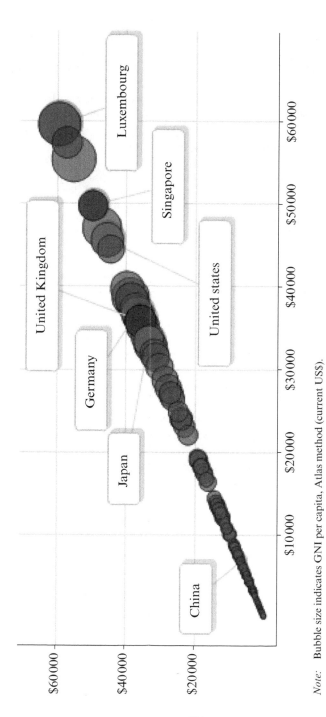

Note: Bubble size indicates GNI per capita, Atlas method (current US$).

Source: The World Bank.

Figure A2.8 2009 gross national income per capita (in purchasing power parity dollars)

179

and psychological framework, which encourages entrepreneurship at every level of the economy. Despite some concern about Singapore's ability to foster entrepreneurial growth within the nation, its leaders are increasingly building the case for entrepreneurship domestically.

Singapore's Minister of State for the Ministry of Trade and Industry, Teo Ser Luck, demonstrated the state's commitment to developing domestic entrepreneurship in his August 2011 speech at a conference for start-up enterprises. Addressing the nation's potential entrepreneurs he said:

> As you advance in your career as an entrepreneur, I encourage you to dream big and think global, and not be constrained by our small domestic market ... the world is your oyster. Having global ambitions will help you to seize opportunities out there. To build a vibrant start-up community, we need entrepreneurs who are ambitious, innovative, and able to provide good solutions to the market.

Mr Teo continued his address by reminding his audience that start-up enterprises are an important part of Singapore's economy because they 'form the pipeline for great companies to emerge'. He went on to say that the government recognizes that entrepreneurship is a key pillar of growth for its economy, and as a result has committed to a pro-enterprise environment. 'By changing mindsets towards entrepreneurship, building up the infrastructure to support entrepreneurs, and reducing the regulatory burden on businesses, we have fostered a strong environment for businesses to thrive'.[46]

Given its history, perhaps Singapore's greatest strength is its ability to adapt to the global environment. Only time will tell if this innovative nation-state is able to leverage its resources and successfully build a sustainable entrepreneurial environment able to compete in the rapidly changing global economy. But if history repeats itself, it will find a way.

NOTES

1. Library of Congress, *Singapore: A Country Study* (Washington DC: Library of Congress, 1989).
2. Ministry of Information, Communication and the Arts, *Founding of Modern Singapore* (Singapore: Ministry of Information, Communication and the Arts, 2011).
3. Library of Congress, 1989.
4. R. Vietor, *How Countries Compete* (Boston: Harvard Business School Press, 2007).
5. B. Leitch Lepoer, *Singapore as Part of Malaysia* (Washington DC: Library of Congress, 1989).
6. Foreign Policy Magazine, 'Measuring globalization', *Foreign Policy* (2001), 56–65.
7. Central Intelligence Agency (2010), *The World Factbook: Singapore*, Washington DC: Library of Congress.
8. Economist Intelligence Unit, 'Country Profile: Singapore', 2008, accessed 23 July 2012 at: http://www.eiu.com.

9. L. K. Yew, *From Third World to First* (New York: Harper Collins, 2000).
10. Yew, 2000.
11. 'Expanding US–India Commercial Relationship: Frank Lavin', *States News Service*, 3 December 2006.
12. Library of Congress (1989).
13. Yew, 2000, p. 58.
14. US–ASEAN Business Council Interview with United States Ambassador to Singapore, Mr Frank Lavin and Singapore Ambassador to the United States Chan Heng Chee. 28 January 2003. Accessed 6 April 2012 at: http://singapore.usembassy.gov/012803.html.
15. Vietor, 2007, p. 44.
16. 'Asset-backed insecurity', *The Economist*, 17 January 2008.
17. Temasek Holdings, 'Media letters and responses', accessed 23 July 2012 at: http://www.temasek.com.sg/media_centre_responses_16Aug2011.html.
18. L. Yunhua, *Economic Competition and Co-operation between ASEAN-5 and China in Trade* (Singapore: Nanyang Technological University, 2004).
19. Y. Lee, 'Singapore falls behind Hong Kong in fight to diversify economy', *Bloomberg*, 14 March 2007.
20. 'Keeping the Inc. in Singapore Inc.', *Institutional Investor*, 2002.
21. J. Burton, 'Singapore Seeks a Nation of Risk-takers', *Financial Times*, 2004.
22. K. Hamlin, 'Remaking Singapore', *Institutional Investor*, 2002.
23. Kevin Hamlin, 'Remade in Singapore', *Institutional Investor*, September 2006.
24. Bhagyashree Garekar, 'Singapore resilient: outgoing US envoy', *The Straits Times*, 12 October 2005.
25. W. Mellor, 'The risks of playing it safe', *Asiaweek*, 2001.
26. Ministry of Manpower, 'Employment Situation in Fourth Quarter 2010', Press Release. Singapore, 31 January 2011.
27. The Boston Consulting Group (31 May 2011).
28. 'Singapore not "high risk" country, says US ambassador', Channel NewsAsia, 24 October 2002.
29. Ginnie Teo 'No American idle', *The Straits Times*, 6 June 2004.
30. S. Oh, 'Giving Singapore a Silicon Valley mindset', *Asian Entrepreneur*, 2000.
31. S. Elegant, 'The lion in winter', *Time Asia*, 2003.
32. Mellor, 2001.
33. Amit Roy Choudhury, 'FTA will help S'pore transform into an IT hub, says US envoy', *The Business Times Singapore*, 23 July 2003.
34. J. Lerner, *Boulevard of Broken Dreams* (Princeton, NJ: Princeton University Press, 2009).
35. Mellor, 2001.
36. Burton, 2004.
37. 'Singapore's big gamble', *Foreign Policy: The Magazine of Global Politics, Economics and Ideas*, 2002.
38. Burton, 2004.
39. Lerner, 2009.
40. Mellor, 2001.
41. Vietor, 2007.
42. Lerner, 2009.
43. Lee, 2007.
44. *Foreign Policy Magazine*, 2002.
45. Hamlin, 2002.
46. 'Singaporean entrepreneurs urged to take global market share', *Asia Pulse*, 22 August 2011.

Appendix 3   Entrepreneurship in the Saudi public sector

Amr Al-Dabbagh

THE FORMS AND COLORS OF GOLD

Gold has always been a standard metaphor, and as a metaphor, can come in many forms and colors.

We have, 'good as gold'.

We have, 'more precious than gold'.

'A heart of gold', 'a golden touch', 'the golden age', 'the golden rules', all ten of them.

Metaphors are valuable because they allow us to see beyond the surface, or to see how everything is connected in one way or another to our experience as human beings.

As a metaphor, then, *gold* can be seen as more than a metallic substance, and can take many forms and colors, *liquid* and *black* being some of them.

Gold can be a fragrance, too.

THE HUB

Perfectly situated between the literal and metaphoric 'East' and 'West', and determined the twain shall meet, what is present day Saudi Arabia grew from the trading activities of the Nabataeans, ancient Bedouins whose influence as much as 2500 years ago stretched north from modern Yemen into present day Syria, over a 2-million-square kilometer ocean of sand. On the backs of their camels and horses were conveyed agricultural items from Mesopotamia to the east, dates from scattered oases on the peninsula, almonds from modern Taif, and frankincense and myrrh from the Tihama plain, modern Oman and Yemen. What came out of South Asia, especially present day India, Thailand, China and Korea, trickled slowly across the Arabian Sea, over the forbidding deserts of Al Dahna in the east, the Rub al-Khali in the south, and in the west, the fiery Al-Nafūd. From there it was onward to the Nile River Valley, or modern day

Egypt, Palestine and Jordan, with stops along the way at outposts such as Hegra, and cities such as Petra, until when they reached Gaza, they sailed for Rome.

For much of unrecorded history through the early nineteenth century the traders of the Arabian Peninsula merely joined two ends of a growing demand, caught in the middle of a surrounding world thoroughly embroiled in battle after battle for domination – Babylon, Egypt, Persia, Greece, Rome – while the peninsula's great expanse of deserts and associated semi-desert shrubland, where temperatures can reach 129°F, kept most of its neighbors at a distance, powerful as they were.

THE HOME OF ISLAM

The Prophet Muhammad (PBUH) was born around AD 570 in the then thriving center of commerce, Mecca, where around 40 years later he began spreading the message that would become Islam. By the time of his death in 632, this message succeeded in uniting all the tribes of Arabia under a single religion, and only a century would pass before this new religion spread as far west as Spain, and as far east as India and China. At the height of its influence, Islam inspired an age of learning in philosophy, arts, culture and science referred to as 'golden' in the modern era.

After the Prophet Muhammad's (PBUH) death until early in the twentieth century, what is present day Saudi Arabia exchanged hands between local dynastic ruling Arabs in the Hejaz who were under allegiance to the Umayyad and Abbasid caliphates ruling from the Islamic empires of Baghdad, Cairo or Istanbul; local dynastic leaders in the Nejd, or Riyadh in central Arabia, and the ever expanding Ottoman Empire, which would finally lose its claims over Arabia at the end World War I.

THE BIRTH OF SAUDI ARABIA

The origins of modern Saudi Arabia begin in 1902, when the 21-year-old Abdulaziz bin Saud and 50 followers captured modern day Riyadh in a celebrated nighttime raid that would set the stage for three decades of conquests and diplomacy. On 22 September 1932, the various and scattered Arab tribes of the Peninsula would finally be united in modern day Saudi Arabia, the largest country in the Middle East, and the 14th largest country in the world, larger even than Western Europe.

The territory is dominated by desert and semi-desert, including the 250000 m² square mile Empty Quarter in the south, the largest sand area in the world, the 40000 m² Al-Nafud in the north, made famous in the film Lawrence of Arabia, and the Al-Dhana in the east. Saudi Arabia occupies 80 percent of the Arabian Peninsula, has over 1600 miles of coastline, with the Red Sea on the west and the Arabian Gulf to the east. It is bordered by Yemen on the south, Oman to the southeast, Kuwait to the northeast, Qatar and UAE on the east, and Jordan and Iraq to the north and northeast.

When Abdulaziz became King of this new and forbidding territory, with no permanent lakes or rivers, it was given the name Al Mamlaka al 'Arabiyya as Su'ūdiyya, or 'The Kingdom of Saudi Arabia'.

Since 1932 when it was formed, still perfectly poised between the West and East, successive Saudi leaders have followed the footsteps of King Abdulaziz, by consistently dedicating themselves to preserving Arab traditions and culture in the process of forming a modern and competitive nation.

BLACK GOLD AND THE 'SEVEN SISTERS'

Few countries were poorer in 1932. State income was derived from limited agriculture, date exports and pilgrimage revenues, and the staple diet, at least for many, was dates and water. Conditions would begin to change quickly, however, when after oil was discovered in 1933, the Saudi government signed a concessionary agreement on 29 May with the California–Arabian Standard Oil Co. (Casoc), an affiliate of Standard Oil of California (Socal), now Chevron. Four years would pass and more oil companies become engaged before the most famous find in the global history of oil exploration would take place on the eastern coast, the infamous oil well Dammam #7, discovered in 1938.

Three more years would pass before full scale development began in 1941, the concession of oil companies grow to seven, the infamous 'Seven Sisters',[1] and in 1944 Casoc would change its name to Aramco, an acronym for the Arabian American Oil Company (considered by some to be the single most valuable company in the world, with estimated worth of between US$2.2 to $7 trillion dollars).

Oil exports grew throughout World War II, and would soar afterwards, providing the resources Saudi Arabia needed to build the basic infrastructure it lacked until that time, such as schools, hospitals, roads, airports and seaports.

Starting in the 1970s, while Aramco was investing heavily in developing the oil industry with new production facilities, pipelines, plants, shipping facilities and continued exploration, the Kingdom invested most of its resources in developing its basic infrastructure through a series of 5-year development plans that would lead to the creation of a modern economy. From 1976 onward Saudi Arabia become the largest oil producer in the world, with urbanization, mass public education and huge investment in infrastructure as a result.

THE KINGDOM

Following the death of King Abdullaziz in 1953, a series of Saudi Kings would begin laying the foundation for the modern and very entrepreneurial present day leader, King Abdullah bin Abdullaziz.

From 1953 to 1964, King Saud began the process of forming a modern government with the creation of the Council of Ministers and establishment of the Ministries of Health, Education and Commerce, and his investments in education included the first institute of higher education, King Saud University, in 1957.

He was followed by King Faisal bin Abdulaziz (1964–75), who initiated the first of a series of economic and social development plans that would transform Saudi Arabia's infrastructure, especially industry, and set the Kingdom on a path of rapid growth. He also established the first public schools for girls.

He was followed by King Khalid (1975–82) whose emphasis on development during a period of enormous wealth and prosperity for Saudi Arabia, lead to an explosive growth in the country's physical infrastructure.

From 1982 to 2005 King Fahd, who adopted the title Custodian of the Two Holy Mosques, lead the Kingdom to diversify its economy and promote private enterprise and investment. He restructured the Saudi government, approved the first nationwide municipal elections for 2005 through then Crown Prince Abdullah, and worked actively in the international arena promoting peace and reconciliation, and resolving humanitarian issues caused by political turmoil and natural disasters, such as the 2004 tsunami that hit Southeast Asia.

THE CHIEF ARCHITECT OF REFORMS

Custodian of the Two Holy Mosques King Abdullah bin Abdullaziz took the throne after the death of King Fahd on 1 August 2005. He was born in Riyadh in 1924, and there received his early education as well as a profound respect for history, religion and Arab heritage. These combined into creating a leader whose well-informed desire to bring sustainable prosperity to his nation and its people would materialize in the greatest series of dedicated reforms ever taken in the Kingdom. The process began as early as 2000 while he was still Crown Prince, acting in that role as the major champion of reforms.

In 2003, he created the National Dialogue that would allow selected professionals and intellectuals to publicly debate current national issues. In February to April 2005 he created the conditions for the first municipal elections to promote increased political participation for half the members of 179 municipal councils, and in December 2005, completed the process by appointing the remaining members of the advisory municipal councils. Also in December 2005, the Kingdom joined the WTO, making it a part of the global trading world. In 2007, the Allegiance Council was created to regulate the succession. In 2008 he established an Inter-Faith Dialogue initiative to encourage religious tolerance on a global level. He also led the Kingdom to secure a membership to the G-20.

In February 2009, he reshuffled the cabinet, leading to a more rapid pace of reform, and also appointed the first female with a ministerial ranking. In 2011 he announced a series of benefits to Saudi citizens including funds to build affordable housing, salary increases for government workers, unemployment benefits, and to women the right to become members of the governing Shoura Council, and the right to vote in and stand for municipal elections.

BIRTH OF SAGIA

Arguably one of King Abdullah's greatest acts of economic reform dates back to April 2000, while still Crown Prince, when the Council of Ministers enacted the new Foreign Investment Law, the first major Foreign Direct Investments (FDI) reform in over 20 years. The new Foreign Investment Law allowed investors 100 percent ownership of their projects as well as the property required for projects, including housing for company personnel; on par national treatment; multiple investment licenses; direct sponsorship of foreign investors and their non-Saudi employees; reduction in the corporate tax rate from 45 percent to 20 percent for foreign companies with profits over US$27000 a year; loans for 100 percent foreign owned projects from the Saudi Industrial Development Fund (SIDF); and finally, the foreign investment created the Saudi Arabian General Investment Authority (SAGIA), an agency responsible for licensing all new foreign investment, streamlining application processes, promoting investments, managing the investment climate, making policy recommendations to the Head of the Supreme Economic Council, facilitating changes in state policies and administration, labor regulations, the tax system, government subsidies, privatization, commercial registration, and ultimately making the Kingdom a hub for international business. The leader of SAGIA would report directly to the Head of the Supreme Economic Council, or in other words, the King himself.

The agency was created as a quasi-government agency, outside ministerial and government bureaucracy with a measure of administrative and financial autonomy in order to facilitate quick decision making, rapid communication and execution, and the flexibility required to develop an efficient organization.

SAGIA was one of the government bodies that benefitted from the new ecosystem of reforms created by the chief architect of reforms, King Abdullah bin Abdulaziz.

'NATION, FAITH, AND PATIENCE'

On 22 March 2004, while Crown Prince at the time, King Abdullah would appoint a new Chairman and Governor to lead SAGIA, Amr Al-Dabbagh, who at 36 would be one of the youngest Saudi leaders appointed with the rank of Minister. Al-Dabbagh joined from the private sector, with no government experience behind him.

Soon after his appointment, the new Governor had the opportunity to meet with HM King Abdullah, and after thanking him for his trust, asked for his guidance.

'Three words,' King Abdullah said, 'nation, faith, patience. Anything that contributes positively to the nation and doesn't conflict with our faith, you should work hard and pursue patiently until it is delivered.'

For the newly hired private sector leader, this level of empowerment opened the gates of entrepreneurship, 'because it basically established that not even the sky is the limit. There were no boundaries for improvement or progress within the parameters of nation, faith and patience.'

The three-word endorsement is what inspired SAGIA to do things differently, to do big things differently. The greatest momentum began as early as 2005 when SAGIA announced a pivotal new goal called 10 × 10, an initiative established to lead the Kingdom to a top ten position in global competitiveness rankings for its business and investment climates by the end of 2010. They started from a ranking of 67 in the World Bank/ International Monetary Fund's (WB/IMF) 'Ease of Doing Business Report' and in 2005 and 2006 jumped in the rankings to 38; in 2007 to 23;

in 2008 to 16; in 2009 to 13 and finally, in 2010, the Kingdom was ranked by WB/IMF Ease of Doing Business Report the 11th most competitive nation in the world, and the most competitive nation in the Arab World and Middle East with no exception.

From a ranking of 67 to 11 in 5 years meant it was the fastest reforming country in the history of reforming countries.

The rise in rankings would lead to a corresponding rise in the value of Foreign Direct investment (FDI) inflows. Between 2005 and 2010 the annual average FDI inflow soared to US$25 billion, when from 1995 to 2004 the annual average was $478 million. The result was that the Kingdom became one of the biggest recipients of FDI in the world between 2005 and 2010 according to the United Nations Conference on Trade and Development (UNCTAD) World Investment Report 2011. During the same period the Kingdom increased its FDI stock 831 percent, from US$20.5 billion end of 2004 to $170.5 billion in 2010, which was nearly 40 percent of its GDP.

HOW DID SAGIA ACHIEVE THESE NUMBERS?

The Ten Golden Rules for Entrepreneurship in the Public Sector.

SAGIA'S TEN GOLDEN RULES FOR ENTREPRENEURSHIP IN THE PUBLIC SECTOR

The Saudi Arabian General Investment Authority (SAGIA) devised Ten Golden Rules in their process of stimulating entrepreneurship in a public sector organization. They hope that by sharing these rules others in similar positions, as well as interested readers, might benefit from an understanding of their story.

1. I Aim, Therefore I am
2. The Greatest Among You
3. Execution, Execution, Execution
4. Organic Tastes Better
5. Collaboration Cures
6. Customer is King
7. The Next Big Thing
8. Reaching Out
9. Honey, No Money
10. No Risk, No Gain

1.   I AIM, THEREFORE I AM

'It is important to link the purpose of existence with a goal.'

A new leadership in place, SAGIA began immediately to define the organization's purpose of existence through the long-term strategic planning process. The first 100 days were devoted to developing a 5-year strategy that would define the organization's big goal, its vision, its mission, the roles and value proposition, and the organizational values. The strategy was as much about organizational building as it was about launching big initiatives around competitiveness and about creating an environment pro-business enough to facilitate a flow of investments to produce a GDP that would grow at twice the rate of the population. The challenges of growing unemployment and deterioration of per-capita GDP were the two most pressing issues at the time.

'Overpromise, and Over Deliver'

Ask any politician, government employee or advisor, or all the former, for advice, and one is likely to hear, 'under promise, and over deliver'.

Ask any government entrepreneur and he/she most certainly likely to say, 'overpromise and over deliver'.

From the start of the strategy creation process, the SAGIA leadership knew it would have to think big, or think the Next Big Thing, a process ideally free from boundaries in thinking or imagining. The ultimate goal of the process would be to spell out the direction, which once shared by all members of the organization, would give it its meaning for life. 'If we don't deliver on our meaning for life,' the leadership said, 'we aren't living.'

Pressure Purifies

The SAGIA leadership believed that people often function better and achieve new heights when under pressure. Since promises made by government are promises made in public to citizens, overpromising is synonymous with over delivering, and once a public promise is made, pressure to deliver is created on the promising party and the promising party's collaborators. Overpromising thereby induces a purifying pressure by stretching individuals in the organization to go beyond their comfortable limits, not to unhealthy lengths, but in the 'no pain, no gain fashion', means the bar is raised and records often established.

A Living Creature

For SAGIA, a strategy was a living creature that would evolve through a process of adjusting and fine-tuning as the organization moved forward and the internal and external environments developed over time. The strategy, they believed, should always be treated therefore as a draft in progress and likewise be developed quickly. SAGIA developed its strategy over 3 months of intense work, after which it would continue to be adjusted through the process of innovation and creativity. The mandate of any government agency, they would argue, should also be viewed in the same way, as a living organism open to creative interpretations.

The Process

Partnering with a group of consultants[2] and academics, SAGIA began the 3-month process of information gathering and analysis. They held over a hundred personal interviews with ministers, senior government officials, local and international business leaders, and academics to discuss items related to Kingdom's business environment. They held more than 15 workshops around the country, attended by more than 250 senior level representatives and experts from the public and private sectors and different industries, and academics from a variety of fields, and analyzed over 50 major domestic, regional and international studies and reports on investment, the Saudi economy, the global economy, and related topics.

SAGIA also benchmarked Saudi Arabia against countries successful for attracting FDI, and against countries that had the most competitive and successful business and investment climates, such as Singapore. This process resulted in a strategy, the key components of which will be highlighted below, including the vision, the mission and the key roles that SAGIA would play in the 5 years of the strategy.

Vision and Mission

The amount of time spent on developing these two ingredients alone was considerable and included dedicated workshops, the engagement of leaders from the public and private sectors in dedicated brainstorming sessions and debates. The end result was known internally as the first page of an organization's strategy book, its reason for existence.

Vision

'To achieve rapid economic growth in Saudi Arabia by capitalizing on the Kingdom's competitive strengths as the global capital of energy, and as a major hub between East and West'.

Mission

'To position Saudi Arabia among the top ten most competitive nations by 2010 through the creation of a pro-business environment, a knowledge-based society, and by developing world-class "Economic Cities"'.

Values

Leadership, Trust, Integrity, Results-Driven, Respect, Teamwork, Empowerment, Continuous Improvement.

Jack of All Trades

Once the process of information gathering was complete, the hundred personal interviews, the workshops, and the benchmarking, analysis was conducted on the collated information, combined with the macroeconomics of Saudi Arabia, lessons learned from SAGIA's current state evaluation, and against stakeholder engagement. From the data a list of 100 possible roles were identified, which if were adopted in total, would make SAGIA a Jack of All Trades, but a Master of None.

The Filter

To become a master, SAGIA screened and filtered the one hundred roles according to five criteria: (1) those that would generate the greatest economic impact; (2) would be most complementary to existing efforts and capitalize on SAGIA's core objective; (3) that could be implemented quickly; (4) be cost-effective; and (5) have the necessary capabilities, such as human resources, developed or acquired most swiftly.

Six roles would be identified at the outcome of that process.

1. Investor services
What began as a One-Stop-Shop (OSS) for investor services, would become a series of ever more refined initiatives that would ultimately bring investor services right to the customer's door.

2. Marketing and promotion
Not in the business of mass communication, the marketing and promotion plan SAGIA developed was a highly focused and segmented plan

of communicating specific investment opportunities in line with the Kingdom's core competencies and competitive advantages to a specific investor audience, globally, regionally and locally, matched to fit that specific profile.

3.   Regional development
SAGIA tracked the lack of investment flows to regions north and south of the so-called 'wealthy corridor' that links the eastern province city of Dammam through the central city of Riyadh and then to the western region city of Jeddah.

4.   Startup stimulation
SAGIA believed it was not enough to attract investors, but participate in the creation of new investors, and introduced a number of solutions to help the start up stimulation process in the Kingdom.

5.   Sector focus
There isn't a single country in the world with all the core competencies and competitive advantages needed to host all forms of investments, so SAGIA adopted a sector focused approach.

6.   Creating a pro-business environment
This would quickly evolve into an enormous competitiveness stimulation play branded under the umbrella of the 10 × 10 program.

2.   THE GREATEST AMONG YOU

'Under every great leader, is an even greater one.'

Once SAGIA had defined its strategy – the vision, mission, goals, values and value proposition – it set out to define the kind of individuals it would need to deliver each and every one of the strategic components, and to define what kind of organizational structure it would need to ensure delivery of the strategy.

The Criteria

Two criteria would guide the process of recruiting new talent.
One, it was necessary to ensure that the people being brought on board would align with the organizational values as spelled out in the strategy.
Two, it was necessary to ensure that the people being brought on board,

were stronger than the people who were bringing them in, the Governor included. Recruiting leaders who were stronger than the Governor, he claimed, would have the effect of freeing him from a load of non-strategic issues, and would serve as a catalyst for lifting the organization up as opposed to pulling it down. It was therefore important not to 'shy away' from people who were obviously strong leaders.

'Mr Yes'

There are problems with weak leaders. A weak leader always tries to recruit people weaker so he can influence them. Weak leaders also get the management entangled in the micro- and nano-managing process, so the stronger the recruit the more time the management has free for thinking about big, strategic things, especially The Next Big Thing. For SAGIA it was about getting the right DNA, and though a stronger leader would introduce other challenges, such as ego, etc., it was preferable to a 'Mr Yes', whose tendency to agree across the board would cost the leadership the healthy refining effect challenging and critiquing normally has.

One characteristic of a good, or even great leader, was that a good leader would never come to the Governor with a problem, but only with a solution. It was in fact forbidden for leaders to come to the Governor with problems without solutions, and the best leader, he argued, would never come to him at all. 'It might even seem at a certain point that he didn't exist.'

How Far Are You Willing To Go

To find leaders stronger than themselves, SAGIA's new leadership first looked internally among the existing pool of its inherited staff of approximately 200 for talent that would fit the new profile, and provided exit opportunities for those who didn't.

The next step was to go outside.

After a lengthy process of headhunting locally, regionally and internationally, SAGIA succeeded in attracting people from some of the world's largest and most successful companies, including P&G and Unilever, and from some local giants such as Aramco, in which case the desired recruit came with a price, and a lesson.

The Governor came across an executive from Aramco who was at the time nearly finished with his MBA at Stanford University. After interviewing him, the Governor found him ideal to lead the Finance Department and approached the Ministry of Oil, whose head was also the Chairman of Aramco, with a request for secondment, believing that since Aramco was state-owned, it would be easy. The Ministry's response was that if they were to accommodate all requests for secondment they received, there would be no people left at Aramco, a company that invests heavily in developing its human resources. If the Governor were willing to pay the costs Aramco had invested in educating this candidate at one of the finest schools in the world, however, they would grant an exception. The Governor agreed, and afterwards spoke to the CEO of Aramco, informing him of his conversation with the Ministry of Oil. The Aramco CEO responded by saying the release would not be possible unless SAGIA agreed to pay the costs invested in the desired recruit.

The Governor asked, 'how much?'

Likely under the impression he was joking, the Aramco CEO sent an invoice to SAGIA, perhaps to call the Governor's bluff, and within 48 hours a check was sent for the amount specified in the invoice. It wasn't cheap.

The lesson is: No distance is too far for the right person.

SAGIA never regretted the decision or the investment, which paid off.

Logic Limits

In most cases the SAGIA leadership did not look to the public sector for leaders, but wanted leaders with no previous government experience. Given the kind of entrepreneurial organization they were trying to build, SAGIA believed it would be better to start with experienced private sector leaders who could then be trained in more conventional governmental processes than the inverse. Government officials were often limited by their experience, and likely to see new challenges as various forms of old ones, and possible solutions in the same way. Three common phrases of government officials included:

> 'We already tried this before and it didn't work.'
> 'There is no reference in the mandate for doing it that way.'
> 'We don't have the budget for that.'

Given the mindset of a government official was based upon government experience, any decision made would likely stem from a process that had been used before, thereby limiting possibilities, and opportunities for innovation and entrepreneurship.

When SAGIA recruited its staff with this in mind, it laid down one fundamental prohibition from the start: 'We don't want to hear any of those sentences from you.'

DNA of a SAGIA Leader

The majority of SAGIA's new staff was chosen for a mix of discipline, commitment, enthusiasm, willingness to take big risks, to think outside of the box, and for the right mix of right attitude and openness, the very values of an entrepreneurial organization. Of course, SAGIA understood that risk varied from one position in government to another, and certain areas within politics and government might require people with more experience. Some additional attributes the SAGIA leadership looked for in its new recruits, and would continue to develop during the grooming process included: humility, drive, innovativeness, self-confidence, optimism, creativity, motivation, courage, achievement and future orientation, a tendency to think big, strategically, in visionary terms, and to deal well with ambiguity and limitations.

The Storyline

Typically the kind of stars and talent SAGIA was looking for would have big career ambitions, big salary expectations, and would be seeking to join organizations similarly ambitious. To get these stars the SAGIA leadership would need to tell a compelling story by packaging the opportunity in an attractive way, and delivering on their promises.

The first story SAGIA would tell its potential recruits was the entrepreneurial public sector one, described as an opportunity to learn from a very corporate minded and entrepreneurial organization seeking to define a completely new territory, what SAGIA would later call 'governpreneurship'. The opportunity to get exposed to the more complex and exciting world this opportunity would entail, included the opportunity to make a difference that would be recognized and remembered for generations. It was very important for SAGIA that the targeted recruit would feel as if he/she could in fact change the world.

Packaging the position in this way tackled the negative image associated with government organizations, known typically as environments with massive levels of existing structure and refinement of scope that prohibited people from dreaming or thinking too far outside of the box. The environment SAGIA offered was the opportunity to dream, perhaps one of the biggest attractions for new recruits.

The employees would also be given opportunities to innovate and network which, given SAGIA was an agency where global business and political elites were part of daily communications, was an appealing possibility.

Finally, SAGIA understood it would need to provide positions with career paths. This meant recruits would need grooming and polishing and given a chance to participate in delivering huge objectives that would be globally recognized, with the possible outcome of their being head hunted to lead a top organization in the future. SAGIA's basic understanding was that all positions should be viewed as stepping-stones to bigger and more challenging opportunities, and SAGIA devoted itself to furthering, and even expanding, new recruits' ambitions. Three of the grooming tools the organization could offer are included below, though it must first be noted that coupled with all the above were compensation packages competitive with the private sector, something SAGIA was able to do through a series of public private partnership mechanisms and creating flexible structures.

1. The Shadow Governor
    If privacy is a virtue, there is no virtue for the member of SAGIA chosen randomly from the pool of human resources to function for a day as a Shadow Governor. Literally following the Governor throughout his entire routine on the chosen day, the Shadow Governor attends every meeting, listens to every phone call, and is privy to every action taken during the 12 hours they are connected. The day starts at 8:00 a.m. sharp, with the first 10 minutes being spent describing the rules of engagement. One is that the Shadow Governor will be exposed to everything, including all conversations, all calls, all letters and emails either read or signed, and all meetings, internal or external. Two is that the Shadow Governor is responsible for keeping adequate records and being prepared to discuss honestly her or his thoughts at the end of the day.
    Once the rules of engagement are shared, the day begins by studying the daily calendar, and ends by reviewing the day's events during a meeting in which the Governor acts as a dedicated listener reflecting with the Shadow Governor on the day. He might ask how the Shadow Governor would have done things differently, or what recommendations does he/she have, or what concerns. The Governor then asks the Shadow Governor to spend a few days digesting the experience and to come back with formal recommendations within a few days, including a more detailed reflection on the closing discussion.

2. The Rotating Chairmanship of the Executive Board
    During the monthly Executive Board meeting, an executive team member was chosen to serve as Chairman for the next monthly meeting, excluding the Governor himself, who was never a chairman, and the new Chairman was required to use the interval before the next meeting to plan and communicate with all parties until the time of his chairmanship day.

3. The Acting Governor

The Governor was very much involved in sales, and often referred to himself as a salesman who enjoyed getting involved in the initiation stage as well as the deal closing stage of an investment license. But a salesman travels a lot, which for the Governor of SAGIA could be as many as a dozen times a year. Being out of the office so frequently became an opportunity for grooming recruits and became the 'Acting Governor' program.

When the Governor of SAGIA was out of town, an Acting Governor would be chosen to fill his place, with all the powers, rights and entitlements of the official Governor, short of, as the joke goes, the option of 'selling SAGIA'. The Acting Governor sat in the Governor's office, at his desk, in his chair, logged onto his desktop, and with full authority to make decisions, but no obligation to communicate with the Governor for authority or decisions needed to be made.

This act of empowerment exemplified SAGIA's view of leadership overall, i.e. giving employees the freedom, authority and support needed to deliver.

Galaxy and Stars

All organizations have their awards and all organizations understand the value in recognizing success publically. For SAGIA it was the Galaxy Award, given for outstanding performance at the end of every year. Galaxy and Stars were chosen as symbols for the annual awards in order to maintain a sense among employees of the vast space of possibility within each of them, reflected in the oft-cited motto held in high esteem in SAGIA, 'The sky is NOT the limit.'

The Galaxy Award was given to the best performing unit, whereas the Stars Award was given to individuals. The latter was chosen through a process of voting by all staff, and the former was determined against Key Performance Indicators (KPIs).

Chief Happiness Officer

The SAGIA leadership understood how important it was for staff to wake up in the morning eager to come to the office, that a happy work culture was likely to increase retention, so they appointed a Chief Happiness Officer to promote the wellbeing and personal growth of the SAGIA staff members.

SAGIA's Chief Happiness Officer was often heard saying, 'Happy Hour is from 8 to 4.'

She was also often heard saying:

Happiness at work is about happiness for today and tomorrow and next year and 10 years from now. It's about realizing that without long-term happiness and enjoyment at work, you will not be your best, contribute as much, make as many people smile, or make as much of a difference.

The level of happiness at work has a huge impact on individual performance and personal lives. People who are happy at work not only enjoy work more, they have a much higher quality of life overall. They also perform much better while on the job. Happy companies exist in every industry and in every country, and while happiness is not the main focus of most businesses, and certainly most governments, SAGIA decided to go happy right from the start.

The Chief Happiness Officer's aim, or reason for existence, was to ensure a cultural of happiness with the outcomes of increasing employee drive and motivation, improving relations with co-workers, empowering more successes, inspiring more creativity, good ideas, energy and less stress in the end.

Or in other words, better health.

3.   EXECUTION, EXECUTION, EXECUTION

A study was conducted on 200 successful company CEOs, who were asked to report their level of satisfaction with their corporate strategies. The results revealed that though 80 percent reported being satisfied with their corporate strategies, only 20 percent reported being satisfied with the level of execution.

What, How, When, Who

Employing tools normally used in the corporate world, SAGIA engaged an external facilitator[3] to manage the process of creating the meticulous execution plan, which would take the form of a 1-page, detailed encapsulation of the entire strategy as a 5-year plan, the SAGIA Balanced Business Strategy (BBS), and as a 1-year Balanced Business Plan (BBP). Whether starting from scratch year one, as they would in 2004, or revisiting the BBP as a '0-based review' during the 3-day annual meeting in the last week of December every year and accompanied by their second and third in command, the entire focus of the SAGIA leadership throughout the year would be to ensure execution of the BBP, and with a view toward ensuring individual and collective ownership.

The BBS and BBP essentially take all the real meat of the strategy and encapsulate it into the two, 1-page documents, each with nine components: vision, mission, must win battles, values, what is being done for customers (goals and targets), what is being done, how and when, for operations (goals and targets), what is going to be done for SAGIA's people (goals and targets), the impact of what is being done in customers, operations and people, and finally, specific projects under each category, with each project bearing the name of a champion, and each project backed with a detailed project brief consisting of timelines and milestones for delivery.

The 1-page document spelled out the entire strategy, including goals for customers, operations, and people distilled to five from an original list of 30 or 40, through a process of voting. These five would be voted upon again, or prioritized with a process of stars placed on the breakthrough ones.

The Rotating Chairman

The more than 25 SAGIA leaders met as an Executive Board on a monthly basis in the so-called '10 × 10' room, a conference room in the center of which was a large round table. The room was given the name '10 × 10' as a reminder of the umbrella 10 × 10 program, and was decorated with a contemporary painting specially created for the room by a famous Saudi contemporary artist. The numbers 10 × 10 are repeated in various forms and colors.

The purpose of the round table, in the center of which were many built in screens to give participants convenient and equal access to visuals, was to equalize all leaders by eliminating the power seat. The Governor himself, who attended the monthly meetings, was an equal member of the board, with no special rights or privileges, and a rule allowing him to speak for only 5 minutes at the end of the 2-hour sessions. It was the opinion of the leadership that leaders should listen more than talk. If a leader talked more and his listeners failed to deliver, then it became the leader's ideas that failed. If everyone participated equally, then everyone was responsible for outcomes. A leader may be tempted by the desire to call the shots, instruct, do all the talking, but a good governpreneur doesn't.

Every month at the end of the meeting a new chairman of the Executive Board was chosen randomly through a standard process in which each of the Executive Board members' names were written on small pieces of paper and placed in a pot. Out of that pot only one name would be drawn, and from that moment onward the newly elected Chair was responsible for preparing for the next month's meeting. Preparations included obtaining feedback from each of the champions of previous meetings, as well as the status of each of the initiatives that would be discussed. All members of the executive board were champions of initiatives of projects.

The Traffic Light

The Executive Board meeting opens with the chairman of the board talking for no more than 10 minutes about an idea of the month, which could be a lesson from a book or a clip from a movie, or any inspiring or informative item the rotating chairman has been inspired by. Following the opening 10-minute talk, the chair directs his attention one by one to the members around the table, giving each 2 minutes to inform the entire board on the status of the project as spelled out in the BBP. Projects can have one of three statuses: green, which means the project is on track according to timelines and milestones spelled out in the project brief; yellow, which means it's slightly off track, and red, which means it's way off track. The champion of that project then has to spell out in detail the status of the project, and if the color is either yellow or red, explain how he or she will get it back on track by the next meeting. The criterion for membership is being a champion of at least one initiative or project.

The dynamics of having everyone spelling out the color and status of the project is to create healthy competition among the various team members. No team member wants to be in the position of having to report a status of red to the more than 25 colleagues in any meeting, or even worse, having to repeat that a project is still off track in a following meeting.

On the other hand, a project that is green represents an opportunity to celebrate a success, and when announced in the presence of the leadership, is a confidence booster for the other team members who report feeling that, 'if he can do it, I can do it'. This creates enthusiasm and a sense of competition.

Once each member has reported on the status of their projects, the chair invites the Governor to close the meeting with a few remarks, most often about local, regional or global trends in investment or business, and then the meeting closes with a new name being pulled from the pot of names.

One month later, it starts all over again.

4. ORGANIC TASTES BETTER

'In general,' it was once said, 'an organic organization is more adaptable, more openly communicating, more consensual, and more loosely controlled.'

Specifically, we are saying, it's also far more effective.

From 67 to 11 in 5

In September 2010, the World Bank/IFC's Doing Business Report ranked Saudi Arabia as the 11th most competitive nation in the world for doing business and the most competitive nation in the Arab World and Middle East with no exception. The progress was consistent, beginning with a rank of 67 in 2004, Saudi jumped to 38th in 2005 and 2006, to 23rd in 2007, to 16th in 2008, 13th in 2009 and 11th in 2010.

As a result of the enhancement of competitiveness, Saudi experienced a corresponding rise in the value of Foreign Direct investment (FDI) inflows. Between 2005 and 2010 the annual average FDI inflow soared to US$25 billion, when from 1995 to 2004 the annual average was US$478 million, making the Kingdom one of the biggest recipients of FDI in the world according to the United Nations Conference on Trade and Development (UNCTAD) World Investment Report 2011. The result was that the Kingdom became one of the biggest recipients of FDI in the world between 2005 and 2010 according to the United Nations Conference on Trade and Development (UNCTAD) World Investment Report 2011. During the same period the Kingdom increased its FDI stock 831 percent, from US$20.5 billion end of 2004 to $170.5 billion in 2010, which was nearly 40 percent of its GDP.

Mothers

To its leadership SAGIA was a mother company whose greatest impact can be derived from incubating certain initiatives in an independent fashion and allowing each to grow and expand, and empowering each to flourish, rather than trying to maintain initiatives as part of the organization's structure. Creating fragmented multi-initiatives in the form of independent units with specific, but ultimately collective goals, SAGIA argued, would lead in delivering the overall goal for the organization and adding to its overall value proposition.

Traditional government centralization means all levels of the organization are constrained by the same rules and structures, leading to many layers of bureaucracy and reduced opportunities for innovation. Fragmented initiatives offer more creative possibilities with regard to compensation packages, funding, organization structure, human resources, and organizational culture. In order to flourish in one area it is necessary to design the whole environment around a specific goal and give it independence and focus it with specific targets.

Daughters

The idea, standard in the corporate world, is that Special Purpose Vehicles (SPVs), established to serve or focus on a specific goal and with eventual spin off (venturing) in mind, changes the whole dynamic from one of dependency and financial predictability to one with the freedoms and pressures associated with independently operating companies. This is the case with SAGIA's eldest daughter, the National Competitiveness Center (NCC). It was created in 2005 when SAGIA announced the 10 × 10 goal, which was to position the Kingdom among the top ten most competitive investment destinations globally in the WB/IMF Ease of Doing Business Report for its business and investment climates by the end of 2010. The NCC is an evolutionary outcome of creatively interpreting SAGIA's strategy, specifically its pro-business environment role.

The NCC would make a common language out of competitiveness to promote the aggressive goals of the 10 × 10 nationally, which put pressure on the team members to become more focused, especially when it was learned that the announcement to move from 67th to 10th in 5 years, was received cynically by some of the public.

The National Competitiveness Center

The NCC is the classic daughter organization established by SAGIA, who through it converted a subjective approach to dealing with competitiveness, i.e. various and scattered reports, articles and papers written here and tossed there plus disconnected fragments of feedback from stakeholders, to an institutionalized approach encompassing everything they wanted to do in competitiveness. The NCC was designed to monitor, assess, and support competitiveness enhancement throughout the Kingdom of Saudi Arabia and was established as a 'think tank' for competitiveness enhancement by conducting and developing competitiveness assessments and monitoring the implementation and results of specially designed programs. It would also systematically address the issues related to regulatory processes, using over three hundred different indicators to judge the competitiveness of the business and investment climate. SAGIA partnered with an international consulting advisory group[4] with expertise in global competitiveness to create the NCC.

The programs focus on two main areas: improving the ease of doing business in the Kingdom through spurring modernization of the general business environment; and improving the microeconomic fundamentals of competitiveness through mobilizing development of world-class clusters.

Over the intervening 5 years from 2005 to 2010, when the Kingdom achieved a ranking just one point shy of its 2005 goal of a top ten placement, the NCC played a key role in advocating for a range of improvements to Saudi Arabia's business environment. It also worked as a facilitator of competitiveness by supporting the creation of focuses councils with members from both the public and private sectors.

Ease of Doing Business

Competitiveness is comprised of a myriad of complex elements,[5] and international agencies that assess it adopt unique definitions. These agencies have developed benchmarking criteria against which countries are ranked objectively. To measure Saudi Arabia's competitiveness, the NCC employed primary indexes, which measured, at a detailed level, the drivers of competitiveness in the countries they cover.

One of the most important measures of competitiveness used by the NCC is the World Bank and the International Finance Corporation Ease of Doing Business Report. It compares the ease of performing various business processes across 183 countries, using standardized indicators to assess activities such as starting a business, getting credit, dealing with construction permits, and enforcing contracts. The NCC uses the WB/IMF methodology to benchmark the legal and regulatory environment in which businesses operate and to initiate reforms based on other countries' best practices.

At the start of the 10 × 10 initiative, the NCC recognized that in order to advance further and compete with the world's best economies, Saudi Arabia's business environment would need to consistently meet or exceed international standards. As a result of introducing 48 reforms between 2005 and 2010, targeting areas such as contract enforcement, dealing with construction permits, getting credit, trading across borders and starting a business, Saudi Arabia made larger strides in competitiveness than any other country. The Kingdom went through remarkable changes in those 5 years, the end result being a far superior and supportive environment for private sector participation, with an 'Ease of Doing Business' ranking that would leap from 67th in 2004 to 11th globally in 2010, and number one in the entire Arab world and MENA region.

Highest to Lowest

The reforms made it easier for start up stimulation and for doing business in Saudi Arabia by reducing the number of steps, time and cost of starting a business. As an example of how this has effected start up stimulation, the

NCC introduced reforms to reduce the minimum capital requirement for starting a Limited Liability Company from the highest of any country in the world at the time, US$150000, to one of the lowest in the world, and the result was that the number of companies formed almost immediately skyrocketed. This contributed hugely to one of SAGIA's key six roles in its strategy, Start-up Stimulation.

Granddaughters

Competitiveness in the area of regulations and procedures, cost and number of steps, etc., was not enough. SAGIA's NCC set out to make competitiveness as contagious as possible and spread it around the Kingdom by introducing various initiatives that would address the whole value chain of competitiveness, resulting in additional organic organizations, or in other words granddaughters, each with dedicated and focused goals and organizational structures.

The Competitiveness Gathering

The Annual Global Competitiveness Forum (GCF) became the venue for accomplishing this. Known informally as SAGIA's 'Annual General Assembly', the GCF is held every January and hosts global business leaders, international political leaders, and selected intellectuals and journalists from around the world who gather to discuss key issues of the competitiveness agenda, and each year under a different theme, such as 'Sustainable Competitiveness', 'Responsible Competitiveness', 'Innovation as a Means to Competitiveness' and the inaugural year, launched by Bill Gates, 'ICT as an Enabler of Competitiveness'. The 3-day event hosts as many as 21 sessions, and over a thousand attendees each year. Since its origins, the GCF has grown to become the global think tank for competitiveness, with an average of 100 global speakers attending every year, including some of the most well known and respected global leaders, including political leaders such as Lee Kwan Yew, Minister Mentor of the Republic of Singapore; Tun Dr Mahathir bin Mohamad, 4th Prime Minister of Malaysia; William Jefferson Clinton, 42nd President of the United States; Mary Robinson, 7th President of Ireland; Jean Chretien, 20th Prime Minister of Canada; Shinzo Abe, 90th Prime Minister of Japan; Tony Blair, Former Prime Minister of the UK; Corporate leaders have included Bill Gates, Chairman, Microsoft Corporation; Jeffrey Immelt, Chairman and CEO, GE; Michael Dell, Founder and CEO, Dell Inc.; Carlos Ghosn, President and CEO, Nissan Motor Company; John Chambers, Chairman and CEO, Cisco Systems; and Peter Brabeck-Letmathe, Chairman and

CEO, Nestlé. From the world of NGOs, the GCF has hosted leaders such as Allison Chin, President, Sierra Club; Julie Marton-Lefevre, Director General, IUCN; and from the world of international sports, icons such as Michael Phelps, Olympic Gold Medalist; Carl Lewis, Olympic Gold Medalist. Finally, the GCF has also attracted leading academicians, including Michael Porter of Harvard University, whose work on competitiveness is well known globally.

Private Sector Competitiveness

The Saudi Fast Growth 100 (SFG) is an annual ranking of the fastest-growing and most competitive companies in the Kingdom in two categories: companies over 5 years and startups. The program awards and highlights a new generation of fast-growing Saudi companies that represent the future of the Kingdom, by creating jobs and spurring innovation and growth. They are the Kingdom's 'leading indicator' of competitiveness. By highlighting these companies, the SFG seeks to ignite the imagination of the country's entrepreneurs, encourage them to take the risks and start the next generation of small- and medium-size companies to ensure the Kingdom's future prosperity. Each year the NCC ranks these companies according to their performance and practices over the last 3 years. In addition, they recognize companies that are less than 5 years old with the Saudi Fast Growth Start-up Award. For the Start-up award, the NCC ranks companies according to their revenue growth over the last two years. Regional companies and companies owned by women and young entrepreneurs are also recognized. The application process is rigorous, including verification of financial figures provided by applicant companies, ensuring awardees are real companies, and with real growth and real success.

Responsible Competitiveness

The Saudi Responsible Competitiveness Index (SARCI) is a multi-year program to help companies in the Kingdom increase their competitiveness through responsible business practices. It does this by identifying ways to manage social and environmental issues to reduce risk, increase revenue and build brand.

SARCI analyses how Saudi companies are building competitive advantage by managing their social and environmental impacts. It looks beyond community projects and corporate responsibility programs to understand how firms are attracting and retaining employees, implementing strong environmental policies and working with suppliers and creating awareness on how responsible competitiveness strategies are enabling companies to manage risks, enhance productivity, build brand value and unlock new sources of innovation.

SARCI engages a wide range of companies from all sectors and regions of the Kingdom, and analyzes them against those areas of Corporate Social Responsibility (CSR) that have a proven business case, appeal to investors and are adopted by international peers. Participation is voluntary, and the three strongest performing companies on the Index win the award for Responsible Competitiveness, but all participants receive confidential benchmarking and strategic advice on how to enhance performance. After 4 years of the Saudi Responsible Competitiveness Index, hundreds of companies have joined and the resulting critical mass of businesses is successfully promoting responsible business practices across the Kingdom.

Competitive Youth

The NCC launched a new platform for developing, recognizing, and nurturing the most competitive youth in Saudi Arabia, the Most Competitive Youth Awards (MCY). The MCY is a strategic initiative that engages youth in Saudi Arabia (Saudi nationals and Saudi residents) in applying twenty-first century skill sets to improving their communities, inspiring creativity, promoting innovation and helping to bring Saudi Arabia's economy to the forefront of competitiveness.

The MCY serves competitiveness by recognizing talent as an increasingly key strategic asset for both nations and corporations, and publically showcases and acknowledges the achievements of young people and rewards their creative and innovative excellence driven by the growing imperatives of entrepreneurship, innovation and competitiveness, as well as sustainability concerns.

The MCY accesses youth competitiveness in certain areas such as technology, art (painting, drawing, collage or digital artwork), film and photography, and continually adds other areas.

Winners take part in an exhibition, work with professional artists, designers, social entrepreneurs, museum curators and filmmakers to develop the key skills of leadership, communication and creativity, and are sent to various international creative and cultural destinations and museums.

Some evaluation criteria include creativity, inspiration factor, social responsibility, artistic skill, artistic presentation, originality and authenticity, relevance to creative industries, content, innovation and entrepreneurial spirit and presentation skills.

Competitive Leaders

The Saudi Oxford Leadership Program at Oxford University was launched for the purpose of developing the competitiveness of Saudi leaders from public and private sector organizations through the creation of a compelling context for the participants to share views on key global and Saudi trends and pressures and how these challenges are influencing Saudi and international organizations. It also gives them the opportunity to acquire strategic perspectives and tools organizations require to develop capabilities and strategies that enhance competitiveness and employee engagement to create higher value for the stakeholders. Leaders step back and reflect on their leadership experiences and skills, which helps them to successfully lead and make a difference in their organization, Saudi society, and the region.

Every year 40 leaders join the program, 20 from the public and 20 from the private sector.

Regional Competitiveness

Given Saudi's size, with 13 different regions, each with a different set of core competencies and areas of strength and weakness, the NCC came up with regional competitiveness indexes and reports, or annual diagnostic studies conducted on each region to spell out road maps for what is needed to be done to enhance its competitiveness.

0-Tax Formula

As one of the tools to enhance the competitiveness of the investment climate in less developed regions, one of the six roles of SAGIA's strategy, SAGIA negotiated with the Ministry of Finance for a tax credit for less developed regions with 50 percent of Cap Ex and 50 percent of the R&D spending, and 50 percent of the cost for employing Saudis to be deducted from the tax base, which meant in the end SAGIA would show investors how to have the right mix of ingredients for what would essentially become a 0-tax formula.

5.   COLLABORATION CURES

In order to create an environment where collaboration is the name of the game, two things are needed. It has to be clear to the other party how they will benefit from collaboration, and a common language of collaboration has to be created.

Just as no country can be competitive in every sector, or possess all possible core competencies and competitive advantages, SAGIA understood that no single organization had all the core competencies and resources needed to deliver everything within its scope of objectives. It therefore set out immediately to collaborate with partners from the public and private sectors to proactively facilitate the delivery of its main objectives, most of which could be subsumed under the goal of competitiveness. Within the first year of launching their collaboration drive, SAGIA signed 17 agreements with sister agencies and ministries around eliminating the most obvious investment obstacles from the private sector perspective, the first phase of the competitive process that would lead to 10 × 10.

Collaboration was fundamental for ensuring progress in the competitiveness arena, so in order to achieve its goals, SAGIA collaborated with the Supreme Economic Council early on in the process. This would result in the 10 × 10 becoming a national program with full support of the government's highest economic body, and a mandate for other governmental agencies to become 10 × 10 compliant. A list of deliverables was formulated for each agency, with the result that SAGIA would become the main driver in a larger and more comprehensive national initiative. Some of the agencies whose support would be essential included the Ministry of Commerce and Industry, Ministry of Labor, Ministry of Information, Ministry of Finance, The Capital Market Authority, The Saudi Port Authority, The Board of Grievances, The Chambers of Commerce and a number of private sector partners.

Understanding Your Partner

It is important to understand and define who the parties you wish to collaborate with are, place them in categories that spell out the level of cooperation and engagement desired, create a common language around that possible collaboration, and that includes set specific goals to be delivered with clear timelines and milestones.

What's In It For Me?

After identifying whom SAGIA would collaborate with, it was essential to understand how the other party would benefit, and before explaining to that party what would be in it for SAGIA, clarify to the other party what was in it for them. The message to other agencies was that the benefits of collaborating on 10 × 10 included:

- Increased productivity
- Local and international recognition.

In other words, the collaboration would increase the other party's efficiencies, thereby making them look good. SAGIA would share the burden by providing a handholding service to facilitate the process, while likewise assuring the other party SAGIA would remain in the back seat and that the credit would be given to the other party for the improvement of efficiency.

The Common Language

To make any form of collaboration a success it is important to create a common language that the collaborating partner speaks and understands clearly. The common language SAGIA created and would promulgate was the language of competitiveness, including the language of benchmarking against indicators that are based upon best practices.

SLAs

The parameters of the collaboration have to be defined, which SAGIA did in some cases with Service Level Agreements. The beauty of SLA agreements for SAGIA was that the objectives of the collaborations were well defined in the SLA, with timelines, milestones and champions from both parties being explicitly spelled out to ensure optimal collaboration. It was also necessary to assess the SLA satisfaction level by both parties regularly to ensure a healthy and sustainable collaboration. The agreement must indicate what each party would do for the other. For example, SAGIA entered into SLAs with multiple government agencies to handle their investment promotion activities to ensure a common message is given to the targeted audiences to avoid or eliminate duplication of efforts. It was done according to targets both parties agreed upon.

Forcing Collaboration

Sometimes it's not enough to say you need to collaborate. Sometimes the conditions need to be created which will lead to collaboration taking place by necessity. For example, capping the number of employees to 50 in one of SAGIA's spin offs, the Economic Cities Authority (ECA) would limit what the ECA could do on its own, which would force them to collaborate with those who have the core competencies the ECA did not have.

When the ECA instructed the authors of the Economic City regulations to find the best practices in the world, they didn't say, for example, 'find and adopt, or adapt'. They said, 'find and evolve, or exceed', introduce the next and better evolution of the process, which stimulates innovation. This forced collaboration with centers of excellence to raise the bar.

Cadre

Give me people and I'll give you my next factory.

This is what Mark Hurd, former Chairman and CEO, HP, said after the Governor finished giving his storyline on the investment opportunity of Saudi Arabia. They were sitting in the corporate HQ on a beautiful sunny day in Palo Alto, California, less than an hour after the Governor shared the same story with another Silicon Valley leader. Mark's reply would reconfirm something the SAGIA leadership had already understood, that the flow of FDI does not only go hand-in-hand with a pro-business environment and competitive advantages, but also with the availability of adequate talent to meet the requirements of the investor.

So important was this to SAGIA, they bore another organic daughter.

Her name is Cadre and she's a human capital initiative formed in cooperation between SAGIA and the Ministry of Labor (MOL). It was created to function as a private company from day one, with all the flexibilities of the private sector brought to the table.

Cadre's added values are to:

- Facilitate the SAGIA/Ministry of Labor (MoL) relationship to deliver efficient investor labor solutions to the Economic Cities;
- Offer Saudization (developing Saudis for positions occupied by non Saudis) solutions to One-Step-Shop customers;
- Deliver a higher Economic Cities' value proposition via leading 60/24/7 labor accessibility services;
- Drive the building of mega training cities within the Economic Cities through attracting centers of excellence.

With respect to the last point, Cadre partnered with Algonquin College out of Canada toward the development of a training institute in the southern Jazan Economic City (JEC), called JEC Polytechnic. Algonquin provided the entire curriculum and instructors to produce electrical and mechanical engineers who would graduate with diplomas from the state of Ontario, without ever having to travel to Canada.

Cadre has internal and external customers, the latter being the private sector and tenants in the Economic Cities, and the former the Ministry of Labor and SAGIA, to whom Cadre delivers value-adding HR solutions such as secondment, and learning and development solutions such as conducting in house training seminars, such as 'War for Talent' and 'Harassment Prevention'.

Human Resources Competitiveness Council and 15 × 15

In cooperation with the MOL, SAGIA established a Human Resources Competitiveness Council to focus on enhancing the competitiveness and efficiency of the labor market in Saudi Arabia. The vision was to establish Saudi Arabia as one of the 15 most competitive and efficient labor markets globally by 2015 (15 × 15), through making progress against a number of identified challenges, such as high rates of unemployment, growing working age population, low rates of Saudization and labor productivity, low rates of female participation, a rigid regulatory environment, a mismatch in the skills required and the skills available and in the supply and the demand of labor.

Strategic objectives included the conducting of in-depth assessments to identify the key challenges and priorities and areas in need of reform, to assess the impact of current and proposed reforms and to serve as an advisory group to the Ministry of Labor in identifying appropriate reforms that might achieve the broader labor objectives of KSA. The Council would also seek to raise the level of awareness on key labor and human resources issues and challenges facing the Kingdom, while serving as a catalyst for dialogue. The Council is co-chaired by the Minister of Labor and the Governor of SAGIA, and meets religiously for 2 hours on the last Monday of every month at 4 p.m.

The ICT Competitiveness Council and Broadband

For Saudi Arabia to achieve its objective of becoming one of the most competitive countries in the world, it must successfully transition to a knowledge-based economy. To do so, the Kingdom must grow its nascent ICT cluster by addressing related major challenges, including bridging the digital divide, stimulating ICT entrepreneurship and innovation, and encouraging the use of advanced ICTs in other clusters. This will require strong leadership, substantial investment, and public and private sector cooperation. SAGIA formed the ICT Cluster Advisory Council to bring together the private sector, government and other key stakeholders to address the major issues in the cluster to increase its overall competitiveness. Collaboration is fostered between private sector ICT firms and key public sector stakeholders, such as the Ministry of Communications and Information Technology, the Commission for

Information Technology and Communication, the King Abdullaziz City for Science and Technology, and the Ministries of Education and Higher Education. Their efforts will ensure Saudi Arabia's ICT cluster matures into a highly competitive and dynamic entity and a significant contributor to the economy. The 15 members of the ICT Competitiveness Advisory Council work together to affirm cluster objectives and value propositions, to formulate cluster competitiveness enhancement initiatives, to co-ordinate common cluster initiatives, to address overarching cluster issues and to support implementation of reforms through lobbying and/ or actual reform implementation.

One of the first initiatives they would launch was the broadband initiative to expand broadband penetration in the Kingdom with a view to using it as a tool for stimulating the economy.

6. CUSTOMER IS KING

The development of SAGIA's service oriented value proposition is a history of refining a concept from more fragmentation to less, from less fragmentation to none, and from no fragmentation to a complete service package in which the concept of service can no longer be distinguished from the concept of living.

OSS

The early One-Stop-Shop (OSS), where 120 government services were supposedly available under one roof, had, in light of a more refined understanding of service, the qualities of a real estate proposition where space had been created for representatives of various government agencies. When an investor or customer entered the facility, he was given the opportunity to visit each and every government representative without having to leave the building, which saved them the time and costs of having to navigate a whole city. In this 'post office' model, the various representatives located in the OSS did not have the authority to make decisions, so they would have to return to their head offices for approvals or decisions on investor issues, again, saving customers and investors time and costs of doing it themselves.

The business community grew a bit skeptical about this process and began to criticize the SAGIA One-Stop-Shop with the less flattering and cynically creative, 'Yet Another Stop'. Instead of getting the job done on the first visit, customers and investors would have to go through this post-office like operation, which though better than driving around the city, lead to a prolonged process and bureaucratic implications.

The New OSS

The solution, SAGIA decided, was to convert this real estate proposition into a service proposition, to make the operation function more like a bank, where customers are not privy to the back office paper-processing operations, but deal only with Customer Relations Managers, or CRMs sitting at front desks.

In the new version, what would be called One-Step-Shops, customers would not be required to visit each and every government agency themselves, getting their papers stamped at as many as a dozen offices around the building, as in the One-Stop-Shop design. Like in a bank, the new SAGIA OSS consisted of four to five CRMs, smiling and dealing with customer issues face-to-face, and then acting as a liaison and managing all the back office process on behalf of the customer. Any rounds that needed to be made were made by the CRM. The customer only needed to take that one step that would ultimately encompass all the steps they would ever need, which is how the name evolved from 'Stop' to 'Step.'

To reflect the new value proposition and brand it publically, SAGIA rebranded 'One-Stop-Shop' as 'One-Step-Shop,' and to ensure that the OSS delivered on the promised quality of services, it implemented a variety of quality assurance practices, such as mystery shoppers to measure the amount of time a transaction would take, assist the quality of the service, and help refine the behavior of the CRMs. SAGIA also came up with an incentive scheme based upon the number of transactions processed each day. The more transactions, the more the individual CRMs and the back office government representatives earned.

0-Traffic

The operations of the OSSs began improving as a result, so much so, that traffic in the OSSs began to increase dramatically. The upside to this was increased revenue generation, the down side all the issues associated with increased traffic in limited space, such as delayed transaction times. When asked for potential solutions to the increasing inconveniences associated with increased traffic, the OSS leadership requested the logical and well thought out, 'we need more staff, and more space'.

The SAGIA leadership responded even more logically, by saying 'we will reduce the staff, and the space'.

'Why generate traffic anyway?'

'We'd rather deliver the service to the door.'

This is when '0-traffic' was born.

The main purpose of the '0-traffic' initiative was the same as the main purpose of the original OSS, to ensure a positive and exceptional customer experience through the provision of exemplary services. The difference is that the provision of exemplary customer services would be electronic and via home delivery, thereby eliminating the need for customers to visit the OSS branches, which would have the effect of reducing traffic in the OSS. In order to be effective the new operations would require maintaining a standard of operational excellence, automating investor services and promotion, consolidating information and databases, and providing real time reporting. To realize this new value proposition, SAGIA collaborated with sister government agencies to ensure the necessary alignment and integration that would maximize efficiency and prevent duplication of work.

The project was designed around a number of principles, the main one being that customer experience would be the umbrella objective, and to achieve such a comprehensive objective SAGIA brought experts on board to re-engineer the process and deliver the 0-traffic finish line.

SAGIA also agreed that it would not 'reinvent the wheel' for any already existing available electronic service, but would act as the portal of portals toward integrating the various services, and that this portal of portals would become the portal of choice for foreigners and Saudis seeking government services.

It was decided that the new OSS would go the organic route, and eventually be spun off through an IPO into a standalone company, which would mean viability could only be established through benchmarking current services against best practices, including their costs and profit margins. It also meant a focus on identifying ideal potential partners.

Of course, as in all SAGIA initiatives, collaboration is the best-known cure, so during the implementation phase SAGIA outsourced some of the tasks that were done in the OSS to external parties.

To manage the 0-traffic initiative the Governor chose a woman from the IT department to lead the initiative, while appointing himself as a simple member of the team. The idea of making himself a member of the team was to achieve two goals: one, to stress the importance of the initiative, and two, to give full support and full empowerment to the leader of the initiative. Another, perhaps latent effect of making himself a member of the team would be the purifying pressure to perform and deliver on objectives.

Making Family: 'Project 1000'

With 0-traffic in the full swing of planning, the leadership decided upon another customer king initiative, 'Project 1000', which had the objective of making family out of clients. The targeted leaders choose from the most relevant 1000 international and national leading companies whose relationships with SAGIA would be enhanced by 'pampering' them with a regular stream of information and updates with regard to SAGIA activities. The objective was to facilitate a more proactive approach to relationship building through a series of deep and ongoing communications built on trust and exchanged with heads of organizations at the Governor's level.

The process of developing Project 1000 was comprehensive, and included consolidating all the scattered information across SAGIA into one accessible document in addition to managing contact lists. From that they created a clear tracking system to monitor the flow of correspondence, communication, and follow up to maximize and leverage relevant relationships toward mutually beneficial outcomes.

Every month the Governor would communicate via email in an informal and friendly fashion. Below is the first correspondence sent.

Dear John,

Hope all is well, and that you've been innovating, keeping busy, and feeling happy.

We at SAGIA have been exploring the entrepreneurial edge ourselves lately, and thought it might be valuable if we kept some of our friends apprised of our activities (and we'd like to know about yours, too).

In June we participated in the 2011 Venice Biennale, as part of our arts and culture strategy. For the past three years, SAGIA has been championing, developing and investing in arts and culture programming as part of a broader ecosystem in Saudi leveraging the Economic Cities. SAGIA's role as one of the sponsors of the first Saudi Arabian National Pavilion in Venice came as part of our vision for KSA to be globally recognized as an advocate for culture and creativity. SAGIA's participation also informs our belief in the spirit of innovation and entrepreneurship that Saudi has come to represent on various levels in line with our core mission to attract investments. The Pavilion, co-curated by Mona Khazindar and Robin Start, hosted the work of two Saudi female artists Shadia and Raja Alem with their piece, 'The Black Arch'. The Pavilion received a lot of positive feedback from the global arts community and press. It was a great success from our perspective, but then, perhaps we are biased?

If you are interested in learning more about the Saudi Pavilion and the work shown, do let me know and I will be sure to send you a copy of 'The Black Arch' – a book that was created by the Steering Committee.

I also thought it would be good to share a copy of the latest edition of *THINK* magazine, which is our quarterly publication we developed to challenge readers to re-evaluate their current perception of business and lifestyle in KSA. I hope this gives you a sense of where we are and where we are going.

And finally, on a 'happy note', we have recently appointed a CHO, that's Chief Happiness Officer to be exact, who has the tall order of bringing and maintaining positive energy to each and every SAGIA employee. We are strongly committed to the emotional wellbeing of our employees and believe that creating an environment conducive to professional happiness will go a long way in serving

our employees and investors alike. I'll be sure to share some of our happiness related projects in our future correspondence.
Please consider this a two-sided conversation – I would love to hear back from you with any ideas or thoughts you may have.
Very best,
Amr

The Annual General Assembly

As is common in the corporate world, SAGIA introduced another customer focused event, its own form of the annual stakeholders meeting, the end of the year gathering to discuss areas of common interest and provide networking opportunities and educational platform to hear words of wisdom from the who's who of the private and public sector worlds.

The Global Competitiveness Forum, as the annual gathering was called, would become the region's most important and prestigious networking and educational event, and a global think tank for competitiveness.

Party Time

To recognize and highlight their contribution to the Kingdom, every year SAGIA publically recognized their top customers, the 100 biggest investors of the year licensed by SAGIA. The 'Top 100 FDI' initiative as it was known used the UNCTAD methodology to determine the value of FDI annually. The initiative also recognized the top FDI contributors to job creation as well as the top FDI exporters. The aim was to recognize publically the role of international companies in increasing the country's competitiveness, while creating a direct dialogue with investors that would encourage expansion of their contribution and increase public awareness on the benefits of FDI.

Predicting the Future

Given the success of SAGIA's evolving strategy with regard to serving customers, the leadership began thinking about customers of the future, businesses whose strategies would eventually lead them to Saudi's or SAGIA's door, and how SAGIA could get to their doors first, saving them the time and energy having to figure it out on their own.

Out of this thinking came 'Provisional Licensing', an initiative designed to proactively serve customers by going to them with Saudi's value proposition. In 2006 the original One-Stop-Shop mutated into a more efficient One-Step-Shop, and the improved OSS lead to '0-traffic'. In 2011, the logically unlimited evolutionary process took a new form as a provisional licensing service taken to the road. With Provisional Licensing SAGIA identified companies whose strategic aims and core competencies were in alignment with the Kingdom's competitive advantages, core competencies and market potential, and to whom teams visited and literally put licenses in targeted investor's laps.

Provisional Licensing proactively read targeted investor's 'strategic' minds, and then provided them with the ultimate tool to fulfill that possibility: a provisional license with no obligations, but full investor rights. The beauty of the provisional licensing process was that it could not fail. In cases where customers declined a provisional license, which were few, SAGIA improved its ability to read strategic minds, to better understand what elements did and did not work in the process of trying to predict customer needs.

At the Customer's Doorstep

The idea of an international representative was that of appointing someone whose background was adequate to the profile of the audience SAGIA was targeting, in a country populated with a number of companies whose profile aligned with SAGIA's targeted ones. The criteria for being an international representative were the ability to speak the industry language, the country language, and to be equipped to focus solely on communicating with the current and future targeted customers in the countries they were based.

8888

SAGIA representatives were not only empowered to give investment licenses to targeted customers, but also to give the licenses in the language and symbolism of the targeted customer. For instance, in Beijing one evening SAGIA issued a large Chinese industrial company an investment license completely written in Mandarin, and because of the size of the investment, SAGIA chose the number 8888 for the license. Eight is an auspicious number in Chinese culture, and the Chinese company leadership were very touched by this act of cultural sensitivity.

The Genie

Forget about formality. Forget about logic and process and convention and the big idea and trying to predict anything. Just go to any investor and say, quite simply, 'your wish is my command'.

The 'wish list' was SAGIA's basic course of action with any potential investor. At the end of every first meeting, SAGIA requested the wish list, the ideal case scenario for collaborating. The wish list once received by SAGIA, became the start of a larger discussion, usually held as a one day workshop and brainstorming session with the top strategic people of both sides engaged. The result of the workshop was an action plan with four to five possible initiatives and well-specified timeframes, milestones and champions, and the appointment of a dedicated staff member from SAGIA whose background aligned in one way or another with the targeted company's, and whose purpose in life would be to serve the client's commands. Finally, and to ensure delivery, quarterly conference calls with the organization's CEO and the Governor of SAGIA were conducted from any two points in the world, to discuss progress on the joint initiatives and deal with any issues or needs the investing party may have had.

SAGIA held dozens of these workshops globally with some of the world's best-known companies and most celebrated leaders.

7.   THE NEXT BIG THING

It's hard to get through life without clichés.

So when SAGIA spoke about the 'Next Big Thing', they were simply using a common language.

Sometimes it's better not to innovate.

On the other hand, they may have borrowed a cliché, but they didn't borrow a message.

The 'Next Big Thing' for SAGIA referred to the activity of institutionalizing a process in the organization that would continually and systematically challenge and critique the status quo in the ongoing and entrepreneurial effort to introduce something to the world or the nation that would 'make a difference', another cliché, granted, but one we all have visions for.

The Next Big Thing for SAGIA would materialize as a new product introduced to the market. It would grow out of existing strategic objectives, as Next Big Things usually do, and out of a mandate for a government agency that might have seemed too limited to some leaders, but to a creative and innovative entrepreneurial organization adept at interpreting for possibilities, the Next Big Thing was there, inside it, all the time.

The Next Big Thing would grow out of 'Nation, Faith and Patience', the place where it all started.

City of the Future

The product is the 'Economic Cities', first introduced in 2005, and in the following paragraphs we will look at the strategy that would inspire and deliver this Big Idea, as well as the strategy that would inform it.

The Economic City concept evolved from seeds planted by the original OSS. If 120 government services could be delivered quickly and efficiently from one smiling customer relations manager sitting at one desk, in one office, and then later from no more than accessing the internet anywhere in connected space, what if every government service an investor ever needed, every service that could ever be provided, more than five hundred of them in all, could be gotten with the same ease in a 0-traffic, 0-waste, 0-hassle way?

Would this not be the ultimate OSS?

That was one of the perspectives in which SAGIA saw the Next Big Thing they needed, the ultimate customer service proposition, the Grand OSS.

Thinking Outside the Box

The process started when SAGIA began examining possibilities for the Next Big Thing that would meet three aspirations: the desire for the ultimate OSS, the desire for the ultimate economic stimulator in less developed regions, and the desire for a pilot project that would enable testing the next generation of everything, and proving it for possible introduction into the base economy. These three aspirations drove them to the phenomena of Special Economic Zones, or SEZs. At the time of SAGIA's strategic planning, approximately 3000 SEZs existed in the world, and those considered successful had doubled the flow of FDI to the areas where they were located every 5 years. The SAGIA leadership would also learn that there were many failures as well, so they focused on understanding what made the successful ones successful, what the critical ingredients were.

SEZs

SAGIA identified three common characteristics of successful SEZs.

One, every successful SEZ had a single regulator that provided all the services in the SEZ (normally these SEZs also have industrial assets and transportation assets).

Two, they found that all successful SEZs had an adequate and ready pool of talent available for the nature of the businesses and industries located in the SEZ.

Three, successful SEZs were located next door to successful cities, with lifestyle and quality of life, such as Jurong Island next to Singapore.

The SAGIA leadership saw the potential in the concept of the SEZ, but took the innovative next step of combining the three success ingredients into one product, and in the process elevated the concept from a zone to a city, and named it accordingly 'Economic City', or EC. The Economic City would encompass the three defining success characteristics of SEZs, while facilitating the national objective of economic diversification into non-oil sectors by the following: providing an innovative 'ecosystem' that would foster innovation as well as creative and cost effective alternatives to fund and operate infrastructure; strengthening the Kingdom's value proposition in attracting FDI and providing DDI attractive options, through jump-starting and sustaining economic progress in the under-developed regions; by offering unique lifestyle options that would attract talent and generate competition between cities municipalities; and finally, by providing attractive jobs to Saudis to stem the emerging problem of urban migration to the major Saudi cities.

60 × 24 × 7

Compared to similar efforts around the world, the Saudi ECs were unique from the start for a number of reasons. One, the initiative was extremely large in scale, involving multiple cities with heterogeneous size, economic focus and geographic locations. Most economic zones being grown in other parts of the world typically focused on a fewer number of sectors and more homogeneous development, and their authorities focused on regulation and to a lesser extent, on service provision.

Two, most economic zones worldwide offered incrementally enhanced conditions as compared to the base economy, whereas in the KSA case, the differentiation was huge, and the ECs were designed to serve as pilots for possible reforms that could be disseminated to the base economy.

Finally, and what was essentially the key differentiator with respect to other, similar development projects worldwide, was that according to the Article 10 of the Economic City Law, or 'General Act' as it was known locally, the Economic Cities were legally required to provide all government services, over 500 in total, in no longer than 60 minutes, 24 hours a day and 7 days week, what has become a branding slogan as the 'World's First 60 × 24 × 7 Cities.'

In other words, if Mrs Citizen wanted a government service at three in the morning on any day, of any week, in any year, it needed to be given to her in no more than 60 minutes.

To stress the importance of $60 \times 24 \times 7$, that it is the purpose of existence for ECA the $60 \times 24 \times 7$ was incorporated into the new logo of ECA.

The Birth of ECA

SAGIA incubated the Economic City initiative for 4 years before spinning it off into a new authority, the Economic Cities Authority (ECA), with a mandate to give it full financial and administrative oversight over all Economic Cities, to capture and retain domestic and foreign capital, and to support the Kingdom's developmental objectives. The role of government in the Economic Cities would be purely regulatory, to design the regulatory and legislative framework with policies and procedures that would make the cities commercially viable and highly attractive investment destinations for the private sector. To ensure that corporate culture was applied to the public sector according to the General Act, the Board of the ECA was comprised of private sector leaders with the exception of the Chairman of the Board, who was the Governor of SAGIA.

Four cities were launched between the years 2005 and 2006, each designed with a unique value proposition and different set of foci, in some sense correlated to location and related core competencies that would result, and also to prevent competition amongst one another.

KAEC

King Abdullah Economic City (KAEC), on the west coast, is approximately 120 km north of Jeddah. At nearly the size of Washington DC, it is the largest of the four cities (168 km^2). Envisioned for KAEC is a future population of 2 million people. The focal sectors are ports, logistics, plastics manufacturing, pharmaceuticals, food, steel industries and services.

PABMEC

Prince Abdul Aziz bin Mousaed Economic City (PABMEC), in the north central part of the Kingdom, is the second largest of the four cities, with a land area of 156 km^2, or nearly the size of the country of Lichtenstein. Envisioned for PABMEC is a future population of 300 000 people. The focal sectors are logistics, agribusiness, minerals and construction materials.

JEC

Jazan Economic City (JEC), on the south west coast, is the third largest of the economic cities, with a land area of 100 km^2, or slightly larger than The Hague. Envisioned for JEC is a future population of 300 000. The focus is on heavy industries such as refining and downstream to refineries.

KEC

Knowledge Economic City (KEC), near the holy city of Madinah, is the smallest of the economic cities, with a land area of 4.8 km^2, or larger than the island of Pitcarin. Envisioned for KEC is a population of 150 000. The focus is on education and knowledge based industries, tourism services, health and medical sciences.

First Step

The first step is always, 'I Aim, therefore I Am.' The ECA engaged a global consultancy firm[6] to facilitate the process of developing its strategy, and they began by developing an aggressive vision and mission that would draw on the goals set in its mandate as defined by The General Act, and that would also reflect its global aspirations for the cities and the Kingdom. The ECA's vision and mission were as follows:

Vision
To create the world's most innovative and competitive cities in which to live, work, play and learn.

Mission
By 2015, the ECA will develop economically vibrant knowledge hubs through innovative partnerships, best in class regulations, and 'around the clock' services in an hour – 60 × 24 × 7.

The Promise

The next step was to come up with the values used to define the DNA of the people and the culture of the organization, in other words the ECA's 'promises to stakeholders'. They were as follows:

1. *Impact*: to contribute to the Saudi economy by developing knowledge-based cities;

2. *Innovation*: to encourage, recognize and reward innovation and creativity;
3. *Collaboration*: to form effective partnerships with the private and public sector;
4. *Engagement*: to involve all stakeholders in a transparent and fair manner, through;
5. *Transparency*: to communicate with openness, clarity and consistency, and out of;
6. *Respect*: embrace and respect local norms and Islamic values.

Must-win Battles

Next was to develop a list of must-win battles, of which there would be two:

The first must-win battle was to ensure that the business model of the master developer was sustainable. Unlike other large scale urban development programs at the time, KSA's Economic Cities relied on an innovative, public–private development model that would make them financially self-sufficient and sustainable, thereby minimizing dependence on government investment. The development of the ECs would be lead entirely by the private sector through the formation of a publicly quoted company considered as the master developer.

The second must-win battle was to ensure the development of the regulations in a timely fashion, and to achieve a competitive advantage for the cities through the legal framework. This would require finalizing the development of laws and regulations in alignment with Saudi laws and with the principle of commercial viability, while taking into account the economic rationale and objectives of the ECs.

The Regulation

The ECA partnered with the world's top law firm[7] in regulatory development, and mandated them to develop the regulations based upon four principles:

1. *Commercial Viability*: Whatever regulations were developed had to be commercially viable, and it would be required that centers of excellence from around the corporate world would be asked to contribute by co-authoring the regulations.
2. *Beyond Best Practices*: Whatever regulations produced should be at a level beyond best practices. For example, if the fastest turnaround time at a globally successful port was 1.5 hours, the ECA would require a turnaround time of less than 1.5 hours.

3. *60 × 24 × 7 Compliance*: Whatever regulations were developed would have to be 60 × 24 × 7 compliant, meaning that all government services would have to be provided in 60 minutes, 24 hours a day and 7 days a week.

4. *Lean and Sweet*: Whatever regulations were developed to ensure commercial viability, the beyond best practice agenda, and 60 × 24 × 7 compliance, should not increase the number of employees working in the ECA beyond 50. This would require choosing third party collaboration and as much outsourcing as possible, and also, that as many centers of excellence as possible would be engaged.

KPIs

To define the ECA's strategy, SAGIA used the key components of the 'Future Cities Index' published by PWC, an international consulting firm with extensive experience working with cities and local government authorities around the world, and whom the ECA had partnered with in the development of the corporate strategy. The holistic, 360 degree approach used would define the ingredients of a successfully run, globally recognized city, the main ones being a local governmental authority dedicated to building the necessary management capabilities, developing the appropriate policies for the building blocks, or 'capitals', and optimizing resources invested according to the vision.

In order for the cities to be ranked among the top cities in the world in 'Future Cities Index', a main objective of theirs, the ECA would be paying most attention to the following eight KPIs:

Economic clout
The first KPI is achieved by the number of global Fortune 500 companies represented in the ECs, by the percentage of financial and business services employment, by the measure of FDI, and DDI; by the number of green field projects; and by the amount of capital investment attracted to the cities. Key to achieving this KPI is the securing of anchor tenants who are in full alignment with the master developer. Anchor businesses established in the cities would create jobs, and jobs would create demand on the rest of the cities' components such as housing, education, health, entertainment and so on, leading to its viability.

The ease and cost of doing business
This is measured in the ease of entry, the number of procedures, the time required to start a business, the business trip index, the cost of business occupancy, and the total tax rate for a business as a percentage of profits.

Infrastructure capital
This is determined by the percentage of trips taken by mass transit, connectivity from nearest airport to city center (time and options), construction activity, and housing index.

Intellectual capital
This is determined by the percentage of residents in the ECs with higher education, the number of libraries per 1000 inhabitants, the number of new business startups, intellectual property rights, and the R&D funding received and commercialized by the ECs.

ICT capital
This is measured by the cities' E-readiness for citizens, its businesses and government, by an ICT competitiveness index, broadband penetration and speeds and mobile phone penetration.

Environmental capital
This is measured by the Green Cities Index, which takes into account air quality, recycled waste, percentage of renewable energy, percentage of green space from total city area, and city carbon footprint.

Social capital
This is evaluated against the number of crimes and violent crimes per 1000 inhabitants, the number of hospitals, healthcare costs, public schools and low-income housing.

Cultural and leisure capital
Finally, this is measured against the entertainment index, which includes the quality and variety of restaurants, performances, and sport and leisure activities within each city, as well as the number of international tourists.

Chief Arts and Cultural Officer

In line with SAGIA's approach to creating world-class ECs, SAGIA had already recognized the integral contribution a cultural strategy would have on the overall success of the ECs quality of life value proposition, and had come up with an arts and culture road map and appointed a Chief Arts and Cultural Officer to lead it. The vision was to stimulate artistic and cultural activity that would contribute to social and economic prosperity, through developing target creative industries and defining and implementing strategic cultural initiatives. The mission was to mobilize artistic and cultural initiatives as part of a broader ecosystem contributing to a better quality of life in the ECs, attracting and retaining a knowledge generating society, and fostering creative and innovative talents.

The first step SAGIA took was to appoint an Arts and Cultural Advisory Council to meet every year to decide on appropriate policy initiatives. Members of the Arts and Culture Advisory Council included the Director of MOMA, the Director of LACMA, the Director of the State Hermitage Museum in St Petersburg, various museum curators, art collectors and financiers and art historians.

Project 60

One of the first projects to grow out of the Arts and Cultural initiative was 'Project 60'. It was inspired by the next generation of government services to be introduced in the four ECs, in which every government service is offered in no more than 60 minutes. Project 60 showcased the best of emerging and established contemporary Saudi art, utilizing public spaces in Economic Cities Authority Headquarters as an exhibition space. Sixty new pieces by a new Saudi contemporary artist were displayed every 60 days in the public spaces.

Stakeholders

Part of the strategic planning process was defining the ECA's value proposition for its stakeholders, and the process resulted in identifying the following:

Residents
To the *city residents* the ECs offered globally competitive lifestyle options for top talent, state-of-the-art infrastructure and connectivity, and a transparent and fair regulatory environment built on world-class standards and respecting cultural norms.

Investors
To the *investors* the ECs offered efficient and effective services through its $60 \times 24 \times 7$ value proposition, special incentives and benefits as permitted by the EC General Act, transparent and consistently implemented regulations and state-of-the-art infrastructure and connectivity. The KSA proposition also offered investors a launch pad for global energy intensive industries, access to capital, domestic and regional markets, unique positioning and reach for Islamic/halal compliant services and products, financial incentives and full foreign ownership.

Master developers
To the *master developers* the ECs offered branding and positioning as part of a world-class project and commercial return on investment that was attractive to shareholders.

ECA staff
To the *ECA staff* was offered the benefit of participating in a national initiative supported by the country's top leadership and with a vision to impact the Kingdom. It also offered the opportunity of learning and training through exposure to the best in class practices, and by belonging to an efficient and flexible team.

Surrounding regions
Finally, to the *regions* surrounding the cities, the ECAs offered local business stimulation, job generation for local community members in the cities, an enhanced profile of the surrounding regions, and infrastructure integration.

2.5 percent
As an example of supporting surrounding regions where the cities are located, in return for the concessions ECA gave to the master developers of the Economic Cities, like PABMEC and JEC, one of the conditions demanded was that 2.5 percent of the paid up capital should be given as free shares to the low income segment of the population. The goal was to include the majority of the regions' population in the ownership of the cities and to help improve the income of this segment.

8.   REACHING OUT

When SAGIA talks about reaching out, they are referring to two targeted audiences, and one question: how to effectively communicate what we are doing well to the internal organization and external world of partners, citizens and investors.

The Internal Audience

With reference to the internal organization, the objective was to achieve awareness in the entire organization and full understanding and alignment on the strategy, the vision, mission, goals and value proposition of the organization. This required a proper communication plan to ensure all messages were communicated throughout the organization effectively.

It was imperative that the people in the organization knew what messages they should be communicating to the external world and how these messages should be communicated. One involved content and the other involved presentation. In the case of content, good governpreneurial leadership will make every effort to ensure its organizational members, from the highest to the lowest, are as well informed on content as is possible.

The danger of team members not having a clear awareness and understanding of what the organization was all about could be a main cause of internal politics, with the outcome that internal politics could be exported externally and converted to external politics. If someone was not satisfied with how things were going, either out of ignorance due to lack of proper methods of disseminating and communicating information or messages, or because of legitimate concerns or complaints improperly managed (lack of mechanisms for so doing), the employee might communicate inaccurate, or even accurate but unnecessary information to external parties. This might grow to larger and more confused messages, or worse, leak to the press, with negative press being plus a growing mass of external politics, or in the worst case, resistance to policies and initiatives the organization may have been trying to deliver on and which were essential for the organization's reason for existence.

The SAGIA language
The basis of a proper communication plan was the common language, or in this case, the SAGIA language for the internal audience. A common language is a language everybody understands, is as simple as possible, and ideally, as simple as one word.

The quarterly gathering
In addition to the annual BBP meeting, and the monthly meeting of the Executive Board, SAGIA also held a quarterly meeting during which the Governor gathered everybody in the organization for two hours to share the latest news and events, as well as updates on progress on the various initiatives and projects.

Quarterly bulletin
SAGIA also published a quarterly digital and hard copy bulletin, in Arabic called *Tawasul* or 'reaching out', through which SAGIA staff could keep tabs on what was happening in the organization.

The online debate
An interactive online forum was established to give staff the opportunity to debate an 'issue of the month'. This forum allowed open expression of

ideas, critical or supportive, to empower individuals through sharing opinions, which reduced the risk of wrong messages being conveyed to external parties with potentially damaging effects on the organization.

One-to-one

Ras-bi-Ras in Arabic literally means 'head to head', a frequently occurring event at SAGIA where an employee is picked randomly to spend 1 hour during a day thinking aloud with the Governor, who during this hour acts as an aggressive listener only. These randomly picked employees can be cleaners, kitchen workers, security staff, receptionists or top leaders. There are two beneficiaries of this process. One, the SAGIA Governor is given the chance to hear an organizational voice that might otherwise never be heard, and from whom something valuable can be learned (there is always something to learn); and the employee is given the chance to share his or her mind, to be heard, which has the very positive psychological effect of boosting morale significantly, leading to increased organization loyalty. During the meeting, which is only attended by the Governor and the selected employee, the Governor takes notes of what is often a talk from the heart. The employee is free to say anything positive or negative about the organization, including issues of personal concern. Should any feedback concern another SAGIA person, such as poor service observed or given in the OSSs, the Governor will reach out to the concerned while keeping the identity of the *Ras-bi-Ras* employee confidential.

Off-site retreats

SAGIA held many informal gatherings outside the SAGIA premises using sports and other activities for team building and to cement the SAGIA messages in the minds of its members or team.

External Audience

Government agencies

When they first began promulgating the language of competitiveness to their collaborators, partners in government and other agencies, SAGIA was greeted with a very short learning curve. The time required from these agencies to grasp the one simple word of their message, competitiveness, and understand what was in it for the nation and for them, was brief, and easy. The message of competitiveness would quickly become a national priority.

Average citizen on the street

Right dose   Given their experience with other government agencies, SAGIA assumed that the term 'competitiveness' and the language of rankings and indicators would be likewise easily understood by the general public, but that assumption was proven wrong. Not only did the average citizen on the street not understand the sophisticated language, they misinterpreted the inaccessible rhetoric to mean quick solutions for just about everything, which resulted in more negativity. SAGIA then committed to delivering the right dose, and a very clear message.

'What's in it for me?' Saudi Arabia's population is very diverse with respect to backgrounds, level of education and interests, and this required a communication platform, or language, that would have to be the right dose, the right words, the right 'me', in the sense that it could be understood quickly, which meant making the message and the 'me' as simple as possible.

Multiplier effect The combination of internal politics becoming external politics by being exported to the public, and the dissatisfaction of the average citizen on the street, would eventually find their way to the press.

The avalanche SAGIA's original assumption, that negative press would fade away if ignored, was found to be 'absolutely wrong'. They would learn that it was important to counter criticism as swiftly and as comprehensively as possible, regardless of the status or visibility of the newspaper or writer or the quality of the article, because bad press would never fade away but instead feed on itself and become even more toxic. Bad press generates bad press, as journalists are always on the lookout for a story in the daily papers and various websites, searching for interesting news and interesting ways to use the ingredients of that news for the next article. Negative press snowballs bigger and bigger until becoming an avalanche with time.

The ping-pong strategy It would take SAGIA some time to figure out that they were doing wrong on two fronts:

One, in the language used with the average citizen on the street.

Two, the assumption that bad press would eventually fade away. After fixing the language and simplifying it for the average citizen on the street, SAGIA decided to adopt a different, what they called 'ping pong' strategy with every single negative article or message that would appear in the media, by countering and explaining its position as clearly as possible.

Targeted investors

Branding SAGIA branded KSA to their customers in the form of a launch pad to three targeted markets:

The Global Energy Launch Pad. First, SAGIA packaged KSA as a global launch pad and most cost effective location in the world for energy intensive industries, due to the nation's obvious core competencies and value proposition. Saudi Arabia hosts one quarter of all proven oil reserves, and has a history of huge investment into the entire energy value chain, including petrochemicals and downstream to petrochemicals. KSA also possess huge raw materials in the form of more than 28 commercially viable mineral deposits such as bauxite for the aluminum industry, and phosphates for the fertilizer industry. To build on this value proposition SAGIA reached out to the external audience through branding KSA as the (future) energy capital of the world, rather than just the oil capital it had been.

The MENA Launch Pad. Second, SAGIA packaged KSA as a regional launch pad to 250 million consumers within a 3-hour flying radius from the center of the country due to its ideal location between East and West. This population of 250 million consumers combined with the additional fact of Saudi's being the fastest growing and the most liquid market in the region, would give investors a market of almost 280 million consumers.

The Islamic World Launch pad. Third, SAGIA packaged KSA as a launch pad to the Islamic world of 1.2 billion Muslims due to Saudi's status as the home of the two most holy sites in Islam, the cities of Mecca and Medinah. This meant a captive audience of 1.2 billion people, or 20 percent of the global population, who would naturally have a preference for products and services that were either halal or shariah compliant and produced in and supplied from Saudi Arabia. This is potentially a multi-hundred billion dollar market, in which Saudi Arabia sits right at the center.

Imagine a chocolate bar, and written very clearly on the package is 'Halal, produced in the holy lands of Mecca and Medinah.' Would this not give the product higher brand equity for the 1.2 billion consumers?

Targeted sectors   Coupled to the above branding strategy, SAGIA adopted a sector focused approach, and created dedicated units for the promotion of three strategic sectors, energy, transportation and knowledge based industries (KBIs).

Energy. By focusing on energy Saudi Arabia sought to transform its status as the global oil capital to the global energy capital, by developing the whole energy value chain and enhancing its market share in the various segments of energy and energy intensive industries.

Transportation. Focusing on transportation to help in achieving KSA's goal to be a launch pad, or a hub, by paying attention to the transportation and logistics industries, and by promoting transportation as a strategic business sector in order to develop a world-class transportation infrastructure, with seaports, railways, airports, logistics hubs, etc., as well as creating best in class legislations.

KBIs (education, ICT, healthcare). Education, ICT and healthcare, though not obviously linked to Saudi's core competencies or competitive advantages, were an important choice because they are enablers for other business sectors.

Education. Education is the backbone of human capital, and investment flow goes hand-in-hand with the availability of adequate human capital. It has therefore become an important area of focus for Saudi Arabia and SAGIA, the latter, which focuses on this sector through attracting centers of excellence and world-class service providers in all segments of the educational value chain.

ICT. ICT has been picked by SAGIA as a strategic subsector. ICT initiatives such as expanding broadband penetration in the Kingdom, would contribute to economic stimulation through introducing additional investment and job opportunities.

Healthcare. Finally, healthcare is critical for a country with one of the highest birth rates in the world, and the focus was to have adequate infrastructure and service providers, not only for catering to the local demand, but also for serving the traffic generated from the Islamic world of 1.2 billion Muslims and the global business community.

3D Saudi

While SAGIA was very focused and segmented in their communication to targeted customers, they were also paying attention to some of the misperceptions about Saudi Arabia that may not have been correlated to the business or investment opportunity, but might represent a concern for some of the targeted investors. SAGIA introduced *THINK*, a magazine in which talk of investment opportunities in the Kingdom was absent. *THINK* focused on the softer aspects of KSA, such as culture, lifestyle, art, and the role of women, blended with elements from the international scene, and with articles written by well-known personalities such as Paulo Coelho.

Each issue presented a concept for the future and a profile of at least one international visionary, to inspire readers to rethink and re-examine opinions on current issues.

9.   HONEY, NO MONEY

While collaboration is essential for the governpreneurial organization, partnering with the private sector is the ingredient for success. Partnering with the private sector means speaking the language of the private sector, the language of profit, and positioning the organization's value proposition around the same language. Doing so shows the private sector that by cooperating with us, you will be cooperating with an organization that understands your language, and we will make you money.

Budget is Never Enough

Government agencies need to show a return on their budget allocation, which should be based on the highest return to the nation, at least in theory, but in practice government agencies should not rely totally on budget allocation. They should be encouraged to find creative and innovative revenue generating opportunities without compromising on the basic service that they should offer. There are certain basics, or bare minimums needed to be provided efficiently without fees, but there are also additional services that could be provided for which fees would be natural, such as offering an instant service at 1 a.m., which might not be obligated by mandate, or forbidden (mandate is a living organism). Call it an 'exception', call it 'creativity', call it whatever is necessary, but charging for an instant service in the wee hours of morning, and making customers happy in the process, is in the end very entrepreneurial.

Funding

Lack of funding is the biggest enemy in government and can be used by a leader in two ways. One, it can be used negatively as an excuse for not delivering, 'we don't have enough financial resources', or two, for being more innovative and entrepreneurial in generating revenues from non conventional sources to execute your plans. When an organization begins thinking about how to generate revenues, it automatically places a great deal of pressure on itself to become innovative in offering new services, and then efficient in offering them in a superior way. Customers will always question why they should pay a fee for a service that is not provided efficiently and in a timely fashion. Lack of funding is therefore an opportunity to improve an organization's offerings and its efficiency.

For example, take a customer who wants a very complex service. The customer knows he must wait for his turn, and second, because it's a complex service it most likely will take time to deliver. But, if an organization decides to offer this service instantly to the customer, there is a good chance he will be happy to pay a fee for it. The organization therefore achieves two goals, one, generates additional funding, and two, becomes more innovative in terms of solving demanding and complex requirements by its customers. This is not discriminating, but offering additional services to those who want or need them and do not have the time to wait, which creates a customer, which then puts pressure on people who will understand they need to offer a superior service simply because people are paying for it.

Win–win

In setting out to achieve its funding needs, SAGIA decided it would provide a variety of services, except for the provision of funds, to a variety of private sector partners, including creating the right policy and regulatory framework for a business environment in which the private sector could flourish; the provision of information and services across the board; the provision of detailed studies to various customers and other government agencies on methods that could be used to improve competitiveness across the whole value chain of the Saudi economy; matchmaking; and the provision of tailor made services that would deal directly with specific needs a private sector company might have, or answer specific questions.

SAGIA had one of the smallest budgets of government agencies in Saudi Arabia, so in order for it to be the entrepreneurial organization it sought to be, it needed funding.

And they got it, 100 percent of it, from the private sector.

Every initiative reviewed in the preceding pages, with no exception, was funded by the private sector, and in every case the private sector would get something in return. To achieve this level of successful partnering, the most important thing was to speak the private sector language and show the private sector what was in it for them, and what was in it for them was almost always profit, of one form or another.

The National Competitiveness Center (NCC), The Global Competitiveness Forum (GCF), CADRE, The Saudi Arabian Responsible Competitiveness Index (SARCI), the Most Competitive Youth (MCY), The Saudi Oxford Leadership Program (SOLP), Regional Competitiveness Reports, the ICT Council, Competitiveness Councils, Top FDI, the Economic Cities, and *THINK* magazine to name a few, were all funded entirely by a private sector who would always get something in return, whether exposure, or branding.

20 × 20

For the ECs, investors were provided the ultimate real estate play whereby the private sector invested in the land and infrastructure and ECA provided legislation that included the best possible practices and enabling policies to enhance the asset value for investors and lead to quicker attainment of objectives, while at the same time achieving the goals of the government by introducing a new product that would function as an economic stimulator in less developed regions.

This typical 'Honey, No Money' scenario worked like this: the ECA would commit to providing the conditions that would make every project within the Economic City viable for private sector investment, and the investor would commit to an agreed upon economic output determined by the ECA. In the case of the concession given to the investors for KAEC's seaport, ECA demanded against the port concession a specific economic output of 20 million TEUs[8] by 2020 (20 × 20) in terms of actual volume. To ensure the delivery of this economic output as well as the viability of the project, ECA went as far as engaging the investors in the development of the legislative environment and seaport processes to make them as sweet as honey toward the best return on the investor's money.

10.   NO RISK, NO GAIN

Risk should be allocated to the party best able to manage it.

Definition

Risk, measured in terms of impact and likelihood, is defined as the possibility of an event occurring that will have an impact, usually negative, on the achievement of objectives. To control risk, or attempt to control it, management must plan, organize, and direct the performance of sufficient actions to provide a reasonable assurance that objectives and goals will be achieved.

Unchartered Territory

Being the governpreneur is like trying to read the future, as well as the minds of others, investors included. It means opening to others about whom you often know very little, no matter how much preparation you might take beforehand. The risk appetite of an entrepreneurial organization is far greater than the risk of a non-entrepreneurial one, and the more entrepreneurial you are as an organization, the more you venture into unknown territories, the higher risk you have. For an organization like SAGIA, that had ventured into the relatively unchartered territory of governpreneurship, and which constantly sought to introduce more organic units and Next Big Things, such as the 10 × 10 goal and the Economic Cities, the amount of possible risk, failure, misconduct, etc., was high.

Chief Governance Officer

This high-risk appetite meant the SAGIA management would need to provide an institutionalized approach to identify, assess, manage, and control potential events or situations. They headhunted and appointed a Chief Governance Officer to lead the governance unit of SAGIA, and who would report directly to the Governor.

Her role would be to establish and lead a department to deal with risk issues such as authorities and operating checks and balances, audit and risk reviews, and board duties.

Colors and Forms of Risk

Some examples of uncalculated and unmanaged risks include:

- Deviation from basic business model due to lack of clear strategy;
- Partners and collaborators disputes due to lack of clear modus operandi;
- Conflict of interest due to lack of segregation of duties;
- Mismanagement of cash flow, or incorrect financial reporting or financial misstatement, which can lead to significant cash shortfall;
- Mismanagement of human capital, which can lead to significant employee turnover and or low caliber staff;
- Poor decisions, including inappropriate expansion;
- Operational risks such as supplier/outsourcing risks, natural disasters, and the inability to keep up with technological advances;
- Fraud and corruption as a result of lack of controls and incomplete or late MIS.

Making Mr Fix It Redundant

SAGIA understood the possibility of someone trying to profit from red tape, and that the more red tape that was involved in a process the more likely corruption would occur, and the more opportunities for an appearance from the so-called 'Mr Fix it', who is always happy to navigate someone through bureaucracy for a fee. The solution for SAGIA was always to ensure its service processes were as transparent and red-tape free as possible.

Making the Process Digital

SAGIA introduced an additional safety valve through digitizing the process and reducing the human component as much as possible, '0-traffic' being a good example.

Incentives

In addition SAGIA introduced in the OSS a system to link productivity to transparent incentive schemes, for example, a clear system for rewarding the number of transactions processed in a day. The more transactions, the more rewards. The fewer transactions, the fewer rewards. 'If you can make money legally, why make it illegally?'

Awareness

SAGIA also concentrated on raising staff awareness by constantly educating them on the subject of conflict of interest, what it means, and in what areas conflict of interest may arise. SAGIA wanted to do more than verbally warn its people against corruption; they wanted to ensure a process was in place that included training people on the policies and procedures, on the whole of SAGIA activities, on culture, and on values, from the recruitment process onward.

Values

One of SAGIA's values was integrity and SAGIA embedded this value in the recruitment process to ensure the integrity of every newcomer. SAGIA was also very thorough in the recruitment process and performed due diligence and carefully checked each candidate's references, and finally, required all accepted recruits to sign full disclosure forms to prevent conflict of interest.

No One Man Shows

SAGIA succeeded in converting itself from an organization that deals with risk on an ad-hoc basis to an organization where risk is embedded in its strategic planning, capital allocation and product development. SAGIA developed an early warning system for detecting risks above established thresholds. They understood the importance of having an effective risk management system that sought to measure and mitigate risk, beginning with reviewing and defining the risk through monitoring it, assessing it, and managing it. SAGIA was constantly seeking to be risk adverse by establishing the basic building blocks, including the right structure, people, reporting lines or systems, the right governance, or checks and balances (no one man shows), the right controls, the right culture – embedded, proactive, board to floor – and performance measurements and monitoring, performance measurement and linking them to rewards, constant reviews and benchmarking.

700

An entrepreneurial organization such as SAGIA has a big appetite for risk by nature, and the most important thing, to mitigate and manage risk, requires enhancing the competitiveness and efficiency of the organization. SAGIA set out to achieve organizational excellence through an initiative called 'SAGIA Excellence', an institutionalized process with the objective of positioning SAGIA as a world-class, or exemplary, public institution.

They chose the EFQM[9] (European Foundation for Quality Management) Excellence Model as the comprehensive 360° framework for identifying and assessing areas in the organization where improvements could be achieved, and to drive its own operations against an applicable model that measures organizational competitiveness. The model is based on the practical experience of organizations across Europe, in both the private and public sectors, and on the concept that an organization will achieve better results, better risk management and better governance through the continuous improvement of processes to achieve efficiencies and external impact. For all award categories EFQM assessors allocate points to arrive at a total score out of 1000 points. The score of the EFQM Excellence Award and prize winners in the past few years were in the range of 660–740. SAGIA's ambition was to score 700 or above to position the organization among the top EFQM award winners globally.

9 + 1

SAGIA argues that unless a government organization is willing to adopt the tenth rule religiously, they should not try to explore the other nine rules.

NOTES

1. A term coined by the Italian Enrico Mattei in reference to the oil companies, Standard Oil of New Jersey, Standard Oil Company of New York (now ExxonMobil); Standard Oil of California, Gulf Oil and Texaco (now Chevron); Royal Dutch Shell; and Anglo-Persian Oil Company (now BP).
2. During the 2004 strategy development process SAGIA engaged Booz Allen Hamilton, and for the 2010 process, PricewaterhouseCoopers.
3. Quest Worldwide.
4. The Monitor Group.
5. The Annual Report of the NCC.
6. PricewaterhouseCoopers.
7. Covington and Burlington.
8. The 'twenty-foot equivalent unit', TEU or teu is an inexact unit of cargo capacity often used to describe the capacity of container ships and container terminals.
9. The EFQM founding members are: AB Electrolux, British Telecommunications Plc., Bull, Ciba-Geigy AG, C. Olivetti & C. SpA, Dassault Aviation, Fiat Auto SpA, KLM, Nestlé, Philips, Renault, Robert Bosch, Sulzer AG, Volkswagen.

BIBLIOGRAPHY

NCC Annual Report 2010.
NCC Labor Competitiveness Council Document, 2010.
NCC National Competitiveness Review, 2008; 2010.
SAGIA Case Study 1962.0, JFK School of Government, Harvard University.
SAGIA and ECA corporate strategy documents.
UNCTAD, World Investment Report 2011; accessed 20 July 2012 at: www.unctad.org/wir or www.unctad.org/fdistatistics.

Websites

Al-Yahya, Khalid O. Managing national competitiveness and institutionalizing reform through collaborative networks: the case of Saudi Arabia General Investment Authority (SAGIA), accessed 20 July 2012 at: http://www.nispa.org/files/conferences/2007/papers/200704182120080.NISPAcee%20SAGIA%20CaseStudy_Khalid%20Al%20Yahya.pdf.
Global Competitiveness Forum, accessed 20 July 2012 at: http://www.gcf.org.sa/.
Lonely Planet Guide, accessed 20 July 2012 at: http://www.lonelyplanet.com/uk.
Most Competitive Youth, accessed 20 July 2012 at: http://mcyonline.com/en/index.aspx?pageid=1.
NCC, accessed 20 July 2012 at: http://www.saudincc.org.sa/.
Saudi Arabian Responsible Competitiveness Index, accessed 20 July 2012 at: http://www.rci.org.sa/.
Saudi Embassy, accessed 20 July 2012 at: http://www.saudiembassy.net/.
Top 100 FDI, accessed 20 July 2012 at: http://www.gcf.org.sa/en/About-GCF/Initiatives/FDI-100/.
Wikipedia, accessed 20 July 2012 at: http://www.wikipedia.org/.

Appendix 4 HUG – Geneva University Hospital

Raphael H. Cohen

In spring 2011, Bernard Gruson, general director of the Hôpitaux Universitaires de Genève (HUG – Geneva University Hospital), was reflecting on what had happened since he had been appointed general manager of this 10 000-employee institution in 1999. His main source of satisfaction was derived from successfully uniting a series of different entities into a coherent and respected organization. He was also very happy to see the cultural change that had taken place.

THE UNIFICATION

It all started with a restructuring of a series of independent public entities active in the health sector of Geneva. Since each entity had its own 'master' with a certain level of power and autonomy, the reunification meant a loss of power for each of them. As is true every time that turf issues are at stake, resistance to change was considerable. The fact that HUG is a public entity governed by public sector rules and influenced by political parties made the challenge even more daunting.

If this was not enough, there was one more parameter adding substantial complexity. A university hospital has a triple mission: treat patients, train doctors and conduct relevant clinical research in medicine. This means that the hospital is financed partially by social security (for the treatments) and partly by the state (for training and research). Another interesting juggling act!

With diplomacy and perseverance, Gruson had nevertheless managed to achieve the transformation. It had been a painful and bumpy road but there was no doubt that the end result was a success even if many issues were not completely resolved. At this point, nobody was referring to the past situation when different entities coexisted but Bernard knew that there were still some challenges.

Since politicians, academics, doctors, nurses, unions, patients, insurance companies and managers do not exactly share the same objectives; Gruson had become an artist at arbitrating between those various stakeholders' aspirations and resistances. He lost some battles, but overall he won the war.

THE STRATEGIC PLAN

In order to channel everyone's energy and get people onboard, Bernard Gruson introduced a 4-year strategic plan. This plan outlined not only the strategic intentions and objectives, but also the managerial philosophy and the different policies which should govern the institution as a whole.

Since such a plan represented a major revolution, one person, Brigitte Rorive-Feytmans, was appointed to manage the process. Together she and Gruson quickly came to the conclusion that a participative approach would be the only way to go. This multilateral consultation process would substantially slow down the design of the strategic plan, but would also increase its acceptance. With all the concessions that had been necessary to deliver the first plan in 2001 that birth turned out to be particularly painful.

Rorive-Feytmans's listening skills and sense of diplomacy were instrumental in dealing with the various stakeholders and key players. Her tenacity, combined with a clear vision and a sense of fairness, contributed to the successful outcome of many negotiations. Thanks to her 'soft skills' and her humble approach, Rorive-Feytmans managed to get the support of many people. She strongly believed that to obtain the engagement of key players, the strategic plan had to become their baby and not hers. And it worked.

Each successive iteration of the plan brought significant improvements and the 2011–15 edition was a real source of satisfaction for her and Gruson. It contained a series of major, coordinated, cross-lateral initiatives that would bring HUG to the next level. Since the plan brought clarity and vision, it was now recognized as an intrinsic part of the managerial process of the hospital. Many executives would even claim that it would be impossible to manage such a complex institution without a strategic plan. This was a comforting success.

THE BURNING PLATFORM

Traditionally, doctors in Switzerland used to prioritize quality of treatment without taking cost into account. Patients were delighted, but insurance companies and the politicians paying the bills were not happy campers. Slashing health-related costs became a political and public issue. By the end of the twentieth century, the health sector in Switzerland had been shaken by several major cost-cutting initiatives.

Sensing that cost management would become a key success factor; in 1999 Bernard Gruson and his management team were the first to introduce a cost accounting system in a Swiss hospital. This was another revolution in the industry, but again to lessen natural resistance to change, the implementation had been done as smoothly as possible. Instead of using cost accounting to police treatments, it was used as an information system to better understand what was happening. The same small-steps participatory approach ensured a friendlier acceptance by the people involved.

With a budget amounting to CHF 1.4 billion and a difficult economic environment, the inevitable happened: in 2005, HUG was asked to dramatically reduce its operating cost. After intense negotiations Gruson agreed to reduce the budget by 100 million within 3 years. Since this was not going to be a piece of cake, Bernard quickly came to the conclusion that he would need the talent of the Boston Consulting Group to implement this new major change in care management that would affect everyone in the institution.

This is how 'Victoria' was born. Victoria was not a pretty baby but the code name for the cost-cutting initiative that would reorganize some departments, reduce the number of full time positions, change some territories, etc. Plenty of losers and few winners. Nothing to look forward to! But here again the objective was eventually achieved.

The good news was that Victoria turned out to be a great opportunity to let all employees realize that cost was a parameter that could not be ignored anymore. Even if almost everyone at HUG still cringes when the word 'Victoria' is mentioned, the 'burning platform' delivered the expected results: processes had been streamlined, efficiency had been increased, quality had been maintained, slackness on the job had been reduced and . . . the cost cutting objectives had been achieved.

THE MANAGERIAL CHALLENGE

While these structural changes were taking place, there was another battle to fight at the same time: the change of culture. Sometimes Bernard Gruson wondered if he was actually a glutton for punishment.

The challenge was to migrate from a hospital culture to a managerial culture. Traditionally, the hospital culture was based on a hierarchy where the hospital management had limited influence. Key medical positions were controlled by the University of Geneva. Since faculty appointment automatically determined the managerial rank in HUG, the main criteria for such nominations was academic performance. The consequence was that doctors were promoted into HUG managerial positions whenever they were promoted in academia. Needless to say, managerial skills were not included in the set of criteria granting academic promotions.

The consequence was that most doctors had little interest in management issues; managing people and budgets was perceived as a necessary pain that was hindering the medical practice. In addition, since many interns had a 1-year employment contract whose renewal depended on the goodwill of their boss, they had no power or opportunity to argue. The bottom-line result was that there were many management problems.

This had been a source of concern for Gruson but he knew that trying to change the system represented a huge task. Direct confrontation could trigger a nuclear reaction. Starting in 2000, he had frequent discussions with his HR director to find a more subtle approach. They both knew that most MDs were reluctant to attend management-training programs. Ultimately, as being a good or bad manager had virtually no impact on the careers of doctors, why should they waste their time learning to become better managers?

A CHANGE OF PARADIGM IN TRAINING

This was one of the central challenges that Bernard Meier, head of the HUG training center, and Antoine Bazin, his right hand man, were struggling with when they met Professor Raphael H. Cohen in 2002. Professor Cohen suggested adapting the course of entrepreneurship he had designed and had been running for both the science faculty of the University of Geneva and EPFL (the Swiss Federal Institute of Technology, the Swiss equivalent of MIT) in Lausanne, a nearby city on Lake Geneva. Their reaction was first of surprise: doctors should not be trained in entrepreneurship, much less those in a public university hospital!

They were nevertheless intrigued by this unusual proposal and agreed to explore its potential. The idea was to propose something radically different to the doctors: something that would suit their own interest rather than training to suit the needs of the institution. This was a practical application of the WiiifT[1] principle: make sure that doctors find enough benefits for themselves.

After some brainstorming a solution emerged: the MicroMBA,[2] a customized version of the study course for entrepreneurship using innovation as a thread. The idea was to teach something exciting enough to attract participants willing to boost their career inside or even outside the hospital. It was targeted to only middle management volunteers. Why volunteers? Simply because they are receptive and willing to learn. If people were forced to attend training courses because their boss told them to do so, they would most likely remain resistant and contaminate the volunteers' level of enthusiasm.

The MicroMBA first taught participants the tools to innovate, then required that they put those tools into practice. After the core theoretical concepts were taught, the class was divided into multidisciplinary groups and each group was asked to identify a real innovation that could support the strategic plan of HUG. Identifying the opportunity was only the first step. Each group then had to produce an Opportunity Case, find a sponsor to support this initiative, and convince upper management to obtain the necessary resources and authorizations to implement at least a pilot program if not the whole project.

Since participants quickly figured out that to implement their idea at field level they would need the tools taught in class, it gave them a compelling incentive to learn as much as possible in order to increase their own chances of success. Taking advantage of this high level of receptiveness, the MicroMBA modules included many managerial tools not directly related to innovation but still useful for the projects. The idea was to indirectly teach management and leadership skills that would improve the management practice of HUG managers.

When the concept was presented to Gruson in 2002, he immediately approved it. He was eager to support anything that could improve management skills even if the approach was outside the box, like this MicroMBA. If such a program could also contribute to the implementation of innovations beneficial to HUG, it would be the icing on the cake. As a general rule he liked audacious projects and he was rather curious to see if this unusual approach would actually keep its promise: low risk with interesting perspectives.

EXECUTIVE EDUCATION AS A VECTOR FOR CHANGE

Gruson now has no regrets because every year the MicroMBA produces a group of agents of change. In addition, the beauty of this program is that it pays for itself: the four to six projects produced yearly by each class are a measurable return on investment. In fact since the returns turned out to be higher than the cost of the MicroMBA, this executive education program has become a virtual profit center.

The recipe that made the EPFL entrepreneurship course one of the most popular of the school was replicated at HUG: teaching by humor. This approach, pioneered in Geneva by Professor Cohen, was one of his 'secret weapons'. Since participants were having fun, these lessons were a nice break for the participants who really enjoyed the overall experience. Another characteristic of his MicroMBA is that all the trainers are pracademics[3] with an entrepreneurial background. This not only gives them the legitimacy to teach the tools to innovate, but they are also a real source of inspiration for the participants.

The first pilot turned out to be a success, even leading to the publication of a peer-reviewed article in French. Over the years the MicroMBA has been improved and has now become a pillar of the executive education strategy at HUG. Bernard Gruson was also proud to know that this concept, first pioneered at HUG, has since been adopted by major corporations including Microsoft, Nestlé and Sanofi Aventis.

ENCOURAGING INNOVATION

Innovation has always been one of Gruson's priorities, but since he had other priorities, it had remained in the back of his mind. Once the Victoria project was behind him, innovation could come back on the agenda. He knew he wanted to promote it but did not have any defined strategy to do so. The MicroMBA focus on innovation was another reason that made the program attractive.

When he saw the quality of the innovative projects that were delivered after each MicroMBA session, as well as some of the other employees' initiatives, he acknowledged that managerial innovation should be recognized and rewarded. He thus decided in 2009 to implement a contest for managerial innovation, in addition to existing contests focusing on scientific innovation and quality improvement innovation.

In 2010 when the first managerial innovation prizes were given, it was interesting to notice that 40 percent of the finalist teams included MicroMBA alumni. This meant that MicroMBA participants who had once been through the process of corporate entrepreneurial innovation continued to be proactive and successful agents of change looking for opportunities to innovate. This confirmed that customized executive education can successfully be used as a lever with a lasting effect to boost innovation and change.

Since one of HUG missions is to produce state-of-the-art research, science-based innovation was always encouraged at HUG and the results were impressive. What was less successful was the ability to deploy those innovations on a larger scale. This prompted the creation in 2009 of a specific HUG Innovation Office dedicated to managing, promoting and capitalizing on innovation. It was staffed by a scientist to assess the scientific merits of technological innovations and by Sandrine Hertzschuch, who had been supervising the MicroMBA after Bernard Meier's departure but who also had obtained the Diploma in Entrepreneurship and Business Development at the University of Geneva designed and managed by Professor Cohen. This dynamic team very quickly boosted the innovation initiatives at HUG. Staffed with the right people, a team focusing on stimulating and supporting innovation can do wonders.

THE RESOURCES BOTTLENECK

In 2010, Bernard Gruson was frustrated by the many requests for resources brought to the board of management that had to be refused because they were not thoroughly analysed and convincing. He asked Gérard Zufferey, head of the training center, and his soon-to-be successor, Didier Jaccard, to find a way to upgrade the standard of those requests. They came to the conclusion that a request for resources was very similar to presenting an Opportunity Case at the pre-project stage of an innovation.

They asked Professor Cohen, an expert of this pre-project stage, to customize an Opportunity Case specifically for HUG requests for resources. He and Brigitte Rorive-Feytmans quickly worked out a template that anyone requesting money or resources had to use to submit a request. This template would have to be used for any kind of request, such as more beds in a unit, the acquisition of new equipment, more staff, more space, a new lab, a new specialized unit, etc.

Since this template requires a robust understanding of the different issues that must be addressed before drafting an Opportunity Case, the obvious thing to do was to teach the IpOp Model[4] to all administrators responsible for submitting new proposals and requests for resources.

When this training took place in 2011, all participants understood that allocating resources or authorizations required a clear document addressing all of the decision-makers' concerns. It also provided a common language to all the participants for the pre-project stage. Since this same terminology was also used by the many MicroMBA participants and the Innovation Office, it allowed better communication between all the HUG innovators now sharing the same methodology.

Another benefit of the HUG Opportunity Case is that it also helps the board of management to allocate resources more effectively. With a more mature presentation of each request, the decision makers can analyse them more thoroughly. A more demanding process also eliminated some requests that could not generate a robust enough Opportunity Case. In other words, the tools normally used by innovators were also helping better allocate resources in general.

THE NEXT MOVE

Bernard Gruson knew that the latest initiative driven by Jacques Hertzschuch, the HUG HR director since 2005, and his right-hand man Antoine Bazin, was going to be another major vector for change. After several months of preparation, they convinced the board of management in December 2010 that appointment of managerial positions, including those in connection with the university, would have to take into account managerial skills. In other words, it will no longer be enough to have the best academic credentials and technical skills to be appointed in a management position.

Until now MDs did not have to make any effort to become better managers. This key prerequisite will bring management skills on the radar of every single doctor who has the ambition to climb the hospital ladder. Now that the decision has been made, his next challenge will be to convey the message that even if management training is not compulsory, doctors are encouraged to proactively learn management skills. Upgrading their management skills should significantly contribute to developing a culture of results that improves quality, processes, collaboration and motivation. In other words, a corporate entrepreneurial culture. This was an exciting perspective.

THE REVIEW

Looking back at what had happened during these last few years, Bernard Gruson was happy with what had been achieved. Three major changes have been implemented: the unification, the strategic plan and Victoria cost-cutting. Since no one-size fits all, each of these used a different and customized change management approach, but all of them ultimately delivered the expected results. One of their beneficial side effects was to let all HUG employees realize that the world had changed and that change inside the institution was inevitable. Many things that may have worked in the past would not work anymore in the future.

In addition, a series of more discrete steps have been taken to change the culture and support corporate entrepreneurial behavior. As Gruson was reflecting on this apparently unstructured approach he found in the 17th chapter of *Winning Opportunities, Proven Tools for Converting Your Projects Into Success (without a business plan)*, a description of the four pillars required to stimulate innovation in a large organization, he was delighted to realize that he had intuitively implemented at HUG not only each of those four pillars but also the Five P's formula for empowerment also depicted in the book.

The first pillar had been the easiest for him: a genuine commitment to innovation. Innovation was in his DNA and he had clearly expressed his support to all convincing innovations or initiatives that would fit with the strategic plan. In addition, he had spontaneously implemented the Five P's formula for empowerment, which states that for Powerful Performance – the first P – the recipe for success requires:

- a Passionate leader: no doubt about it!
- Permission to innovate: with the MicroMBA, the prize for innovation and the Innovation Office, there is no ambiguity that innovation is encouraged
- Protection: no innovator has ever been punished in case of failure
- Process: the tools, i.e. the IpOp Model taught in the MicroMBA and to administrators, give a clear and practical process for innovation.

The second pillar to stimulate innovation: employees' motivation to innovate can only be achieved with a managerial style empowering lower levels to proactively come up with improvement proposals. Several moves have been going in this direction. One of them was the MicroMBA, but the other big one was the recent prerequisite for management skills to be promoted. There is still a lot to do but the process is in motion.

The third pillar: an environment that supports corporate entrepreneurship is also shaping up. Here again, several measures have progressively been introduced to support innovators: the MicroMBA and the Innovation Office but also the prize for innovation and some funding for innovative projects. There is no doubt that more support is needed, but here again the direction is set.

The fourth pillar had introduced the IpOp Model taught to MicroMBA participants and to administrators: provision of easy-to-use innovation tools and corporate entrepreneurship education. Other initiatives that each brought their own tools and processes included the Strategic Plan, the quality improvement initiatives, the cost accounting, a project management office and, of course, Victoria. Overall the tools and processes being deployed throughout the organization are actually making a difference.

Successfully introducing corporate entrepreneurship into a public service organization was a great source of satisfaction for Bernard Gruson. Thanks to a supportive and committed team, he had managed to change the culture of HUG to make it a more agile organization with a corporate entrepreneurial spirit. There is still a long way to completely achieve this objective, but HUG has now passed the point of no return. If the past has been rich and stimulating, the future looks even more exciting.

NOTES

1. What is in it for Them?
2. See www.micromba.org or Chapter 17 of *Winning Opportunities, Proven Tools for Converting Your Projects Into Success (without a business plan)*, 2011, Raphael H Cohen, free download on www.winning-opportunities.org.
3. http://en.wikipedia.org/wiki/Pracademic.
4. See Chapter 16 of *Winning Opportunities, Proven Tools for Converting Your Projects Into Success (without a business plan)*.

Index